Thinking of Seeing A Psychic?
Let
The Psychic Sourcebook
Be Your Guide

You may have walked into a storefront palm reader for fun or have heard of a psychic's abilities from a friend. But before you pay $60, $100, or more for a consultation with a professional psychic, you need to have the facts to make that visit both exciting and fulfilling.

Now this straightforward, authoritative primer gives you the knowledge you need to make your psychic consultation helpful and possibly life-changing.

Plus you'll learn, from America's most renowned psychics themselves, what they honestly can and can't do for their clients ... and how you can use this information to change the course of your own future.

For each step of the way, whether it's your first visit or your fifteenth, *The Psychic Sourcebook* offers the facts and security you need.

ABOUT THE AUTHOR

Frederick G. Levine has been a student of religion and the occult for the past 15 years. He has a degree in Comparative Religion and English from Amherst College, and studied at Trinity College, Oxford, and at Hebrew University in Jerusalem. Formerly a magazine editor for various consumer publications, he is currently a freelance writer and editor specializing in New Age topics.

In researching THE PSYCHIC SOURCEBOOK, he spent more than a year interviewing professional psychics, receiving psychic readings, and talking to people from all walks of life who have visited psychics for a wide range of reasons.

THE
PSYCHIC
SOURCEBOOK:

How to Choose and Use a Psychic

Frederick G. Levine

WARNER BOOKS

A Warner Communications Company

Epigraph excerpt from THE SEARCH FOR SIGNS OF IN-
TELLIGENT LIFE IN THE UNIVERSE by Jane Wagner. Copyright ©
1986 by Jane Wagner Inc. Reprinted by permission of Harper & Row
Publishers, Inc.

Warner Books, Inc., 666 Fifth Avenue, New York, NY 10103

 A Warner Communications Company

Printed in the United States of America

First printing July 1988

10 9 8 7 6 5 4 3 2 1

Library of Congress Cataloging-in-Publication Data

Levine, Frederick G.
  The psychic sourcebook: how to choose and use a
psychic / Frederick G. Levine.
      p.   cm.
  Bibliography: p
  Includes index.
  ISBN 0-446-38729-0. (pbk.) (U.S.A) / 0-446-38730-4 (pbk.) (Canada)
  1. Psychical research.   2. Occultism.   I. Title.
BF1031.L45 1988   87-31732
133.3—dc19   CIP

Cover design by Miriam Campiz

To my parents,
who taught me to believe in my own
vision of reality,
even when it differed from their own

CONTENTS

ACKNOWLEDGMENTS

I would like to thank all the people who helped me with this book, which includes both people who have visited professional psychics and the psychics themselves. In addition, there were many more—some merely acquaintances—who gave me names, telephone numbers, and leads, all of which ultimately blossomed into an impressive data base of people doing work in the field of spiritual growth. As I began to explore this fascinating new world, I was continually impressed by the enthusiasm of the people I met and by the degree of candor they showed in sharing with me what were in some cases very personal experiences.

As for the psychics themselves, I am indebted to them not only for the time and energy they took to sit with me and describe what they do, how they do it, and why they do it, but also for the chance to experience firsthand what psychic ability is all about. It was not only a process of discovery, but an unmatched opportunity for self-growth that continues to this day.

I apologize to those who, due to space and time constraints, are not mentioned directly in the text. Everyone I spoke to, almost without exception, was a source of help and inspiration, not to mention unbounded giving. Without them, this book would still be just a glimmer in its author's (third) eye.

INTRODUCTION

What is reality?
Nothing but a collective hunch.

—Trudy the Bag Lady
*The Search for Signs of Intelligent
Life in the Universe*

Fortune-tellers have always been with us, from the days of the Greek oracles to the palm readers you can find on almost every other street corner of a major city. But in recent years, the nature of psychic consultation has taken on a new twist.

Consider these examples: a successful New York lawyer drops her career when she learns she has psychic abilities and opens a "practice" in which she "channels" spirit guides for $75 an hour; hordes of fast-track young urban professionals line up during lunchtime, briefcases in hand, at a local "tea room" that does a brisk midtown business in 15-minute tarot card readings; major American corporations, including IBM, AT&T, and General Motors, are considering ways in which metaphysics "might help executives compete in the world marketplace"; the Pentagon secretly invests half a million dollars to train psychics to locate the positions of Soviet submarines.

What is going on here? Is this just crystal-ball reading, eighties-style? Or is it symptomatic of a much greater shift in human consciousness, or even the development of a new kind of spirituality? What is it that inspires perfectly rational, successful, productive people—people who have no more personal experience of the occult than you or I—to plunk down $400 and spend a weekend trying to "relive" their past lives?

The simple answer is that they—like most of us in this age of materialism—are looking for something more: something other than the material rewards of a successful career, the emotional satisfaction of a stable home life, and the spiritual trappings of going to church on Sunday. They are looking for a way to get in touch with themselves, with that part of them that they believe is more than just a combination of chemicals, neuroelectrical impulses, and human personality.

We live in an age of information. But we also live at a time when the mountains of facts we are garnering are beginning to point in some startling new directions. We stand at a crossroads in human thought, at a point where science is no longer seen as the answer to all our ills, whether personal or cultural. Science itself has shown that the materialistic model of the universe, in which everything is observable, measurable, and reducible to the simple equation of cause and effect, is no longer adequate to describe the world we live in. In the search for answers, we have found new ways of dealing with both our world and ourselves, and we have rediscovered traditional methods of healing and self-development. Increasingly, we in the West are putting a premium on ancient wisdom, especially that of the East. We are slowly learning that, though there are things we may not be able to explain, we can still benefit from them.

Psychic ability belongs in this category. It represents a form of knowing as old as civilization itself—whether Eastern or Western—and hearkens back to a time when people were more willing to trust their intuition and to look for answers from within, rather than look for proof from without. What all the psychics in this book have in common is that they are part of that ancient tradition, part of an unbroken line of healers who have been given a special gift.

When you decide to visit a psychic, be aware that you are choosing to explore aspects of yourself. What you learn during that exploration may yield profound insights into yourself and may even enable you to make some fundamental changes in the way you relate to your world. For most of us it is a journey that has no end. Consulting a psychic is involved most of all with change, and change is what characterizes life: cease to change and you cease to live. So, at its best, seeing a psychic is concerned with ensuring that your life continues to evolve in a productive, satisfying way.

The process of discovering new aspects of ourselves does not require that we all shed our skepticism and swallow every self-developmental craze that comes down the pike. What it does require is that we take our healthy search for information and extend it to whatever realms of the human experience seem likely to bear fruit. In order to make the most of that search, we need to know as much about the process as possible.

This book will furnish that information. The more you know about psychics and psychic phenomena, the more you will be able to get out of a psychic reading, whether it's your first time or your fifteenth. If you have never been to a psychic, you will want to know what to expect. You may not know, for instance, that there are many different kinds of psychics. Some go into trances and channel spirit guides. Others receive information psychically just by sitting and talking with you about your problems. Some have studied long and hard to develop their abilities, while others simply accept their gift at face value. Knowing the different forms that psychic ability takes will enable you to both enjoy and evaluate your experience more fully.

Even if you're a seasoned veteran when it comes to visiting psychics, it will be a great help if you know a little about the historical and theoretical sides of parapsychology. The formal scientific inquiry into psychic phenomena goes back more than a hundred years, from the early speculations of the famed psychologist William James to the recent psychic ex-

4

periments of astronaut Edgar Mitchell en route to the moon. Historical examples of psychic ability can be traced back to ancient Greece and include some of the world's best known philosophers and artists.

So that you'll have a context in which to put your experience with a psychic, this book will give you a basic understanding of what constitutes psychic ability as well as a look at some scientific theories that seek to explain "psi," as it is known. In addition, you will be able to get an appreciation for the rich and colorful role psychics have played throughout history as well as a small taste of the vast literature that has been compiled on psychical research.

For those who have not yet decided to visit a psychic, this book will clear up a host of misconceptions about what psychics are and what they do and, in the process, will remove the veil of superstition that continues to color public opinion of psychics. The fact that psychics are just human, with all the conflicts and considerations that presumes, will become clear through the process of letting them speak for themselves, Remember: psychics are people too. As in any group of professionals providing a service, there are those who are very gifted, those who are less talented, and those who are outright frauds. If you can define exactly what you hope to gain from visiting a psychic, you'll be more able to detect fact from fraud early on and make a wise, informed choice.

You may also be curious as to why other people visit psychics. It's possible that you have heard of people who consult their tarot card reader before buying a certain stock or ask their astrologer the best time to put their house up for sale. But you may not actually know anyone who has gone to a psychic either to work out emotional conflicts or as part of a deeper spiritual path. You may be shocked to learn that some psychotherapists actually refer their clients to psychics—or that some certified, accredited psychotherapists are psychics themselves!

By reading about others who have found psychic information to be of use to them, you will get a better understanding of what psychics can do and cannot do. Perhaps someone else's experience will ring a bell for you, and you'll decide that visiting a psychic could lead to some new understanding about yourself or about your life. Quite simply, it may just be an option you have not considered before, but, looked at in a new light, now makes sense to you.

The premise of this book is that a psychic consultation depends as much upon the client as upon the psychic and that the success of the reading is an outgrowth of the relationship between the two. Toward the end, there are chapters that deal not only with psychics, but with *you*, the client. After all, if you're paying $75 for a one-hour meeting and you've waited three months for it, you'll want to be sure that you are properly prepared. For example, what sort of questions should you ask? Are different kinds of psychics better suited to different problems? Will you be expected to respond to what the psychic tells you? The more of these questions you can answer, the fewer mysteries will await you, and the more *you* will be able to determine the shape of your psychic reading.

And you may be surprised to learn that the benefits of a reading don't end when the session is over. It's up to you to determine what you will do with the information you have gained. What is the point of spending your time and money if you're going to bury the tape of your reading in the bottom of a drawer and "wait and see" if the predictions come true? You'll want to reevaluate what you have been told and decide if it makes sense for you. Are there changes you should be making in your life that the psychic has identified? Are there aspects of your personality that you are unhappy with? Can you change the course of your own future if the psychic has predicted a specific outcome?

This book will help you find answers to all these questions. You should then be able to construct a framework in which to put psychic phenomena in general and your personal psychic reading in particular. Whether you are interested in visiting a psychic as part of a higher spiritual path or just out of curiosity, this type of analysis will better enable you to define exactly what it is you hope to gain from your experience, and to go out and realize those goals.

In doing so, you will discover that where the psychic leaves off, you must begin. You will find that information that can be gained psychically is little different from any other kind of information: that is, its value lies chiefly in what you do with it. If you take the time to answer the questions posed in this book—and to examine yourself—you'll be able to use the information you gain in the most positive and productive way possible. In that way, this book is really about you.

Those who possess psychic ability have the opportunity to use their gift not only for the benefit of those who come seeking help, but for the betterment of the world as a whole. But they cannot do it alone. The more we *all* know about human consciousness and its potential, the greater the chance that we will begin to see our world in a new light—as more than just the haphazard collision of the natural world and human events. If we choose to explore human potential in all its strange and wonderful guises, we may discover new ways of acquiring information and uncover whole new realms of knowledge in the process. The ability to create the opportunities to change our world is in our hands. Whether we take advantage of those opportunities is purely up to us.

HOW TO USE THIS BOOK

Because this book is written for readers at all levels of involvement with psychic work—from those who are just curious to those who have been frequenting psychic readings for years—it is organized to be used in a number of ways. To begin with, it can be read linearly—that is, from front to back—to give those who are new to psychic phenomena a thorough acquaintance with the subject. It can also be used as a reference work, enabling those who have some experience with the field—who may want to know more about a specific kind of psychic or an aspect of the psychic reading—to home in on a particular subject.

The first three chapters are best read in sequence, since taken together they will give the reader a thorough understanding of what psychic ability is, what its uses are, and the different forms it takes. Chapter One, in particular, will be of interest to the psychic aficionado and the beginner alike, since it examines some of the most recent thinking about the nature of psychic ability and how it fits in with psychology, physics, and theology—all of which are attempts to describe reality from different points of view. By considering the various contexts into which psychic phenomena can be placed, the reader will be better able to understand the mechanisms by which psychic readings operate and the value they have to offer.

Nevertheless, the temptation may be to turn directly to Chapter Four, which is the heart of the book. Here, each type of psychic reading is considered in detail—from what the actual process is like to the historical and philosophical context. The first section, "Clairvoyance, Precognition, and Psychometry," sets the pace for the remainder of the chapter, since it describes in detail a typical psychic reading, from the psychic's opening remarks to the client's final questions. All psychic readings follow this basic format, so it will be useful to become familiar with this entire section, even if you are interested in only one type of psychic reading.

Chapters Five and Six are the "hands-on" chapters. They are best read after you have covered the material presented in the first four. Presumably, by then you will have some sense of what type of psychic would best suit your needs, and you may possibly even have begun your search for an experienced professional. Be sure to read Chapter Five before you call for an appointment, however, since it deals not only with how to prepare yourself for a psychic reading, but also gives advice on how to book your appointment and what to expect from your initial telephone call to your chosen psychic.

Finally, a note about Appendix B, which includes a list of the psychics who are quoted in this book. This list is not provided as a directory of psychic services, but as another tool for the curious reader who wants to know more about the field in general. It is not the intention of this book to recommend particular psychics above others or to create some sort of "star" system among people who work in the field. The psychics quoted here were selected, not for the quality of their readings, but for the quality of their insight. Most of them, having thought long and hard about the work they do, are valuable resources for the interested researcher.

The names of clients—those people who have visited psychics and shared their experiences—have been changed to protect their privacy.

CHAPTER ONE

What Is A Psychic?

Scientific and Theological Foundations for Psi

The word "psychic" invariably carries with it negative connotations. Images come to mind of a gnarled old fortune-teller poring over a tattered deck of tarot cards or of the traveling medicine man in *The Wizard of Oz*, rummaging through Dorothy's handbag as he pretends to read a crystal ball.

Although there is some justification for such images, this view is, for the most part, outdated and limited to the storefront readers who prey on people's fears and curiosity. The fact is that the nature of psychic work has changed considerably in the last decade or so, and in contrast to the stereotypical psychic trappings of séances, ghosts, and mediums, we now have spiritual awakening groups, past-life regressions, and trance channelers.

But it is not just the work that has changed. The psychics themselves are of a different breed today. The reader of the eighties has little in common with her sister of 50 years ago, when the stigma of being psychic meant being branded as at best "different" and at worst mentally unbalanced. Today psychics are seen as people who possess highly developed intuitive abilities—abilities that we all have to one degree or another. Those who practice professionally have chosen to use their skills to help others deal with the uncertainty and difficulties that life entails. This is a far cry from entertaining a Victorian audience with displays of mind reading and attempts to conjure up apparitions from the dead.

Nevertheless, the stigma remains. "Psychic" is still used to refer to anything and everything under the occult sun (or perhaps I should say moon). Perhaps it is for this reason that scientists studying the field of parapsychology prefer the term "psi" to describe paranormal abilities. Such phenomena can include anything from "simple" mind reading and predicting the future to the more metaphysical pursuits of contacting dead spirits and "seeing" people's past lives. We will deal with the different types of psychics in a later chapter, but for now we can define psi as the ability to access information about the past, present, or future in a way that cannot be explained using the known laws of nature.

Parapsychology has existed as a separate discipline since the 1920s, when two psychologists, J.B. Rhine and his wife, Louisa, established the first parapsychology laboratory at Duke University. (Parapsychology was recognized as a component science by the American Association for the Advancement of Science in 1969.) But the formal scientific inquiry into paranormal events goes back more than a century to the establishment of the Society for Psychical Research, in London in 1882. Despite this long and distinguished history, however, research into psychic ability has been unable to answer most of the questions surrounding it. Although experiments conducted under strict scientific controls have established that psi does exist, the question of how it works, and why certain people seem to possess a greater degree of psi than others, continues to baffle parapsychologists.

We still do not know why some people seem to exhibit psi from the time they are born, while others must study for years to develop their skills. Most psychics, and many researchers, believe that everyone possesses psychic ability at least to some extent. Some even claim that psi can be learned by anyone. Work at California's Stanford Research Institute, for instance, has demonstrated that subjects trained in "remote viewing" were able to describe the whereabouts of an unidentified person at an undisclosed location with 80-percent accuracy. These subjects included people who had never experienced any psychic events whatsoever. Similarly, parapsychology pioneer Lawrence LeShan showed more than 20 years ago that anyone could be trained to perform psychic healing on another person.

Another puzzling aspect of psi is that it is not always the result of willful effort. Many people experience precognitive dreams, see apparitions, and hear voices without trying to or even wanting to. Short of such melodramatic instances, however, most of us have experienced minor incidents that seem to involve psi. How many times have you simply "known" that someone was going to call just as the phone rang? Or had a "hunch" about something that proved to be correct? Many psychologists now believe that déjà vu, the feeling of having been in a particular situation before despite knowledge to the contrary, is a type of psychic phenomenon.

In fact, it seems that paranormal experiences are a lot more widespread than anyone previously thought. According to a recent poll conducted by sociologist Andrew Greeley and the University of Chicago's National Opinion Research Council, 67 percent of those questioned reported having "experienced ESP." Perhaps more surprising is the fact that 42 percent of the adults polled in the study stated that they had "had contact with the dead." This type of evidence indicates that although researchers have difficulty observing paranormal events in the laboratory setting, they do, in fact, occur, and not just to professional psychics or mediums.

These figures are also significant because they show that people are finally willing to come forward and admit to having experienced things that cannot be scientifically explained. In the West, at least, there has always been a stigma attached to anything beyond the reach of scientific explanation, and the line between mysticism and insanity has always been drawn as a very thin one. But as more people report their unusual experiences, scientists will be able to take their investigations out of the sterile environment of the laboratory and into the field of human experience.

Thanks to studying case histories gleaned from individuals who wouldn't normally consider themselves psychic, it is becoming apparent that psychic phenomena do not merely represent a sixth sense. Rather, psi seems to belong to a continuum of altered states of consciousness, which ranges from simple intuition on one end to extreme states of mystical awareness on the other. This means that when you have a "gut feeling" about something, or go with a "hunch," you are doing the same thing a psychic does when she gives a reading. It is simply that the psychic has developed her intuition to a much greater degree and has learned to interpret her "feelings" in a clearer and more specific way.

Similarly, when a mystic speaks about having experienced "the oneness of all things," he is referring to a level of knowing where the boundaries of the self have been eliminated, enabling him to know reality from the point of view of others outside himself. This is perhaps why many Eastern adepts, such as Buddhist and Hindu monks, following years of meditation or yoga, reportedly can perform paranormal feats in the same way psychics can.

What links all these different degrees of psychic awareness has to do both with the structure of the human brain and the nature of human consciousness. Basically, scientists now know that there are two halves, or hemispheres, to the human brain, and that these two hemispheres not only handle different neurological functions but, in fact, process information differently. The left brain is the logical, analytical side—the "computer" part of the brain, so to speak. The right brain is the intuitive, creative side—the psychic component. Thus, the left brain processes information in a linear way—in terms of cause and effect, deductive reasoning, and what are essentially the rules of logic. The right brain processes information holistically—in terms of inductive reasoning, drawing conclusions from the whole, and seeing the relationships between parts. Generally, women are thought to be more right-brain oriented, while men are left-brain dependent. This may account for the expression "women's intuition," and may partially explain why most psychics are women.

In conjunction with these neurological findings about the nature of the brain, psychologists are exploring altered states of consciousness. Although the terminology may conjure up memories of Timothy Leary and his experiments with LSD, most current work in this area deals with non-drug-induced states of mind: meditation, dream states, mystical experiences, and the connection between mind and body, for example.

Research into different states of consciousness has identified a particular brain-wave pattern that exists between the states of wakefulness and sleeping. Known as the alpha state, it is characterized as "restful awareness" and seems to be a purely right-brain function. Although an alpha state can be induced through simple meditation techniques, most of us are familiar with it as that moment just before falling asleep or immediately upon waking up, when we are semiconscious and in an almost dreamlike state.

One effect of the alpha state is the ability to control bodily functions that were previously thought to be autonomous, through the process of biofeedback. Metabolic functions such as heartbeat, blood pressure, and skin temperature are among those that can be altered by a subject who is in an alpha state. Indian yogis have been famous for this ability for centuries, but it is only recently that science has been able to find a mechanism to explain such "mystical" feats. This is what researchers such as Harvard cardiologist Herbert Benson have termed "the relaxation response."

Another aspect of the alpha state seems to be the ability to access certain kinds of information. Psychologists have known the value of hypnosis for years, and Sigmund Freud used it extensively to enable his patients to recall distant memories hidden in the subconscious. It now seems as though hypnosis may be nothing more than a way of inducing an alpha state, with the help of a therapist's directions for navigating the inner recesses of the mind.

Some psychologists have gone beyond the boundaries of a single lifetime and used hypnosis to aid patients in recalling memories from previous lifetimes. Whether these people are actually recalling previous incarnations or simply exploring some not yet understood aspect of the subconscious does not lessen the effectiveness of this treatment. It should also be made clear that these "regression" psychologists do not consider this work to be "psychic," or beyond the scope of science. To them, it is merely an effective technique for eliminating blocks to psychological health.

In any case, it seems apparent from this research that the alpha state is one in which the right brain takes over from the left, and where information that was unintelligible to the analytic portion of the mind now flows more freely. Many psychics bring themselves into an alpha state before they are able to receive information about a subject.

A new branch of psychology, known as transpersonal psychology, has grown up around these discoveries. During transpersonal therapy a person is encouraged to access information from his right brain, either through meditation, hypnosis, or even spiritual practice. The insights that result are couched in symbolic language—either visual images or dreamlike experiences. This seems to be the "code" of the right brain, which does not use language (the province of the left brain) as we understand it. This is also the way in which most psychics receive their information and why the accuracy of their readings depends not only upon their psychic ability but also upon how well they interpret the symbolic impressions they receive from the right brain.

Many psychologists look to the work of Carl Jung for an explanation of this right-brain symbology. Jung was extremely interested in psychic phenomena and refused, as he put it, "to commit the fashionable stupidity of regarding everything I cannot explain as a fraud." He postulated the existence of a "collective unconscious," which he described as a level of the mind where we all share common information. According to Jung, this information takes the form of symbols, or "archetypes," which are drawn from mythology and religion. By interpreting these symbols in the correct way, much can be learned about the subconscious mind. Moreover, the collective unconscious provides a mechanism by which one person (e.g., a psychic) can acquire information about another.

Interestingly, some psychics speak about the "Akashic records," which are thought to include all knowledge of the world—past, present, and future. According to them, this "cosmic database" of information exists on a purely spiritual plane and is the mechanism by which spirit guides can find out things about our lives. Some psychics also claim to be able to access information from this database directly, through a process of meditation or visualization. The parallels between the Akashic records and Jung's collective unconscious cannot be overlooked, especially since both seem to be reached through processes involving the right hemisphere of the brain.

If it is true that we all share in some kind of gigantic pool of knowledge at least at some level, why is it that we are not constantly bombarded with information about our destinies and those of others around us? Some parapsychologists have proposed the idea of the mind as a filter. Instead of regarding a psychic insight as a unique event in the realm of perception, let us take the opposite tack and assume that we are constantly being bombarded with psychic information and that our minds have simply learned to tune out all but a very narrow band of frequencies, thereby making it possible for us to function. As Arthur Koestler has pointed out, the "filter theory" follows logically from what we know about ordinary sense perception:

> Our sense organs are like narrow slits which admit only a very narrow frequency-range of electromagnetic and sound waves. But even the amount that does get in through these narrow slits is too much. . . . Thus the nervous system, and above all the brain, functions as a hierarchy of filtering and classifying devices which eliminate a large proportion of the sensory input as irrelevant "noise," and process the relevant information into manageable shape before it is presented to consciousness. . . .[1]

Just as dogs hear frequencies much higher than the human ear can detect, birds see objects in much finer detail, and bats use a form of radar to navigate, so we, too, have learned to perceive our world using very specific parameters of sensation. Those people we label psychic may simply be detecting a wider range of information than is available to the majority of us. And at those moments when the rest of us suddenly get a flash of psychic insight, our own filters may actually be allowing a particularly strong stimulus into our consciousness. This may be why many instances of psi involve emotionally powerful events—the mother who suddenly "knows" her child is in danger, for instance, or the inexplicable feeling of uneasiness that makes us turn around when someone behind us is perceived as threatening.

Again, Jung offers some insight into this reasoning. He coined the term "synchronicity" to describe events that seem to be causally related but cannot be attributed to any known mechanism of cause and effect. For example, the mother seems to know her child is in danger as a direct result of the child's personal experience, and yet there is no apparent means by which the child's situation has been communicated to the mother. According to Jung, such emotionally powerful events stimulate certain ingrained patterns of behavior as a result of the archetypes. Since these archetypes are common to all of us, communication can then take place on the level of the collective unconscious, resulting in a synchronistic—or psychic—event.

Parapsychology deals with those aspects of the human mind that may account for psi. Researchers are just beginning to scratch the surface in charting the mechanisms by which psychic ability works. Even if they should succeed in locating a region of the brain that controls intuitive knowledge, or manage to construct a workable model to explain the accessing of psychic information, the question would remain as to how that information could travel from one person to another using no known means of transmission. For answers to this difficult question, we have to turn to the physicists.

In the same way that parapsychology grew out of the attempt to account for psi within the categories of existing psychological thought, so, too, has another new discipline appeared that seeks to put psi into the framework of contemporary physics—it is known as paraphysics. Most of the work done in this area is so technically oriented it is almost unintelligible to the layperson, especially since it must necessarily cross the borders of psychology, neurology, biochemistry, and electromagnetics. Consequently, it lies beyond the scope of this book. Suffice it to say that in spite of promising research in the area of electromagnetic fields, most physicists believe that "a completely new framework in physics" will be necessary to fully understand the mechanisms of psychic phenomena.[2] That framework has begun to emerge from what is perhaps the most exciting search for the laws of nature since the time of Isaac Newton—quantum physics.

Quantum, or subatomic, physics—the study of matter and energy below the level of the atom—grew out of Albert Einstein's work in the first few decades of this century. By 1927, the term was being used to describe a physics that was so different from the classical physics of Newton that it defied common sense. Perhaps for this reason, and because it cannot be fully understood without the use of mathematical equations, most people are unaware of the shattering implications of this "new" physics—despite the fact that it is more than half a century old.

It is perhaps ironic that the very people who are most likely to reject psi as "unscientific"— physicists—are the same ones who are doing the most to generate explanations for the paranormal. Physicists themselves are seeking a way in which to link all physical phenomena in the universe, which they call a Grand Unified Field Theory—in short, one single law of physics that will encompass all the known laws of nature. In doing so they have come up with some startling conclusions about the nature of the universe and our place in it. Although the equations they use describe a reality that exists either on a subatomic or intergalactic level and deal with matter at exceedingly high velocities and temperatures, their descriptions come very close to offering perhaps the best explanations for paranormal phenomena available.

Very simply—and no one but a physicist could begin to understand these theories on more than a very simple level— physicists are now talking about a universe that is made up of "fields" of energy, in which all matter is interrelated. Whereas we once conceived of matter as being made up of particles, such as electrons, protons, and neutrons, we now know that matter is simply another form of energy and that the world as we know it is the product of interacting fields. More than that, the energy that makes up the "stuff" of the universe seems to be able to communicate across great distances of space and perhaps even time. And because we ourselves are part of that energy, we are intimately bound up with the rest of the universe as well, on a very profound and significant level.

Perhaps the leading theoretician in this area is the physicist David Bohm. Bohm likens the structure of the universe to that of a hologram, which most of us are familiar with as a three-dimensional image. (You may have one on a credit card.) What is unique about a hologram, however, is that each part contains elements of the whole. In other words, if you cut a hologram into two pieces, rather than ending up with two halves of the whole image, you end up with two smaller, but complete, images. In Bohm's model of reality, every element of the entire universe, including ourselves, is somehow represented in each part of the whole, no matter how small or how large.[3]

If this model of the world proves to be true, it is a small step to the possibility that knowledge about someone or something could be gained psychically simply by "reading" the encoded holographic information present in matter itself. And since Bohm's model is not limited by space or time, it follows that information about a distant point in time or a remote location in space could be accessed as easily as an event occurring here and now.

There are those who would argue that the laws of quantum physics are only applicable on a subatomic level, and that the world we live in is clearly made up of concrete, independent bits of matter that we can interact with according to the laws of Newton. But psychic events may, in fact, be the very evidence we have been looking for that Newton's laws do not fully describe reality on the macroscopic level, and it may simply be because psi does not fit those laws that it has been rejected out of hand throughout history. Now that we have the beginnings of some new ideas about physics that might begin to explain psychic phenomena, we should avoid further rationalizations and use these insights in our search for understanding. As Arthur Koestler put it:

> The odour of the alchemist's kitchen is replaced by the smell of quark in the laboratory. The rapprochement between the conceptual world of parapsychology and that of modern physics is an important step towards the demolition of the greatest superstition of our age—the materialistic clockwork universe of early nineteenth-century physics.[4]

It should be obvious by now that quantum physics sounds more like metaphysics than the classical physics of Isaac Newton. Part of our trouble in understanding these concepts—and the evidence supplied by paranormal phenomena—is that our whole way of conceptualizing our world grows out of a strong philosophical tradition, one begun by Aristotle and Plato several thousand years ago and developed into a comprehensive world view by the philosophers of the Enlightenment in the eighteenth century.

Nineteenth-century science was an attempt to describe reality according to that world view, and any phenomenon of nature that did not fit comfortably into that scheme was rejected as unreal. This change in thinking was particularly ironic since metaphysics, which is the branch of philosophy that deals with non-material, spiritual causes, was an accepted branch of science in its own right for most of our history. Our difficulty in coming to terms with the implications of the new physics is merely the result of the limitations imposed upon us by this nineteenth-century shift in thought. In probing the nature of reality itself, the new physics is finally breaking the bonds of Western philosophical thought and searching for new categories to describe previously unexplainable phenomena.

Religion, on the other hand, has always had categories in which to place metaphysical concepts and so did not have to slough off the unexplainable as unreal. By looking at religion from a historical and philosophical viewpoint, we will see some ways in which society has been able to deal with psychic phenomena.

The line between spirituality and spiritualism has always been thin; for many psychics, it does not exist. Thus much that was once considered mystical in a religious sense would now be considered paranormal in a scientific sense. Ever since the ancient Greeks divided the human being into flesh and spirit, it followed that whatever did not belong to the realm of the flesh must, in fact, belong to the realm of the spirit. As a result psychic phenomena learned to cloak itself in the garb of religious experience.

It is very probable that much of what is described in the ancient scriptures as miracles or prophecy is actually psychic ability. Certainly the Bible makes no bones about describing precognitive dreams, foretelling the future, and contacting the dead. Although in some cases these abilities are attributed to the direct intervention of God, in others they are not. Today most religion scholars believe that even the miracles worked by Jesus may have been, at least in some part, the result of his own paranormal abilities resulting from a profound level of spiritual development.

Probably the clearest examples of psychic ability are those cases of biblical prophecy recorded in the Old Testament. In spite of the fact that the scriptures warn against consulting 'soothsayers, enchanters, or sorcerers," and "resorting to ghosts or familiar spirits," there are many examples of such psychic activity taking place. It may be that these injunctions were intended not so much to proscribe against all psychics but only against those who lacked a certain level of spiritual development. One of the most vivid psychic consultations on record appears in the Book of Samuel, when King Saul visits a medium, who in turn conjures up the dead spirit of the prophet Samuel so that Saul can ask his advice.

Others, such as Joseph, received premonitions in the form of dreams; he foresaw his own worldly success and later used his interpretations of the Egyptian pharaoh's dreams to develop a successful economic plan for that country. A good argument can be made that these instances of precognition—as well as most Old Testament prophecies—may have been more the result of individual psi than divine revelation, mainly because they appeared in cryptic symbols, which, as we have seen, are the language of the right brain, or intuitive self. Had God been transmitting information directly to the prophets, it seems likely that it would have been in a clearer form, such as the "voice" that the patriarchs (Abraham, Isaac, and Jacob) and the prophets (Moses, Isaiah, et al.) frequently heard.

We see similar evidence of psychic ability in the New Testament, which records a number of Jesus' miracles, ranging from multiplying the loaves and fishes to raising the dead. Again it is not exactly clear how much of his ability was the result of psi and how much was divinely inspired. The fact that he did perform such miracles is likely, though, because none of the sources of that time—even those that sought to discredit him—refutes that fact. It is also interesting to note that the apostles did not see Jesus' miracle-working as proof of his divinity; they accepted the miracles as part of their normal world view.[5]

The Eastern spiritual traditions, possibly because of their more mystical orientation, have always exhibited elements of the paranormal. As we mentioned earlier, Hindu yogis have long been known for their seemingly superhuman abilities, such as remaining motionless in meditation for days at a time and causing material objects to appear out of thin air. These abilities are called *siddhis* and are the by-product of spiritual development, often resulting from the practice of yoga. Unlike hatha yoga, with which most Westerners are familiar and which is a process of developing the body, such deeper forms of yoga as raja or kundalini are devoted to stilling the mind, focusing the concentration, and opening up the pathways of spiritual energy. Basically yoga is an advanced form of meditation and therefore yields similar results. But unlike hypnosis or meditation, the goals go far beyond merely accessing intuitive, right-brain information or reducing physiological symptoms of stress.

The word "yoga" itself means "the union of the individual self with the supreme self," and the end point is *samadhi*, a superconscious state of mind in which the true nature of reality becomes apparent. The Hindus believe that the world we live in and experience with our reason and senses (left-brain faculties) is made up of *Maya*, or illusion, and that it is only through a process of spiritual discipline that we can experience *Brahma*, the real world. Despite the fact that samadhi implies the complete transcendence of the ego, it shares many characteristics with psychic ability as we know it. As one Hindu swami described it, "There is a vast area outside reason, which is the realm of the superconsciousness and which can be known only by a higher faculty than reason, called *intuition, inspiration, or direct or immediate perception.*"[6] (Italics added.) It would be difficult to distinguish this definition from psi.

Jung, who was quite interested in yoga, albeit from a psychological viewpoint, said much the same thing, calling yoga "the perfect and appropriate method of fusing body and mind together. . . . This unity creates a psychological disposition which makes possible intuitions that transcend consciousness."

Once the mind is calmed, through the process of yoga or meditation, it not only begins to hear the inner, intuitive self, but, according to Hindu teaching, also the thoughts of others. Thus telepathy becomes possible: "All thoughts vibrate eternally in the cosmos. By deep concentration a master is able to detect the thoughts of any man, living or dead. Thoughts are universally, not individually rooted; a truth cannot be created but only perceived."[7] Perhaps it should come as no surprise that this sounds like Jung's collective unconscious.

In addition the Hindu system of thought describes an "energy body" that envelops the human being and that is made up of energy centers, called *chakras*. There are seven major chakras, which correspond to the endocrine system of the physical body, as well as a number of minor ones. Many psychics claim to actually be able to see these chakras, which radiate with different colors of light and vary in intensity depending upon the physical and emotional health of the person. Psychic healings are based on the theory that balancing the different energies of these chakras will restore one's health.[8]

The complete energy body that exists within and throughout the human organism is known in the Hindu system of thought as the astral body. Psychics describe this as a person's "aura," and, like the chakras themselves, it fluctuates in color and intensity depending upon one's emotions and physical health. According to Hindu thought, it is the astral body that survives death and which later joins with a new physical body through the process of reincarnation. It follows that in out-of-body experiences (astral projection) or cases of bilocation (appearing in two places at once), it would be the astral body that journeys beyond the confines of the physical self. Both Hindus and psychics believe that our astral selves regularly leave our physical bodies while we sleep.

The process of death and reincarnation is governed by the Hindu law of karma. Karma is the organizing principle by which one lifetime is connected to another. Although many Westerners interpret this idea to mean that if you do good deeds in one life you will come back better off in your next life and vice versa, this is a simplistic view based mostly on the purely Western notion of spiritual reward and punish-

33

ment. Although this may be a *consequence* of a particular individual's karma, in general the process is much more complex.

For our purposes, we can compare karma to the quantum physics concept of interrelatedness. Just as all matter and energy are interrelated on a fundamental level, so is every action we take, every thought we think, and every emotion we feel—all of which are forms of energy—related to the rest of creation in a profound and fundamental way. Karma is telling us that in the same way a physical event sends out signals through waves and fields into the fabric of matter-energy, so do our lives send out signals that have lasting effects, not just on the world around us but in lives to come.

Many psychics today frequently speak about karma. They see their role, in part, as the ability to psychically perceive the effects of one's past lives, either directly or intuitively, in an effort to give guidance for this life. Past-life regressionists go further and attempt to directly access memories of previous incarnations in order to remove blocks that may have been set in motion long before one was born into the present existence.

It is clear that there is a great deal of variation in the quality and significance of psychic experience and that much of what was previously thought to be either an illusion or the product of mystically-induced hallucination may actually come under the heading of psychic phenomena. In taking into account both the scientific and religious context into which psi fits, we see a continuum that ranges from the relatively mundane to the positively cosmic. At one end we have phenomena such as telephathy, in which information is transferred according to laws of physics we simply have not yet discovered. At the other end we have reports of abilities such as astral projection (leaving the body to travel to a distant location) and dematerialization (vanishing into thin air), which are considered the product of years of rigorous spiritual discipline.

We are not yet at a point in our studies of psychic events where we can hope to discover the true nature of any of these phenomena. Rather we can begin to open up our inquiries to the full range of human experience as it is recorded in history and as it is presented to us every day and examine it in the light of modern scientific thought and traditional spiritual truths. Perhaps in this way we will find that psychic phenomena have much to offer the continuing dialogue between science and religion and the evolution of human thought in general.

The purpose of this chapter has not been to furnish "proof" of psychic phenomena in scientific terms or to construct an apologetic in religious terms. The purpose has been to create an atmosphere of openness, based on the full capabilities of the human mind— whether rational *or* spiritual. If we take our cue from the new physics and cease trying to reduce everything to its smallest parts, we may find that a context

already exists in which to put paranormal occurrences, even though we might not yet understand the
mechanism by which they operate. It may simply be
that we can't see the forest for the trees. If we take
the time to step back and examine the whole picture,
we may find that we are using too small a lens for too
large a landscape.

CHAPTER TWO

How To Use A Psychic

The reasons people go to psychics are as diverse as the psychics themselves. As we have seen, the world of psychic ability covers a broad spectrum of intention and intensity. On the one end, there is the corner fortune-teller, who may or may not be able to tell you what stock to buy. On the other end is the psychically skilled "metaphysician," who sees her role as that of a spiritual counselor and who will not be as interested in telling your fortune as in telling you how you can take a greater responsibility for your life.

Your own reason for visiting a psychic may not be so well defined. If you have never visited a psychic before, your chief motivation will most probably be curiosity. It is difficult to pick up a newspaper or turn on the television these days without seeing something about psychics, and it's likely that you've wondered who these people are and what they actually do. The best way of finding out is to visit one yourself.

If You Are Curious

If you live in a metropolitan area, there's a good chance that you know someone who has had a psychic reading—perhaps you even have a close friend who has been urging you to go. You may have listened to a tape of your friend's reading, agreed that one or two pieces of insight could not have been the result of sheer guessing, and had your curiosity piqued. Yet you still wonder whether it's worth $50 just to satisfy that curiosity.

Or your friend may have gained profound insight into himself as a result of his psychic reading. You may have witnessed a real change in a person you have known well and wondered what actually went on at the reading. Sharon, a New York attorney, listened to the tape of a friend who had visited an astrologer:

> I found a lot of what was on that tape to be very true and also sort of inspiring, subconsciously. It affected me deeply because my friend is the same sign as me, and there were certain similarities. She had a lot of insights into Andrea's character and nailed some pitfalls right on the head. She also gave her a lot of guidance and encouragement. At Andrea's urging, and after listening to her tape, I decided it would be a good thing to do.

You, on the other hand, may not be the same sign as your friend or share any personality aspects at all. As a result you may not be so sure that a psychic has anything to offer you. But you still may be curious.

Use your curiosity as a starting point for your own

inquiry into psychics. Begin by asking your friend what she feels she got out of her reading and why she thinks it would be valuable for you to go. Something she says may strike a chord in you and may just be the extra little push you need. Most people don't decide to visit a psychic purely out of curiosity. Eventually an issue comes up in their lives that they need some guidance with. Whether that guidance takes the shape of just wanting to know the future outcome of a situation or a desire to examine more intimate aspects of their own feelings, it usually provides the spark to pick up the phone and make an appointment.

Examine your own life and see if there isn't a particular issue you've been having trouble resolving— something that would make a good "test case," perhaps. The two major ones are, of course, career and relationships, and the chances are good that one of these areas of your life would benefit from consulting a third party. Even if you are just curious, though, you never know where your reading may lead.

It is interesting that many of us will walk around wondering about psychics for some time and then suddenly get the urge to go and see one. Most psychics will tell you that if you decided to come for a reading, no matter how arbitrarily you think you arrived at the decision, it means that the time is right for you to come and to receive some inner guidance. But if curiosity does nothing but serve to get you in the door, you will have begun your inquiry into the value of psychic information.

Solving Crimes

Psychic ability takes many forms, and the nature of that ability will determine what kind of situations it can be applied to. The simplest form of psi is probably clairvoyance, which is the ability to "see" things or events that are not within the immediate vicinity of the psychic. This is may be the most usable of psychic skills, since it enables the psychic to access information about the world as it is now (as opposed to past lives or future predictions).

Clairvoyance has been used in almost every aspect of human endeavor. One area that has received a great deal of attention is criminology. Various police departments around the world have used psychics at different times to help them solve crimes. Just as often, however, a psychic will simply have a spontaneous vision of some wrongdoing, and may not know exactly where it is taking place or who is involved. Although in many such cases crimes have actually been prevented, a lot of times the outcome is not so happy either for the potential victim or the psychic herself.

For example, one psychic who does a radio show on Long Island responded to a caller's questions by describing a murder that had taken place. She assumed the case had been solved. Later that night, both she and the radio show host received threats at their homes. In another case, a woman came to a psychic to ask about her son. The psychic saw several murders taking place and realized that the woman's son was somehow implicated. When she confronted the client, the woman admitted she was there to use the psychic to help her get her son off the hook.

Contrary to popular opinion, most psychics are not clamoring to work with the police in solving crimes. Yvonne Ciardullo is a Denver-based psychic reader who has her own radio talk show and frequently works with the local police. She is quick to point out, however, that she never contacts the police—they call her. She will only consent to help them if it is understood that there will be no publicity and sensationalization of the work. The police are only too happy to comply, since they are not anxious to have the public know they are using psychics. As Ciardullo explains:

> Sure, they're skeptical. But I've worked with a lot of law enforcement agencies. And there are detectives whom I work with who trust me—*they* call *me*. As long as it doesn't get into all the sensationalism and glamour, it's okay. I've found children who were lost or runaways, I've worked with homicide, I've worked with the bomb squad in the Denver area. And they call me, I don't call them, so I must be doing something right.

The relationship between psychics and police is not always so cordial, however. Several years ago, for instance, a California psychic began seeing visions of a woman's body lying abandoned in a field. Eventually she was able to focus on the general location and found the body in an open field just outside town. When she brought the police to the scene of the crime, they arrested her, assuming she could not have known about it unless she did it herself. She spent several days in jail before the real murderer was found and has subsequently won a considerable lawsuit against the police department.

Locating Missing People

Less sensational, but generally more successful, are those cases involving missing persons, especially children who have disappeared. Often private citizens will contact psychics directly in order to receive help in locating someone whom the police are unable to find, and there are psychics who actually specialize in this kind of work. Yvonne Ciardullo recalls a case in which she was approached by a family to locate a missing girl:

> I became really involved with finding this girl, because I have a son, and I know what that's like. I was so sensitive; I went and I "became" that girl. But it was the first and last time I would ever do that. It was very scary. It was not a possession, but it was my first experience with actually "being" the individual. I was climbing a mountain, and [I saw that] she was decapitated and on the other side of the mountain. So I said I'll never do that again. That was too traumatic for me. It took me about 72 hours to get my own self back, and a long, long time to get over it. So now, if they call—if someone's missing or they ask me a question—if I don't get it right away, I do not get involved.

Divining For Water or Oil

Another kind of clairvoyance, which was once fairly commonplace but which is not found very often today, is divining for water or oil. Using certain branches from a tree, a skilled diviner will be called in to determine the exact location of an underground spring in order to dig a well. The British army supposedly used diviners in North Africa in World War II in order to locate water in the desert. More recently some large oil companies have hired professional diviners to pinpoint the location of substantial oil deposits in order to minimize their risks in digging a new well.

But not all psychic ability of this kind is so lucrative. Often it is a simple matter of making everyday life a little easier. There is the case of a particular spiritual community in upstate New York where many psychically gifted people live and work. Many of these people "channel" spirit guides who give them information. As one psychic recalls:

> Up at the center, they were having trouble with the septic system, and they couldn't find what they were looking for under the ground. So someone said, "Well, ask Frank to go to his channel." And this man just went to his channel, walked out into the back parking lot and stood in a certain place and said, "Well, here's your problem."

Contacting the Dead

Another pragmatic, although somewhat farther-out, use for psychic ability is to contact the dead. Although the practice of "mediumship" was a lot more widespread during the heyday of Spiritualism, from the late nineteenth into the early twentieth century, many psychics still maintain that they can contact dead friends and relatives.

Today the term medium has been replaced by the word "channel," "channeler," or "trance channeler," which implies the ability on the part of the psychic to access not only the spirits of those who may have been close to the client, but all forms of spiritual energy, including "spirit guides," "guardian angels," the spirits of great religious leaders such as Jesus and Buddha (not to mention those of rock stars and political leaders), beings from other planets, and even, in some cases, animals such as whales and dolphins.

Many people have found satisfaction in visiting a psychic in order to contact a friend or relative who may have died suddenly or to whom the person did not have a chance to say good-bye. In most cases, you won't be able to see or hear the spirit of your loved one directly but will have to rely on the perceptions of the channeler to do that for you. Nevertheless many people have found this to be an effective emotional release and a way to handle unfinished emotional business.

Suzanne Kluss, a trance channeler in Sedona, Arizona, originally went to a psychic before she herself began channeling in order to contact her father, who had died suddenly at a relatively young age. As she recalls:

I had never been to a psychic until my father died. It was very traumatic for me, because I was very close to him and he died suddenly. I really felt like I wanted to get in touch with him. So I went to this woman who went into a trance. [My father] didn't actually talk through her, but she talked with him, and relayed how he was feeling at that time. And she gave me messages for other members of my family, which I relayed to them. They were a little taken aback at the perceptiveness of what Daddy had passed along. She amazed me because she tapped into a lot of the dynamics within my family that she could not have known about and about how my father probably would have felt. And it was very comforting to me. I never went back to her, but that sort of catapulted me into trying to find out what was going on, and it lent a certain validity for me to the whole realm of psychic phenomena.

Skeptics have argued that psychics who contact the dead may not actually be communicating with spirit entities as much as they are reading the thoughts and memories a person has about a particular friend or a close relative who has died. The fact remains that, in some cases, the information communicated was totally unknown to the recipient and was later independently verified. Whether the phenomenon of channeling is proof of life after death or not, however, it does seem to serve a purpose for the person who is still living and who desires to make one last connection with someone who had played a significant role in his life.

Similarly, when it comes to contacting the spirits of famous historical figures, whether actual contact is being made may be less important than the message that is being given. If a channeler delivers a message from Jesus that we should all love one another, is it any less useful than if Jesus himself had repeated his words of 2,000 years ago? And indeed, many people who are involved in channeling, whether they are channelers themselves or the recipients of their messages, find a great deal of inspiration in much of what is communicated. For many people who have lost interest in organized religion, such experiences often give them a new context for their belief in some kind of divine force. As one man, a frequent channeler-visitor, recalls:

They confirmed my original feeling that there's lots of big stuff out there. . . . It brought me back into becoming a Christian—I do believe in Christ and that Christ was here and that he was a being who was highly evolved. I had thrown away a lot of that stuff when I was younger, thinking it was all bull. I was agnostic for a number of years. Now I believe in [Jesus Christ] as one of the ascended spirits who were on earth and spent time here helping us out. Exploring what psychics have to offer has also given me a feeling of hopefulness, as opposed to helplessness—that you can ask for help and it is given.

Rather than turning people off to the established religions, psychic information often helps them rediscover the original principles and values upon which those religions were based. For others, it offers an opportunity to explore new spiritual paths, and a renewed desire to work on making themselves more whole and on making the world around them a better place to be.

Predicting the Future

What psychics are perhaps most famous for, besides contacting the dead, is their ability to foretell the future. Known as precognition, the ability to predict is not only one of the few manifestations of psi that is testable in the laboratory, but is also one that has the greatest mass appeal. There is almost no one who has not heard of Jeane Dixon, for instance, mainly because she has made some very accurate predictions during the course of her career. And even today, bookstore shelves are filled with new editions of the predictions of Nostradamus, the sixteenth-century French physician who predicted everything from the French Revolution to the outbreak of World War I.

Although such predictions can be entertaining, and for many people proof of genuine psychic ability, in actuality they make up a very small part of most psychic readings. The problem with using precognition as proof of anything is, of course, that you have to wait until the predictions come true. By then, the psychic has cashed your check, and your original reasons for going may have faded into distant memory. This is not to say that there is no value to learning the outcome of future events (as we shall see later), but prediction *alone* is of little more use than a simple entertainment. Carl, a 41-year-old art director at a major advertising agency, made several visits to a card reader who gave him a number of predictions, none of which came true. As he describes it, it was similar to reading a horoscope in the newspaper. In hindsight, however, he takes a more philosophical view of the process:

> I think she predicted what I wanted to happen. It was as though she were reading my mind, and I was doing my wishful thinking, so she was picking up on things that I wanted to happen. The idea of telling the future is something that I really don't buy into—there are too many variables. We always have free choice in everything that happens—my free choice, someone else's free choice. It's like a chain, and one link depends upon the next.
>
> Maybe there's a fundamental law that says they can't [predict the future]. Otherwise, they would tell us what was going to happen, and we'd all just sit back and let it happen. It would stop mankind from doing anything. So I think there's a flaw in the whole idea [of prediction].

The real value of learning about the future is putting it into the context of the present. Therefore, most psychics will tell you more about yourself as you are now than as you will be in several months' time. Where the future enters the equation is in knowing whether what you are doing right now will have positive future results and whether you are on the right track in the way you pursue a particular aspect of your life.

J. Ronald Havern is a tarot card reader and psychologist, with a master's degree in Divinity, who practices in New York City. As he sees it, the tarot cards give you a kind of blueprint of where you have been and where you are going:

> The cards show you how things are set up to go, sort of the path you are traveling along. I think of it as a road map. It's like the traffic report from a helicopter, where you get above and see where the traffic jams are so you know to avoid them. If you go to a psychic, and they tell you something terrible, I think that is because you have an opportunity to avoid that. If you didn't have the opportunity to avoid that, there wouldn't be any reason to know about it.

Another value of knowing what the future will be is in just knowing that there *is* a future. This doesn't mean that you are worried you are going to die tomorrow, but simply that you need reassurance at those times when you just can't see over the next "hump." We've all experienced these blind spots at certain crucial turning points in our lives: graduating from college, mid-life "crisis," and retirement, for instance. Laverne is a textile designer who lives in New Jersey. She first visited a psychic when she graduated from college. As she explains it:

> I wanted to know I had a destiny. I was just coming out of college and I was really mixed up. What am I going to be? Should I go to grad school? Should I go

into business? I was completely without tools for being able to make a decision. So I went to a psychic to kind of know that my life was going to continue and that there was a path that might be more right for me, based on where I had come from.

The danger is in thinking that the psychic will tell you *what* is going to happen. Although many psychics do make predictions, most are in general terms. More importantly, the reason predictions make sense is that, as Laverne pointed out, they are based on *where you have come from.* For example, if you had just finished up eight years of medical training and were having trouble deciding whether to go into private practice or take a research position, and a psychic told you you would make a great lawyer, it would be of little use, even if it were true.

Instead of such unhelpful advice, a good psychic might say something like, "I see you working with children." If your field were pediatrics, first, you would know that the psychic was accurate, and second, it might make you realize that you would be happier working with people than with test tubes and lab results. It's important to realize that we all have free will and that our future is what we make it. In other words, the future does not just happen to us; it's the product of our desires, talents, and actions. Psychic prediction can tell you only in what direction to focus those talents and whether or not your desires are realistic.

Beth, a 25-year-old musician in a punk band, decided to visit a numerologist to give her more direction with her life. Her expectations, however, went way beyond the scope of where she herself was directing her life. She describes her disappointment:

> I guess I sort of went in expecting to be told that I was wonderful and all these sappy, flattering things that I wasn't told—even though I was told nice things. It's just like nowadays all parents want to be told that their child is gifted. I wanted to be told the same thing—that I was *gifted*, and that I had this golden life in front of me.

Stories like Beth's are not isolated cases. A lot of people think that by visiting a psychic they will be relieving themselves of the responsibility of working toward goals, of accomplishing things through personal effort. One psychic tells the story of a woman who called her up to voice her dissatisfaction with a reading:

"You told me I would sell my house by April!" the woman complained. "And it's now almost June and the house isn't sold."

"Did you run an ad in the paper?" the psychic asked.

"No."

"Did you put a sign on your front lawn?"

"No."

This story sounds silly, but when people hear predictions, this type of reasoning takes place more often than not. Somehow, they think, events are just going to happen to them, like a miraculous intervention from above. The truth is, whatever a psychic tells you is nothing more than a prediction of what you yourself are going to do. You always have the choice of not doing it, and you always can choose how you are going to do it.

One New York psychic who does a good deal of predicting always stresses to her clients that we all have freedom of choice and that nothing is really predetermined:

> People have a very strong misconception: they think that you go to a reader, and they will tell you that A, B, C, and D are going to happen. Yes, a reader will tell you that, but a good reader will tell you if you do this, you will get this; if you decide to do that, you will get that—there is always an option. There are two sides to every coin. Because nothing is "written down." We ultimately make things happen in our lives according to our decisions. You've got to give people options and you've got to nag them to start to make their own decisions.

Similarly, Rock Kenyon, a New York psychic who appears regularly on television and radio, has little sympathy for people who come for readings because they want to hear that their life is going to change by itself. As he puts it:

> If there is nothing happening in your life and you expect to go to a psychic reading and have the psychic tell you that Prince Charming is going to ride up to your door and sweep you away, it may be possible, but that's pretty rare. If you're not doing anything [with the situation], there isn't anything to say what the outcome is going to be. The dice have to be cast in order

to know how they're going to fall. The right situation is if people are doing something [with their lives] and want to know, "Can I do something better with it to make it as I wish?"

Getting Rich Quick

On its simplest level, prediction can be a valuable tool in achieving material success, and many people visit psychics purely to find out what stock to buy or which job to take. But before you rush off to the corner tarot card reader with your Dow Jones listings in hand, you should realize that very few psychics actually do this kind of prediction. Most psychics are not that specific in what they can predict. Others find that trying to access psychic information for purely monetary gain simply does not work; it is like trying to get D.C. power from an A.C. outlet.

There is a famous story about Edgar Cayce, perhaps the best known psychic of this century, who specialized in the diagnosis and healing of illnesses for thousands of people who wrote to him throughout the course of his long career. Cayce believed his ability came directly from God and was uncomfortable with taking much money for the work he did. On the one occasion when he used his ability to predict the outcome of a horse race for a friend, he lost his special ability for a year.

Putting aside the ethical implications of these kinds of readings, the fact remains that there are a lot of psychics doing predictions today, and very few of them are terribly rich. If psychic ability could foretell such things as stock market trends and lottery numbers, presumably many psychics would not bother doing psychic readings for a living.

Without getting into a philosophical examination of this phenomenon, we might observe that if the future is indeed made up of choices we all make (as a result of our free will), then such large-scale mechanisms as the American economy would be the product of so many individual free-will decisions and interactions that predicting the outcome of all of them would be virtually impossible.

A more realistic scenario might be if you were someone who played the stock market extensively, had studied a particular company in depth, and were looking for a little more guidance with your decision to invest. In many cases, what psychics can tell you depends as much upon what you know as upon what they know. Many psychics believe that in doing a reading, they are merely tapping into your own knowledge—either about yourself or about a specific area of expertise that you may have. As a result, it is unlikely that they will be able to just "reach into a hat" and pull out a stock that you should buy or a company that you should apply to for a job. As we already mentioned, it's up to you to put the wheels into motion before you expect to hear what the outcome will be.

All this isn't to say that there haven't been cases where people have made money as the result of psychic ability. Plenty of psychics do offer that service and some actually specialize in business consultations. As part of ongoing research in remote viewing, parapsychology researchers at the Stanford Research Institute (now SRI International) were able to earn $120,000 for a group of investors by dabbling in silver futures. But later repeat trials of the experiment failed to yield successful results. So if you decide to visit a psychic for the purpose of investing, be advised that you are gambling as much as if you were playing the stock market straight.

It should also be pointed out that the majority of people who visit psychics do not do so for purely material ends. According to Michael Goodrich, president of Cosmic Contact, a national psychic referral service, no more than 25 percent of those who come for a psychic reading are looking for "what stock to buy." The other three-quarters are interested in "spiritual awareness" and want to know more about themselves.

Insight Into Yourself

Probably the most valuable asset a psychic can offer you is knowledge about yourself. As we mentioned earlier, most psychics will focus mainly on where you are now in your life and the ways in which you are handling specific situations. And although a responsible psychic won't make decisions for you, she can supply vital information that will aid you in making your own informed decisions.

On the simplest level this information will deal with your personality and the special skills and talents that you bring to the world. For instance, a psychic might tell you that you tend to be too analytical, that you hold yourself back by trying to reduce everything to a simple equation before making a decision. She might point out that you have a strong intuitive capacity that is waiting to be developed and that you should rely more on the hunches that you so often feel but usually ignore.

Although much of this sounds somewhat general, a good psychic will then take this information and relate it to specific issues in your life. For instance, say you decided to visit a psychic because you wanted to know if you were going to get a raise at your job. He might begin by telling you that you are good with people and that you have excellent communication skills. He would then point out that you should rely on this ability more when it comes to getting what you want. With regard to your raise, it would mean speaking to your boss directly and using your verbal skills, rather than writing an interoffice memo in accordance with standard company procedure.

Of course, all this should ring true to you and not sound like something out of left field. It may be an aspect of yourself you haven't thought much about, or a new way of looking at yourself that makes sense once you consider it. Or it may echo something your friends or family have said, but that you felt was coming from a place too close to home. Often simply hear-

ing things from a disinterested observer will give
them much more weight, and you may find yourself
looking closer at aspects of your personality that you
previously shrugged off. As Carl, the art director
whom we mentioned earlier, sees it:

> I guess I see a psychic as someone who can look into
> me and say something that will make me understand
> more about myself. They point out things that make
> other things fall into place, that strike a chord. I tend
> to use psychics as "bigger picture" psychothera-
> pists—in trying to figure out how to deal with the here
> and now; in being able to take that information and
> put it to a positive use. I think that's what I go to them
> for— looking for them to direct me somehow, without
> telling me what to do, but giving me just enough of
> a clue what to do. Actually, I wouldn't mind if some
> of them told me what to do . . . but I most likely
> wouldn't do it.

Visiting a psychic can indeed be similar to seeing
a psychotherapist, especially at those times when you
simply want some disinterested third party to bounce
your thoughts and feelings off. The odd part of it is
that in reality you are not doing any "bouncing"; you
are not telling the psychic things about yourself and
then hearing her response. On the contrary, here is
a complete stranger who has never seen you before
and who has been told nothing about you, uncovering what are in some cases intimate aspects of your
character. Beatrice Rich, a well-known New York
psychic, explains that when people hear details of

57

their life situation described by a total stranger, they sit up and take notice:

> Many times I simply confirm what people already know: they already know about their boyfriend and their job. I am not a friend; I am a total stranger who knows nothing about their life, telling them the most intimate things about them—their feelings, their situations. Frequently, the way people think things are going, for good or ill, are the way things *are* going. I clarify what they already know, let them think about things differently, give them some perspective and insight.

This kind of experience, although at first a little startling, often carries a great deal of impact. If there is value to hearing things about yourself from a person you see once a week and speak to on a therapeutic level, imagine the effect of hearing that sort of information from someone you have never even met, only see once, and who knows nothing about you apart from your name. And that tends to be the case more often than not. The assumption is, of course, that what you hear makes sense to you on a deep level—that it resonates with your sense of self. When this happens, just having heard such truths echoed back to you can be therapeutic in itself.

Career Counseling

In addition to aspects of your personality, a psychic may tell you things that are much more pragmatic, such as whether you have strong business acumen, or that you are good with your hands and should think about taking up a hobby or craft like music or sculpting. Such information may reinforce something you already know about yourself, or it may rekindle a childhood ambition you had but gave up somewhere along the way.

Let's say you work in an insurance company from nine to five, but play in a band at night. Eventually you find yourself with enough bookings that you can consider leaving the office job behind, but you are still unsure about whether you have "what it takes." A psychic would be able to say that you do have genuine musical talent and that perhaps you should experiment with writing your own songs in addition to playing an instrument in the band. She also might point out that you have a poor business aptitude and that, before you decide to rely completely on your music for making a living, you should find yourself a good business manager to handle that side of your affairs.

In many cases a psychic will suggest that you undertake something artistic or creative, not in order to make money or start a new career, but simply to balance out something you are already doing. If you work with computers all day, you might find that a suggestion to go home and work with your hands is much more relaxing than staring at a television screen at night. Eventually you might find that you have been neglecting your intuitive, emotive self, and that by pursuing a creative or artistic endeavor you are discovering another side of your personality.

In many cases this kind of advice may seem no more impressive than just good common sense. But hearing it from someone who you assume has a greater degree of intuitive insight than a friend or relative can give it much more weight. If the information is accurate and true for you, you probably will not find yourself quitting your job, selling your house, and turning your life upside down, but will instead be sparked to go in a direction you might already have been considering. (Of course, if you were *already* considering quitting your job, selling your house, and turning your life upside down, then it may have that effect.)

In the case of astrologers, you will not be told so much *what* you should be doing as when you should be doing it. We will deal with astrology in greater detail in Chapter Four, but for now it is only necessary to understand that this "science" deals with cycles of energies and the times when those energies are manifest on this planet. It therefore offers the opportunity to determine the best times to do certain things. For instance, if you were planning on starting your own business, your astrological chart might indicate that the coming month was a bad time to begin any new projects and that if you simply waited until the following month, you would have a much easier time of it. It's important to note that the astrological interpretation would not necessarily mean that your business would fail if you began at the wrong time, but simply that you might encounter fewer difficulties if you waited until a more auspicious time.

In general, astrology deals with probabilities: if you plan your actions in accordance with planetary movement, you'll have a greater probability of success. It won't tell you what you should be doing with your life or predict the absolute outcome of a situation. As with all psychic information, it assumes that you are creating the events in your life and are working toward specific goals. But within that framework, it can offer you additional guidance with your next step.

In this way, psychic readings can help you get past particularly difficult times in your life, times when you are perhaps having trouble making a decision or when nothing you do seems to come out right. At some point during your reading you might hear something that opens up a new point of view for you or lets you see an aspect of your problem that had previously gone unnoticed. Thus you may have one more bit of information with which to make your own decision, one more piece of the puzzle that you were unable to recognize on your own.

Relationships

A psychic reading can also give you insight into other people, enabling you to better handle your personal and professional relationships. For instance, a reader may be able to look at a photograph of someone and tell you something about that person's character, emotions, and, most significantly, how that person would be likely to act in a particular situation. This can be particularly helpful in a business situation, but it can also go far in suggesting some new ways of dealing with friends, lovers, and family members. As one man recalls:

> I was having major problems with this guy I was doing business with. All he could hear was what *he* wanted to hear. So I asked [the psychic] what the outcome of this particular business deal would be, and the first thing she said was, "You're involved with another person on this—he's a reactor—you've got to watch out for that. You won't get anywhere by confronting him. . . . Instead, make him think whatever you do is in *his* best interest." Now that might sound pretty obvious, but the fact was, I was thinking that I would finally have to get tough with this guy, so she made me realize that that *wouldn't* be the best way to go—that that would just make it worse. She also told me that he was basically an honest person, which I needed to hear at that time.

Even more useful is the way in which a psychic will tap into the aspects of your own personality that you bring to bear on a relationship. By gaining deeper insight into yourself, you may learn about certain patterns of behavior that you tend to repeat, things you do that trigger negative responses in the other person, and perhaps even aspects of your personality that you prefer to ignore. If you're willing to take a realistic look at yourself and work to change existing patterns, then you may find this kind of information invaluable in enabling you to get the responses you want from other people in your life.

Astrology and palmistry are especially useful in working with relationships because you can visit a reader with another person and have your horoscopes compared, or the lines in your hands juxtaposed, to determine areas of conflict and harmony. In the case of astrology, this is known as synastry; often the astrologer will actually prepare a third chart for the relationship itself, in order to better reflect the areas that may need to be worked on. Similarly, palmistry can reveal aspects of people that they might not otherwise admit to themselves or others. Nathaniel Altman, a palm reader and author in Brooklyn, New York, has been reading palms since 1969, and he frequently works with couples. He explains the value of doing comparisons:

> Sometimes people come for counseling—for example, two people come for a hand reading together and they ask, "Should we get married?" "What's going on?" Well, I say, "I'm not going to tell you that, but both of you are stubborn, and neither of you is going to give way, and this could become a source of problems. A positive thing here, though, is that both of you are very sexually oriented and that you have the potential for a good sex life. However, you have an eye for other men, and you like to be very domestic, so you won't like it, you'll be very jealous." And then I'll tell them, "Maybe you do need counseling," or "You don't need counseling, you need to talk more."

In the end a psychic reading may not be able to tell you something you don't know about yourself or your mate, but it may open up avenues of communication between you. Hearing something about yourself that you've previously been hesitant to bring up may be the catalyst you need to express your feelings. Similarly, hearing someone else describe something about another person in your life that you sensed was there but always had difficulty putting into words could give you a starting point for fruitful discussion. Lastly, as Nat Altman points out, a psychic reading might just convince you that you would do well to seek out professional counseling.

Creative Problem Solving

If we go along with the theory that psychic information is right-brain, or intuitive, and that most of us process experiences (and try to solve our problems) using our left brain, or analytical mind, then going to a psychic is merely a way of accessing information that is otherwise not easily available to the majority of us. It is a way of considering a problem or question in a totally new light, similar to the stories of sudden creative insight we often hear about. Many scientists, for instance, will recall that their greatest breakthroughs came about only after they had stopped trying to solve a problem analytically. That sudden flash of "Aha!" seems to be a right-brain function.

This is not to say that solutions to complex scientific problems are the result of psychic intuition, but only that after the analytical mind is loaded with all the data about the problem, the intuitive mind can reprocess the information in a way entirely different from logical thought. Many solutions are the result of long, hard analysis, of course. But if we are trying to look at something in a completely new way and not simply as a function of everything that came before, then a nonlinear, nonlogical process seems to be required. This may be why many thinkers who have had such brilliant moments of insight report that they received the information in a dream or awoke from a deep sleep with the solution before them. Sleep is one of the few times when our analytical minds are shut down, opening the gateway to the subconscious, intuitive self.

If we take this model to be an effective method of problem solving, then we could say that by going to a psychic you are availing yourself of the opportunity for creative problem solving—of seeing a situation in a wholly new way. The psychic becomes your gateway to the intuitive self, and by drawing upon your own knowledge of the problem, the psychic can reprocess that information in such a way that may let you see it in a new light, offering totally new, creative solutions.

Andrea Hinda is a psychic counselor who lives in Boulder, Colorado. As she sees it, creative problem solving grows out of the ability to see that you have choices, options you may not have considered previously:

> Sometimes what it comes down to is showing people that they have a choice. You can choose to stay in this situation or you can choose to move out of it—you do have a choice. We get involved in our own stuff. We

forget how many choices we actually have, how many options are available to us. And as much as we think and run something through our minds and come up with all the options and all the different perceptions, there are always others. That's been one of my greatest learning lessons—that there are always other perceptions and options.

In some cases, it may not be that a person is so much unable to see things in a new light as he is un-*willing*. The fact that we can always make a choice in a situation is a frightening realization for many people, bringing with it the weight of responsibility. One psychic-goer put it this way: "No one wants to make a choice—choices are hard, choices put you on the line. They challenge you, and basically we don't want to be challenged, we want to be taken care of." Your visit to a psychic could indeed be a gentle introduction to the art of making choices and therefore controlling the direction you want your life to move in.

Personal Development

The reprocessing of left-brain information is not the only creative aspect of the right brain. Many psychologists as well as psychics believe that the right brain is the source of all genuine creativity, whether it be a piece of art, a musical composition, or a new way of looking at a problem. For this reason, many people will visit a psychic in order to enhance their own creativity. This can take the form of identifying particular areas of talent, or it can take the form of removing blocks to the creative process itself.

By accessing your subconscious, intuitive self, a psychic may be able to see ways in which you are blocking the expression of that self. This might take the form of personality characteristics or emotional difficulties that are holding you back, or it might mean finding new ways in which to express a particular talent.

Laverne went to a psychic who told her that she had great talent as a writer and that she should begin writing, at least for her own personal fulfillment. She had heard this before from other people but never knew where to begin. The psychic suggested she start a "wish book," in which she could write down anything that she desired, no matter how preposterous it might seem. She had "seen" that Laverne was holding herself back by thinking that whatever she wrote would have to be "important" and logical. As a result, she was always too intimidated to write. The psychic had also seen, however, that Laverne had a very strong fantasy side to her imagination and that by tapping into that aspect of her creativity, her writing ability would flow more easily.

This type of analysis can go much deeper, not only into the psychological realm, but into the realm of the spiritual as well. And, indeed, many people consult psychics for the same reasons they would see a traditional psychotherapist or spiritual counselor.

Psychic-Therapy

In the relatively new field of therapy known as transpersonal psychology, more and more psychologists are incorporating psychic or spiritual elements in their work. Some psychologists are themselves psychic, others work closely with psychics in their practices. It is interesting to note that Sigmund Freud felt that his best insights into patients were those that came intuitively. And Carl Jung was convinced that the *only* meaningful exchanges between therapist and patient were those that took place on the subconscious level. Peter Janney, a licensed psychotherapist and nutrition counselor in Cambridge, Massachusetts, points out that it has been only in the last couple of decades that psychological theory has begun to take into account the importance of a person's spiritual nature:

> In theory, the more traditional therapies are limited in their perspective in terms of how they look at and understand human beings. Most of them pay little attention to man's higher quest for wanting to evolve to higher and higher levels of organization and expression and evolution. That really wasn't opened up until Abraham Maslow came along. Until then, psychotherapy was oriented by the Western medical model—you've got something wrong with you and I am going to fix it. That sort of mechanistic point of view has in essence worn itself out; it's so limited in terms of what we know is available today.
>
> People are more than just a bunch of needs and drives. People have whole other dimensions of themselves that they're eager to develop, and I don't think that the kind of mental health practices that we saw in the 1950s and the early '60s really were ad-

dressing what I would call some of the deeper needs, some of the deeper desires of expression.

A lot of people visit psychics for the same reason they visit psychologists: they like the attention. On a very basic level, we all have a need to be listened to and we all like attention. More than one person has told me that the best part of seeing a psychic was being the center of attention for an hour or so. As one woman put it:

> The first thing I noticed when I went to a psychic was that it's about ego. I'm sitting here, and this person is using all these powers and all this unknown stuff, and it's all about me! Tell me that's not colossal ego!

Of course, such visits are usually more than just ego trips. A good psychic will deliver her information in a way that is both constructive and comforting. More than one person described the psychic he had visited as an "earth mother"—someone who was nurturing as well as insightful. In some cases, the affirming quality of the reading is due less to the information given than to the energy surrounding the psychic herself.

The range of psychological help that is available through psychic means is wide and varied. It includes everything from psychologists who occasionally use psychic information in treating a patient to professional psychics who are essentially practicing psychotherapy. Clearly, if you desire this kind of a reading, you must choose a psychic with great care—preferably selecting one who has been recommended by a close friend whose judgment you trust.

Susan Edwards, a tarot card reader in Boulder, Colorado, and a teacher at the Naropa Institute, frequently works with a psychologist in order to help the therapist isolate the specific issues a client needs to deal with. According to Susan, one reading is enough to save both therapist and patient time and money:

> It's like getting a prescription for the person as to what they should be working on in therapy. I'm like a surgeon—I can cut into whatever the [issue] is. I'm considered to be someone who drives the point home, who gets right to the heart of the matter. [The therapist] almost always calls me in right away, because I save her a lot of time. I say, "Here's the thing that's most on the surface." And then she just works on that. She doesn't have to listen to all the hoo-ha the person is trying to sort through. It saves her maybe ten sessions or something.

Many psychics, Edwards included, feel that traditional psychotherapy fails to take into account the whole person—physical, emotional, and spiritual—and that reading someone psychically is an effective way of addressing all the aspects of the total person—what might be called "psychic-therapy." In addition, proponents of psychic work feel that traditional psychotherapy tends to pigeonhole people according to fixed diagnoses and that it ignores the fact that each of us is a unique individual with particular spiritual and emotional issues. They also maintain that most health problems—whether psychological or physical—are the result of spiritual problems, and that unless these are dealt with on a spiritual level, they will continue to recur.

As Susan Edwards sees it, the psychic is a "metaphysician" who treats the spirit in the same way a medical doctor treats the body:

> I want to start a metaphysical checkup business. You just come in every six months to see whether you are working with your emotions, your karmic situation. "Yes, you're fine—keep going," or "No, you're really off the track." And if you have a problem, you could catch it before you do something like destroy your marriage or run away from your children. A lot of times I see people who are emergency cases and I ask them, "Why didn't you come in a year ago?" And they say something like, "Well, I just didn't want to spend the money." A year ago they should have spent the money, because now it's going to cost them more [than just money].

Some psychics maintain that traditional forms of therapy don't go far enough in accessing information about a person. They feel that psychic awareness is a tool that can't be matched by other modalities for tuning into the self. Margo Schmidt, a psychic counselor and healer in the Boston area who has a master's degree in education, was trained in the traditional psychoanalytic method but now finds the standard clinical approach too restrictive:

> Part of the problem with clinical [psychology] is it focuses only on the problems, it doesn't focus enough

on the emerging wellness. The other thing about standard therapy is that it's much too passive. People enjoy being engaged. The nature of healing is interactive; it's "in relationship" to wholeness and interaction.

I think the whole scientific modality in ancient times was much more interfaced with spirit and metaphysics, and I think we're going to come back to that in some ways. I think that therapy is going to go through a lot of changes by necessity. There's a lot of fear and competition around the standard medical community and the standard therapy community. Sure, it's to their benefit to dismiss this stuff. It becomes a very political issue, unfortunately, but what's in danger here is the healing of the human spirit, which is not a place to do battle.

Treating a Physical Ailment

Many people go to psychics to be healed of physical illnesses. These can range from something as simple as food allergies to such life-threatening conditions as cancer and AIDS. Most of these people go out of desperation: they have been to a conventional medical doctor and been told either that their condition is incurable or that it will require debilitating invasive procedures, such as surgery or chemotherapy. In deciding to visit a psychic healer, many of these patients are making a choice to take a much greater responsibility for their own health.

Psychic healers should not be confused with faith healers. They provide no miracle cures and cannot simply "fix" what is wrong in a single visit. Although in some cases successful results are achieved quickly, don't think you'll find any magic bullet at a psychic healer. Anyone who promises you miraculous results is probably a fraud and should be avoided at all costs, since you are dealing with your health.

Marilyn, a psychologist who lives in rural New Hampshire, was suffering from a debilitating inner ear condition. After being treated by conventional medical doctors for some time, she decided to "balance out" the standard Western approach by visiting an aura and chakra healer who works with energy fields. As she recalls, however, she was expecting miracles:

> I wanted her to fix me, which she thought was really amusing. And of course that's not what happened. I had heard stories about her—how she had been able to dissolve brain tumors in a week, and how she cured the cancer of a 75-year-old woman. So I knew that she was powerful. And I thought: Well, gee, maybe I have a chance to get an instant healing from her. There were no instant results, but I felt much calmer and more collected and more in control of my healing processes after she left. It was an important thing for all of me, not just my inner ear. It wasn't magic, but it was kind of a kick in the butt to get going and heal myself.

It should also be pointed out that a psychic healer is not a substitute for good, competent medical care. Any reputable psychic healer will insist that you continue to visit your doctor to have your condition monitored and your progress checked. Some healers work closely with doctors in trying to diagnose a difficult or hidden condition, and they will sometimes recommend specific treatment that only a medical doctor is qualified to administer.

Above all, a good psychic healer will teach you to heal yourself. That may involve anything from altering your diet, taking nutritional supplements, and using herbs, to changing your sleep habits, learning to meditate, doing visualizations, and chanting. The bottom line is self-responsibility. No psychic can heal you unless you take responsibility for your own well-being and decide to heal yourself.

Spiritual Development

To most psychics, the task of healing begins on a spiritual level. They feel that everyone eventually has to deal with the issue of unifying the physical self with the spiritual self and that in doing so we will discover that truth lies within each and every one of us. To these psychics, or "spiritual counselors," as many prefer to be called, the issue of responsibility is central to the process of self-discovery: when you visit this type of psychic, you are taking on the responsibility for discovering who you are and what your purpose in life is.

This type of psychic is best suited to those people who are either already on a spiritual path and seeking further guidance or those who wish to begin a process of spiritual development. Many of these people are seeking a spiritual component in their lives but have been unable to find it within the confines of organized religion. Psychic work offers them the opportunity to explore their spiritual selves without taking on the trappings of traditional religion or conforming to someone else's idea of spirituality.

Suzanne Kluss, who practices trance channeling, prefers the label "spiritual counselor" because she sees her job as empowering people to discover their own inner selves:

> I consider my work to be that of a teacher. I see myself as a communicator, really sharing skills—the techniques of how to let people get in touch with themselves and to find a balance for themselves—of the intellectual, the emotional, the physical, and the spiritual. The society we live in is not really supportive of individual spiritual growth. And people really need to claim their own spirituality now.

Many psychics who deal with spiritual development, Kluss included, utilize techniques such as past-life regression to remove blocks. They feel that we are all born into a certain karma, which we have chosen before birth, and that it is only by working with that karma that we can express ourselves as fully actualized human beings on this planet. Through the process of remembering past lives, issues crucial to this lifetime are uncovered, eventually leading us to knowledge about who we are and why we are here. Martin, a computer software salesperson in Boston, recalls a channeling session in which he was told about his past lives:

> The channeler spoke about reincarnation, Atlantis, Lemuria, Greece, Rome. . . . He said, "In all your past lives you were a teacher, a minister, a healer—all of that, and you may find that you identify with that, with instructing people. You will find sometimes that when you're talking about something, you'll say more than you thought you knew." When he said that, a little light bulb went off—bing! Because that does happen a lot. There's an inner source that I tap into when I get going. And I have always identified with teachers and ministers. My mother once told my grandmother that the first questions I was asking were about God and religion, and that I once got very upset when my father went to church without me!

Of course, many psychics will pass on past-life information that in most cases does not ring a bell. As one woman recalls, however, it can at least be entertaining to speculate on who you might have been and who, from this life, might have been there with you:

> A couple of psychics have told my mother and me that we're very old souls and that in an earlier life I was my mother's mother, and that she opted to come back as my mother to thank me, to return the favor. And we love that, because we don't have a real classic mother/daughter relationship. We have more of a friend relationship, and we always have, instinctively. So to us, that just seemed perfectly understandable. Do I really believe that I was her mother? Probably

not. But it's a fun thing to think, because we love our relationship. And anyway, it's a whole lot better than if they had told her she was an ax murderer four lives ago. What's the harm? I don't walk around saying that 8,000 years ago I was my mother's mother, but it's a pleasant thought.

There are certain psychics who specialize in past-life work. Some of them use their psychic ability to tell you about your past lives and the significance they have for this life, while others will use a guided meditation to allow you to "regress" or remember particular past lives for yourself so that you can make your own discoveries. The method you choose will depend upon your own spiritual development and the degree to which you want to become involved in working with your own personal awareness.

Suzanne Kluss, who had been meditating regularly and was no stranger to psychic insight, recalls her first experience of a past-life regression workshop:

A very good friend of mine came across this group and she suggested I come to a weekend. She called it a "spiritual empowerment weekend." I didn't really know what this weekend was about, but I talked to two people who had gone to it, and they said it was one of the most constructive weekends they'd ever had as far as opening up the blocks to their own spiritual growth. It felt right to me, and instinctually I said, okay, I'll sign up for that.

The teacher talked about rebirthing and past-life regressions. And she constructed topics of past-life regressions specifically to help us remove blocks to our spiritual growth. Almost everybody was channeling by the end of the weekend. The energy was palpable. You could really feel it. And there was a lot of great stuff happening in the room.

For example, there were two people who were friends—they'd come to class together. We had just come out of one regression, and this woman was sobbing. She had remembered being thrown off a cliff [in a past life]. And you relive this—you let all the emotion out and that's the release. Well, her friend turned to her and he said, "Oh, my God. I'm the one who threw you off the cliff!" *He* had regressed to throwing someone off a cliff. Well, they both sat there, and they looked at each other, and they cracked up. They cried, they let it all out, and they gave each other a hug. It was like this huge karmic release right there in the room.

I feel like I've been put on an accelerator after that weekend because all the blocks that were keeping me from growing were sort of pushed away. I said to my friend afterward that I felt like I wasn't carrying around all this baggage anymore. I felt like I had taken a great big spiritual "dump."

Eventually you may find yourself developing your own psychic ability, whether that means being better able to know your intuitive self or being able to predict future events. All psychics agree that every person possesses some psychic ability to one degree or another and that the process of developing that ability is generally the outgrowth of spiritual development.

You may already sense that you have some psychic ability and wish to develop it further or gain a better understanding of it so that you can use it to help you in life. There are psychics who will help you with this process as well. Many offer classes in psychic development and in such related areas as learning to channel, establishing a better connection between mind and body, and discovering techniques to heal both yourself and others. According to most psychics, we are all both students and teachers. Visiting a psychic for the first time, you may find that you have something to give that teacher in return, and by putting yourself in the position of a student who wishes to learn more about yourself, you may take on the role of teacher for a small part of the time you are together.

As Peter Janney explains, the main purpose of gaining spiritual insight into yourself is the total integration of *all* the aspects of being human. When you reach that point, you know who you are, what your task is, and where you are going:

> What it means for someone to be open spiritually is that they have a sense of what the big picture is; they have a sense of what it is they're supposed to be doing in their life—what kind of experiences they're supposed to be going after. When people start to get that, they're able to take in spiritual energy—they're able to use it in terms of helping their body to open up and use their mind more appropriately to get their needs met, to get where they want to go, to get the things that their soul really wants.

It is a difficult task for us as human beings to peel back the various layers of our selves, whether psychological or spiritual, and discover the true motivations that drive us and the real goals that would fulfill us. Like any skilled, caring counselors, psychics can help us with that challenge. Whether we need just a little more information in order to make a decision or a full-fledged spiritual analysis of where we are, where we've been, and where we are going, ultimately it is we who must do the work. Psychics are simply additional resources for us to tap when we feel that a little more input is needed. Looked at in a balanced, sober way—not as people with miraculous powers, but as catalysts for self-healing and life changes—psychics can truly fulfill their role as guides and advisors.

CHAPTER THREE

How To Choose A Psychic

I: What To Look For in a Good Psychic

Choosing a Method of Divination

Once you have decided why you want to visit a psychic, your next task is to locate one who will be able to meet your needs and with whom you will feel comfortable. Different types of psychics are suited to different needs, so you will first need to acquaint yourself with the different methods of psychic reading to find what each is capable of revealing.

It's difficult to draw clear lines between the various types of psychics, mainly because many psychic readers combine more than one method of divination. If a person has psychic ability, he will most often choose the specific approach to reading that affords him a comfortable vehicle for expressing his ability. Certain approaches may work better in particular situations, and a psychic may find that as his own ability develops during the course of his career, the ways in which that ability is manifested also change.

We can nevertheless categorize most psychics by the primary method or methods they choose to use. The particular title by which a psychic chooses to call herself will also reveal certain aspects about how she sees herself in relation to her clients and her work. That title will give you an indication of where the psychic is coming from. Obviously someone who is known as a "fortune-teller" is going to be doing very different work than someone who calls herself a "spiritual counselor." As we have already seen, psychic ability covers a broad range of skills and intention, and the more you know about where an individual psychic is located on that continuum, the more informed a choice you'll be able to make about whether she is right for you.

We can divide professional psychics into the following basic categories:

Clairvoyants
Card Readers
Astrologers, Numerologists, and Palm Readers
Channelers
Psychic Healers

We will go into each of these in depth in the following chapter, but for now it will be sufficient to briefly describe the type of work that each group is best suited to.

Clairvoyants are people who possess what we might call the "simplest" level of psychic ability—straight psi, or extrasensory perception (ESP), as it used to be called. In parapsychological terms, psi is purely a "sixth sense," that is, totally a function of the human mind. As such, it doesn't involve belief in life after death, spirit guides, or extraterrestrials. Most of us have experienced some form of psi at one time or another, and many of us know someone whom we would call psychic, as it is meant here.

If you are visiting a psychic for the first time, you will probably be most comfortable with a clairvoyant reader. There are no special rituals involved, one visit is usually enough to have your needs met, and you don't necessarily have to believe in psychic ability in order to have a successful reading. If you're interested in knowing the future or the outcome of a particular situation in which you are involved, then this type of psychic would be your best choice.

If you are seeking information about another person, many clairvoyants, using a process called psychometry, will be able to tell you something about that person either from a photograph or an object that was once in his possession. So this type of reader would also be a good choice if you have questions about your relationships with other people—either personal or professional (although finding a photograph of your boss may be more of a challenge than finding a good psychic).

Similarly, the "pragmatic" uses for psychics that were discussed in the last chapter would fall under the aegis of a psychic reader. Solving crimes, locating missing persons, divining for water or oil, or locating ailing septic tanks are all specialties of people with these abilities.

Card readers are similar to clairvoyants in that their work stems directly from their own ability and not from spirits from another world, altered states of consciousness, or elaborate rituals. This category includes not only tarot card readers, but people who read regular playing cards, rune stones, the *I Ching*, and dice—in other words, any kind of apparatus that is used to reveal an answer to a question or a particular problem.

Card readers would be good for foretelling the future, predicting the outcome of present events, and giving you information about another person. The strength of a good card reader, however, is his ability to see the whole situation at once. Most tarot spreads deal with every aspect of a particular question—past, present, and future—enabling a good reader to put the issue into a larger context, both in terms of your own life and your relationship to others who may be involved.

The next group of psychics includes astrologers, numerologists, and palm readers. These three methods are grouped together because in their purest form they are really "sciences." That is to say, they reveal information solely on the basis of set formulas or physical data (such as the movement of the planets or the lines of your hand).

If you are interested in seeing what is coming up for you in the next year or so, in a somewhat broad scope, then astrology or numerology would be a good choice for a reading. Palmistry can deal with an even longer time span, since the lines on your hand contain information about your entire life. The degree of detail, however, is much less than is available using the other two methods. Numerology, which is based upon the interpretation of the numbers in your birth date and the numerical equivalents of the letters in your name, is similar in that it often deals with larger patterns than astrology, but in less detail.

Astrology and numerology are very effective in analyzing the energy cycles that surround us. In other words, if you wanted to know the best time to sell your house or look for a new job, these techniques could chart that out for you very specifically. (In one case, a woman who wanted to sell her house was told to put a "For Sale" sign on her front lawn at exactly 3:45 A.M. on a particular day.) Or, if you simply felt that your life was "not going anywhere," a good reading would be able to show you how that slump was part of a larger cycle of energy, how long it was likely to last, and ways in which you could better deal with it.

The other value of astrology, numerology, and palmistry is in revealing to you where your own abilities and talents lie. According to this way of thinking, special skills or aptitudes are the result of when you were born. The assumption is that the time you entered the world determines not only the direction your life will take, but specific problems and issues you will have to face along the way. The astrologer's job is to isolate those aspects of your character that you have to work with to try to solve your problems and achieve your goals during the course of your life.

Palmistry is not used alone in many cases, and there

are very few really good palmists who specialize in hand analysis. Very often an astrologer or numerologist may just want to glance at the lines in your hand as a sort of second opinion on what is revealed using the other methods. These lines will reveal aspects of your personality or character, which the reader will then tie in with your desires, achievements, and future goals.

For most people seeking psychic help, channeling, or "trance channeling," as it is sometimes called, will require the biggest leap of faith. Until recently, channelers were known as mediums, and they specialized in contacting spirits of the dead. Today channelers still deal with contacting spirits, but those spirits can range anywhere from those of dead friends and relatives to extraterrestrials, dolphins, or whales. A bit more belief on your part will be required should you decide to visit a channeler.

One of the reasons people go to channelers is to find out about their past lives. Because spirit guides can access information from the Akashic records (mentioned in Chapter One), they can supposedly find out everything about anyone in the world—including who you were in past lives. Thus, if you want to know more about who you were before and how it has affected the way you are now, you would probably want to visit a channeler. (Other psychics may access past-life information, but it seems to be most common among channelers.)

Psychic healers are perhaps the most straightforward group of practitioners because they deal in physical ailments. Although their methods vary greatly and in some cases may seem pretty far out, their work always centers around treating a particular physical condition. If you have a physical problem that you feel has not been successfully treated by standard medical treatment, you might want to consider a psychic healer. Or you may have a condition that is being held in check by the use of drugs or invasive therapies that you would prefer to handle in a more natural way and, in doing so, take more direct control of your own health.

Whatever your reason for visiting a psychic healer, be advised that you thereby decide to take *more* responsibility for your own health than if you stay with standard treatment. It is a lot easier to take a handful of pills each day than discipline yourself to meditate regularly, eat right, and work toward uncovering the spiritual or emotional causes of your disease.

Most psychic healers feel that their job is not so much to focus on curing disease as on the process of getting well. In this way, their services are valuable to anyone who wants to improve his total well-being. Unlike Western medicine, which is built entirely around curing illness, psychic healing—as well as the Eastern model of health care upon which it is based—is devoted to maintaining health.

Although there are many theories as to how psychic healing works and a wide range of non-Western modalities upon which they are based, belief in a particular system or philosophy is not necessary in order to benefit from a psychic healing. The beauty of the treatment is that the results are very tangible: if you feel better, you know it has worked. Thus, more than with any other form of psychic ability, you will know if you have got what you paid for.

Know Yourself

Knowing the nuts and bolts of psychic work is important in choosing a good reader, but like any successful learning experience, the quality of the teacher is more important than the subject being taught. You will want to look carefully at some of the more personal aspects of the psychic you visit, rather than being influenced unduly by important-sounding titles and esoteric methodologies. Before you do, however, you should take a good look at yourself.

The success of your psychic reading will depend a great deal on the degree to which you are comfortable with the person doing the reading and the method he is using. It is important to know what aspects of your own personality or belief system may get in the way of achieving results. As we will see later, your visit to a psychic depends as much upon you as upon the reader, and ultimately it is only what you do with the information that will determine the value of the reading. If you are too skeptical of the process or if you are just uncomfortable with the psychic, you will find it difficult to open yourself up to the guidance you are seeking.

For instance, if you tend to doubt most psychic phenomena but are curious enough to investigate firsthand, you will not want to visit a channeler right off the bat. It's a long leap from being a skeptical observer to believing in guardian angels and spirit guides and most people cannot make the leap easily. Carl, whom we mentioned in the previous chapter, has visited a number of different kinds of psychics, including channelers:

> I get the same kind of babble out of all the channelers I've been to—it's channel-babble—all this "love and light" stuff. They all basically say the same thing. You're looking for an indication of a way to go, or how [to improve your life], and they just tell you, "You already know; [the answers] are all within you." They're like that kind of shrink who answers your question with a question.

If you're like Carl, you would probably be much happier going to a clairvoyant for your first visit. There you may hear things about yourself that are more specific and more accurate, which will reinforce your belief rather than strengthen your defenses. As a result you may find yourself more willing to accept the possibility that channeling is also a valid phenomenon.

On the other hand, you may be the type of person who is very rational and who doesn't want to be confronted with anything too "flaky." In that case, you might be more comfortable with the more analytical approaches offered by astrology and numerology. Not only do these systems have a long and respected history, but you can clearly see the way in which the information they convey has been derived from astrological charts or numerical calculations. Most astrologers will be happy to show you exactly how they arrived at their conclusions. Many have regular clients who know a great deal about astrology and want to share in the process as much as the conclusions.

Numerology and astrology are so logical that a number of computer programs have been developed to help calculate the planetary movements and "crunch" the numbers in order to save time. If you are someone who tends to be mathematical or likes numerical puzzles, you may find yourself taking more than just a casual interest in the numerological process.

The scientific nature of astrology and numerology cuts both ways, of course. It may not make any sense to you to shell out good money just to have someone "do calculations." Instead you may prefer to know that you are paying for a unique service—one that is based upon someone's personal psychic ability. One woman recalled visiting an astrologer and thinking it was a waste of money. "Everything she told me came out of book," she complained. "I could have done that myself!" (As we shall see in the next chapter, astrology is not quite that simple.)

In terms of your own personality, you may be someone who is very emotional, very sensitive, and feels a little psychic yourself. In that case, you would probably prefer the more "personal" touch of a clairvoyant—someone with whom you can experience a connection that goes beyond the purely professional relationship of psychic and client. Many good readers combine their psychic ability to see with a strong nurturing quality to deliver the information in a caring way. The feeling that someone not only has special insight into you but also cares about how it affects you may be an important part of your psychic reading.

Another aspect of yourself you might pay attention to before choosing a psychic is whether you like to talk or to listen. Most psychics would rather you listen to what they have to say before bombarding them with questions or asking for clarifications, but many realize that they are involved in a therapeutic relationship and that you may have a need to voice what is on your mind. It is very important to find a reader who can accommodate that need, since many psychics find that it breaks their concentration to have to stop frequently during a reading to listen to a client's responses.

Similarly, if you tend to be reticent, and are a little nervous about opening yourself up to a perfect stranger, you will want to find a psychic who likes to talk and who does not require that you show up with a list of prepared questions. There are psychics who would just as soon not be bothered answering specific questions, since they feel that whatever is of significance in your life at that moment will come out in the reading anyway. Or you might just find that going to a group meeting and listening to a few people channel spiritual information is the right place for you to begin. A group setting will also give you the luxury of observing from a distance before becoming personally involved. If you feel like asking a question, you can always do so from the safety of the back of the room. (Rest assured the lights are usually turned down low at these soirees.)

You will also want to examine your own attitudes toward the psychic process itself. For instance, you may have more respect for a traditional means of reading, such as tarot cards or the *I Ching*, than for someone just speaking off the top of her head. Since nobody understands the process of accessing psychic information, you may find it a lot easier to attribute it to the cards themselves than to a person's purely psychic ability.

On the other hand, you may think that using psychic apparatus is just silly. Many of us have played with ouija boards and fooled around with tarot cards during the course of growing up, and you may simply remember these things as toys, not as something to be taken seriously. In that case you may want to go to someone who tells you what she sees by directly accessing the information. Or you may find that the process of channeling makes sense to you or fits in with your spiritual beliefs, and that the idea of information coming from the higher self seems more valid to you than the idea of it coming from a deck of playing cards.

Finally, ask yourself if you are someone who respects tradition. Because of the explosion of spiritual work in recent years, what comes under the guise of psychic ability includes every new self-developmental technique under the sun. The word "channeling," for instance, has become a new buzz-word of the psychic movement, and you may be too sick of hearing about it to want to visit a channeler. In that case, try to find someone who calls herself a "medium," or who does good, old-fashioned "séances." Someone using this language probably has her roots in the traditional Spiritualism movement and would be less likely to have incorporated any new fads or trendy ways of working.

The long history of the tarot, and the fact that it has a very respected side as a mystical text as well as a means of divination, may be reassuring to you. Similarly, the *I Ching*, which dates back to the earliest roots of Taoism and Confucianism in ancient China, may command your respect and therefore your attention. If you take the time to find out where a psychic is coming from, you may be surprised by the degree to which he is rooted in tradition.

These roots may have very spiritual aspects. Many psychics see their ability as a gift from God, which may be something that is important to you. A lot of people are afraid to visit a psychic because they have been told it is ungodly or "the Devil's work," or because it was prohibited in the Bible. You may be surprised to learn that many psychics are very religious people and that they take their own spiritual growth quite seriously. If you have strong religious affiliations yourself, you may find it helpful to voice those feelings and try to locate someone who seems to share your sensibilities and can put your reading into a traditional religious context.

It is important to remember that there is no religious component per se to psychic readings and that psychic phenomena do not conflict with traditional religious beliefs. Brian Hurst is a channeler in Los Angeles who has worked with clients in Europe as well as this country. He explains the conflict that many people perceive between religion and psychic work:

> I have a friend who's a born-again Christian. Now our basic desire for people to love each other is the same. But she has a real strong belief in Satan. And she says that Jesus and Satan are doing battle for my soul. And I say, "Let 'em fight." Because I know who I am. I told her what I thought of Satan, and she said, "You're just being deceived. And Satan is deceiving you." Somewhere in the Bible it says that psychics and soothsayers are tools of the Devil. I don't know how you differentiate between a visionary and a psychic, since visionaries are blessed in the Bible.

Hurst's own experiences with the spiritual aspects of channeling have led him to the belief in a universality shared by all religions:

> My biggest problem in what I do is in trying to describe it. I think that religion is a form that people create to make themselves right, to make themselves righteous. I think that eventually religion will topple

in favor of the universal faith. I'm Jewish, and I totally believe in the teachings of Jesus Christ. I wear a little Joan of Arc medallion to remind me not to be a martyr, and I wear a mezuzah, which contains passages from the Old Testament. But I really believe in Christ consciousness, which teaches universal love and unconditional love. So in that respect, God is in all of us.

Your Psychic's Personality

Even if you are not concerned about religious orientation, there are a number of things you should try to find out about a psychic before deciding where to go. Just as your own personality may affect the quality of the reading you get, so, too, will the psychic's demeanor greatly influence your response to what you hear. If you have received a recommendation for a specific psychic, ask the source of that recommendation to describe the personality of the psychic a little bit. Is she nurturing and sensitive? Is she very businesslike? One style will probably appeal to you more than another. Carl recalls having felt put off by the appearance of a card reader he visited, only to find that she was a very different person underneath:

She was totally not like what I thought I would like— she was heavy, didn't seem to have much style, and talked with a heavy Brooklyn accent—all these "Carl-judgmental" things. But in spite of these outwardly stupid judgments, I liked this woman. She appealed to me on a personal level because she had some sort of earth-mother quality. I felt good around her. There was some energy or something there. I went back to her because I needed a pump-up, and she did that— she has a calming effect—she's nice in that way.

I think it's very important to feel that I just like this person, and that's why I would go back to one. It's totally subjective. I've gone to people who friends have recommended, and sometimes they're good for one person and not for others. And some psychics I've liked, other people haven't liked.

You may feel that a psychic should be sensitive to you as a person and not simply view you as an object to be bombarded with information. Psychic ability itself often implies a much greater degree of sensitivity when it comes to relating to people. Many psychics have had to work very hard at learning to disentangle themselves from the emotional makeup of a client following a reading. As was already mentioned, many people who visit psychics look for a certain nurturing quality and want to feel that they mean more to a psychic than just a source of income.

There are types of psychic ability, however, in which sensitivity is not important and can actually be detrimental. A psychic healer, for instance, may need to distance herself from her clients to a certain extent so that she does not take on the illnesses or symptoms of those whom she is treating. Some psychic healers run their offices very much like regular medical doctors, with a reception area, a treatment room, and a medical-history questionnaire. This can be reassuring to many people, since it implies a certain degree of professionalism and experience, but it can also put off those who expect more of a personal approach than that of a conventional medical doctor or psychotherapist. Anne is an insulin-dependent diabetic who visited a psychic healer, but she was uncomfortable with the healer's "professional" approach:

> When you don't know someone, you're always looking for clues as to who they are. I couldn't help noticing that she was wearing a 300-dollar dress and very expensive shoes. Not only did I have to send her a check for $150 two weeks in advance [of my appointment], but she had the nerve to charge me another $10 for the healing tape she gave me to take home—not to mention tax!

The important thing is to know your own sensibilities enough to avoid putting yourself in an uncomfortable situation. These differences in style will also vary with the type of psychic you visit. Just as there are healers who try to run their practices the way medical doctors do, so is it possible that a channeler may not strike you as an especially warm person. But, particularly if he is a trance channeler (someone who goes into a trance to allow a spirit entity to "use" his body), his own personality may not matter as much as that of, say, a clairvoyant. Once a spirit entity comes through, a whole new personality may emerge and you may witness changes in mannerisms and even speech patterns. In most cases, it is preferable for a channeler to be able to remove his own ego from the process in order to assure that the information you receive is totally a function of spirit and not mixed in with the channeler's own emotional makeup.

Again, if you prefer a little distance between you and the psychic, then astrology, numerology, or perhaps card reading would be your best choice. If you are looking for affirmation and more of a therapeutic experience, then you might opt for a clairvoyant who can sense things about you directly, or even consider experiencing some form of spiritual growth process firsthand.

The bottom line, however, is how you feel about the psychic on a gut level. Every psychic I spoke to agreed that the most important factor in choosing a reader is that you feel comfortable with that person, that you are both on the same wavelength, so to speak, that you "resonate" with her. As Susan Edwards explains:

> I think you need to pick someone you can be comfortable with, whom you have a good feeling about, to heal yourself. If you're interested in healing, there has to be a relationship. It's not something that happens arbitrarily.

It's strange the way some people will put aside their emotional response to a psychic they are visiting because they feel that on some level this person is bound to be strange or mysterious. By all means take your emotional responses in with you and, above all, *trust your own intuition*. If you don't feel connected with this person even on a superficial level, it's unlikely that you will be connected with her on a psychic level. Barbara Rollinson, a trance channeler in Broomfield, Colorado, explains that this connection is integral to the channeling process:

> You need a trust level [in which] you are totally in sync with that person when you go for a personal reading. There is a vibrational connection that is there. And I think it's very important that you feel comfortable with that person—with the channeler's own personality and with the channeler's [spirit] guides. Sometimes people will feel comfortable with them, sometimes they won't.

You should also be aware of a psychic's own biases and try to discern whether she allows those to affect the quality of her reading. One psychic told me she received several clients who were emotional wrecks because of readings they had had from a particular male psychic with whom she was familiar. Apparently this man was very hostile toward women and was using his sessions as a way of expressing deep psychological problems of his own. As a result, all his women clients would invariably leave his readings in tears.

I visited a psychic myself whose anger was so strong I could sense it the minute he entered the room. Not surprisingly, his reading was far from uplifting, and he seemed to want to preach only doom and gloom. When I showed him photographs of friends and relatives for brief comments, he had nothing good to say about any of them, focusing only on character flaws and dissatisfactions with their lives (most of which were totally inaccurate).

Don't be afraid to admit to yourself that you just don't like this person and that you want to leave. Your own critical faculties are your best guide to finding a good psychic, and although you may have to make one or two visits before you find one you feel really good about, it will be well worth it when you do. One psychic explains the importance of being sensitive to the client:

I have a client who's from the Mafia, who's put out contracts on people. And he sits in front of me and confesses his life story, and I forgive him. I'm not scared of him. He wanted out; he wanted to love. Unless he forgave himself, he was probably going to end up back in jail. And by some miracle he stayed out of jail, he's out of the Mafia, and they left him alone. If I judged him for murdering people, instead of offering forgiveness, he never would be where he is now. He never would have been able to forgive himself and get rid of his anger. Everywhere else he turned he was getting judgment.

But for me, that was a real discovery about myself— that I didn't sit there and judge this man for murdering people. I guess there really is no such thing as being a psychic. I guess it's just being sensitive enough to see what is in other people—past your own value systems and your own belief systems of what is right or wrong.

Even though you'll want to ask your friends for recommendations, be sure they are telling you to go not just because the reading was accurate, but because they liked the reader as a person. Also bear in mind that every person is unique, and one person's likes differ from those of another. Just because your friend felt he had a rapport with a psychic doesn't mean you have to feel the same. People relate on various levels, and you may be looking for something totally different than your friend when you go for a reading.

Credentials

Another important aspect to consider when choosing a psychic is his professional background. Was he born with psychic ability (or did it emerge early in childhood) or did he develop it by study and practice? There are many people today who give classes in psychic development, and it's not unusual to find people whose ability is purely the result of having taken classes. This is not necessarily better or worse than innate ability—it depends more on the type of training. Even people who are naturally psychic often need some form of training in order to use it in the most constructive way.

Some people have discovered psychic ability well into adulthood as the result of some sort of spiritual awakening. Since we all have psychic ability to some extent, it may take just a certain stimulus to bring that ability to the surface. Deep religious conviction or sustained spiritual practice, such as meditation or contemplation, may result in a strong psychic awareness.

Other people seem to have been "chosen" and simply start picking up things psychically from others around them.

In all these cases, however, some spiritual or psychic training is usually essential in order for psychics to hone their skills, make it easier to access their intuitive self, and enable them to shut off their awareness when they prefer not to access things psychically about people around them. If a psychic doesn't have such training, chances are she will have to learn her lessons the hard way—by practicing on clients. A lot of issues come up during the course of psychic work, and these will have to be dealt with at some point or another during a career.

Bear in mind that if you visit a person who has not had any formal training, she should at least have a number of years of experience behind her before going professional. Doing psychic readings is playing with people's heads, if not with their emotions, and no one is qualified to hang up a shingle simply because she has innate ability. That ability is only one small part of what is involved in doing psychic readings, and it is only through years of practice, personal exploration, and guidance from others who have trodden that path that a person can consider herself ready to work professionally. There are strong psychological and spiritual components to psychic work, and these should be treated with caution and respect.

There are, in fact, some psychics who are qualified psychologists or who have a lot of experience with some form of therapy, such as transpersonal psychology or bodywork-oriented therapy. Although more "conventional" backgrounds such as these are hardly essential (and in some cases may actually prevent someone from letting go of standard modalities), they are at least good indications of a reputable professional.

It's not unusual to find cases where someone who was practicing psychotherapy began to tune in to her patients psychically, accessing information intuitively as well as analytically. Many of these people found that their best work was being done on the psychic rather than emotional level and decided to develop their intuitive faculty even further, eventually giving up conventional modes of treatment.

There are also a number of traditionally trained therapists who, over the course of their work, came to feel that the more conventional therapeutic models focus more on illness than wellness. Many of them got to the point where they wanted not so much to make emotionally sick people well as to make mentally healthy people spiritually whole. Thus their work went from psychological counseling to psychic counseling. Margo Schmidt, although not a licensed therapist, worked extensively with disturbed children and their psychological issues. She recalls her own journey from psychological to psychic work:

> Increasingly I became aware that the [standard] modalities of healing were maintenance at best, and that you can't heal the part without healing the whole. The real awakening to this was my own inner

journey . . . a major vision I had ten years ago at the Edgar Cayce Foundation. Basically the vision was a sense of personal contact with Christ . . . In it, I was holding onto his hand, and he was leading me to a tower—it was something between a church steeple and a minaret—and he said, "You have to go on your own now." And I got onto the balcony and I looked out, and there were thousands of people there. And I thought, "Wait a minute! Whoa!" And this voice said, "This will be your destiny some day. Now it is time to go into a long sleep." And I did.

Right after that was when my life fell apart. Without any warning, in a two-week period, I lost my job, I lost my relationship, I lost everything but the house I was living in. Just like that. It was almost as if all the [physical] forms literally had to be mushed. And that's happened two or three times to me since. It's been just a massive source of transformation and letting go . . . I feel that the vehicle of the soul is an experiential one, and that we cannot teach what we are not. That is why a lot of people in the healing/helping professions—and myself—are going through such an intensified practicum. What I'm looking to teach people is what is involved in opening to [spiritual energy] and grounding [it]. Because I say to people, you can't plug 220 volts in a 110 socket—you'll blow your fuses.

Spiritual Development

At some point or another in a psychic's career, he is going to have to confront the issue of spirituality. As we have seen, psychic ability is really an expression of the spiritual side of a person. Although many people can use their ability in very helpful ways solely as a function of psi, if they are to continue to grow psychically, they will almost invariably have to grow spiritually. Similarly, many people who visit psychics are interested in working on the spiritual part of themselves, and if a psychic has not worked on his own spiritual side, he will be of little use to a client who is seeking guidance in that area.

Although you are not going to try to pry into someone's spiritual beliefs before making an appointment for a psychic reading, if you have the opportunity to speak to the psychic when making your appointment, or even when you first arrive for your visit, you might simply ask him if there is a "spiritual component" to what he does. The answer might range anywhere from an affirmation of very traditional religious beliefs to a brief discussion on the value of meditation and knowing one's inner self. Whatever the nature of the response, it will go far in telling you where that reader is coming from. Ellen Hendrick, a psychic healer in New Orleans, believes that healing, and even ritual magic, comes directly from God:

I believe it's the power of suggestion from God, because He can move anybody or anything. He's letting us know that He is within us, and that we have the same powers—not as much, but we're like a battery. God is within us, yet we do not become Him. He is the power source, we are the batteries. We have to go back and get recharged. But He's showing us we have the power to do anything we want to. He's showing us that He is everywhere; that He has dominion over everything and everybody.

I believe that's what the Holy Spirit is: if you open your mind and your heart to receive what God gives you, or the Force, or whatever you want to call it, it will come to you. And it will talk to you in ways that you will never believe. And you will be able to do all kinds of things. I'm talking about getting in touch with your inner self to help others. You cannot help your inner self until you help others.

Above all, don't be afraid to ask a psychic about her spiritual beliefs. I have met psychics who gave me readings, then spoke with me for several hours, whom I thought were just "straight" psychics—people with psi. It was only when we were wrapping up our interview that they revealed themselves to be deeply spiritual people. In the same way, just because some people wear their spirituality on their sleeve, constantly talking about the "higher self" and "divine energies," it doesn't mean that they are any more spiritual than you or I. There is a lot of jargon being flung around these days, and much of it is being used to sell a product. It's up to you as a discriminating consumer to weed out the hype from the genuine article.

Finally, it is important not only to know a psychic's degree of spiritual development, but to be aware of how "grounded" she is. Grounding means that despite spending a lot of time accessing intuitive or spiritual information, the psychic has not lost the ability to apply that knowledge to the material world—either yours or her own. Many people expect a psychic to be a little "far out," but it's too easy for someone to get lost in the metaphysical aspects of psychic work, forgetting that the role of a professional is to be able to use that information in a concrete and helpful way.

You might also find that a psychic who is not properly grounded is difficult to communicate with, and therefore it is hard to make yourself understood. Someone who has lost touch with the material plane will also have lost touch with people and the dynamics of interpersonal relationships. If you encounter someone like this, obviously it will be a great handicap in getting the most out of your reading; in the end it will simply prove frustrating. Don't be fooled by someone who hides under the cover of "otherworldliness": a good psychic should be able to relate to you as well as any other skilled professional.

II: Where To Look For a Good Psychic
Personal Recommendations

Now that you are ready to interrogate your prospective psychic, you need to go about finding one. The best way to locate a good psychic is through a personal recommendation from a friend. Someone who knows both you and the psychic will obviously be a great help in determining whether that psychic will be able to meet your needs—on all levels. If you're interested in having a reading simply out of curiosity, then a simple "Go!" will probably be enough of an endorsement. But if you are looking to delve a little deeper into yourself, it's a good idea to ask your friend all the questions you can think of that may affect the quality of the reading.

Many people will go to a particular psychic simply because she's the one their friend went to. But an individual psychic may be better suited to your friend than to you—or you may be looking for a different kind of information. Be patient. If you are really interested in getting a quality reading, you'll have to shop around, the same way you would shop around for a good therapist before settling on one. Today it is easier than ever to locate a good psychic, and there is no reason to go to someone simply because it's the only name you have. After all, why go to an astrologer if you really think you would enjoy a channeling session? By now it should be clear that there really is no such thing as a "generic psychic." If you are willing to put in a little extra time and effort, you'll be able to compile a substantial list of several names under each category.

In addition to your close friends, you'll want to broaden your search by putting out feelers. Mention to other people that you are looking for the name of a good psychic. If you're sure that you want to see an astrologer or psychic healer, make it clear what kind of psychic you are looking for. Otherwise, don't limit your search. Although you may think you want to see a channeler, you won't want to miss a sterling recommendation for a great tarot card reader either.

If you're a little shy about telling people you want to visit a psychic, be subtle. Shooting the breeze over the coffee machine at work with a group of coworkers might be a good time simply to mention the word "psychic." You'll be surprised how fast someone will take the bait. And it will probably be someone you had least suspected of having an interest in psychic phenomena. Almost everyone knows somebody who has been to a psychic, and they will be only too happy to start talking about it, even if it's only to poke fun at the whole idea. If you really want to keep a low profile, simply say, "Shirley MacLaine." That should blow the lid off the whole subject. Keep your ears open and follow up any leads. After a while you'll become very adept at separating the ones who sound a little questionable from those who are doing serious work. And guaranteed, before long, you'll have more names than you know what to do with.

Psychic Referral Services

If you are having trouble coming up with a satisfactory recommendation simply by word of mouth, don't despair. There are still several ways to locate psychics who have been screened, without having to resort to blind ads. Probably the best way is through something that has just recently started cropping up—psychic referral services. These are agencies you can call to get the names of reputable psychics who have been carefully screened and tested before being put on a referral list. A markup or commission is sometimes charged, but many referrals are offered as a free service by concerned people who are trying to weed out the frauds from the genuine readers. Be advised, however, that not all referral services apply equally strict standards to the psychics they represent. Choose a referral service as carefully as you would choose an individual psychic.

Ellen Hendrick runs The Psychic Connection, an international organization made up of professional psychics, people doing spiritual work, and those who are just interested in the field. The organization acts as a clearinghouse for information, and referrals are free to any person who wishes to call. She explains some of the reasons for starting such an organization:

We're trying to create psychic awareness throughout the world. By doing this, by getting everyone together who is a true psychic—through this power we can create peace, we can create plenty in the world. No more hunger. Changing the world through the power of the mind. We all share what we have with other people, whether it be food, or spiritual food, or knowledge.

One of the other features of using a referral service is that they may interview you first, in order to get a good idea of what you want to get out of a psychic reading and who might best suit your personality. If the service has done an adequate job of screening its psychics, then you are insured of at least a minimal level of compatibility between you and the psychic reader. Michael Goodrich is president of Cosmic Contact Psychic Services in New York, which, for a fee, offers referrals to people searching for reputable psychics. He describes the screening process he uses to select those he will represent:

> We use people who show exceptional ability. If they're coming out of the cold, they have to send at least 15 or 20 letters of recommendation, just to see that they are serious. And I have them give people cold readings, people they've never seen before. Then I check on those readings. Then I have them give my staff psychics readings—people who have been certified by Lily Dale [a community for psychics in upstate New York], who I've worked with over a long period of time. That's really one of the best ways to tell. And then if they pass that test, I have them give me a reading, and I guess at this point I'm intuitive enough to know whether I want to work with this person or not.

A psychic referral service is probably as close as you can get to "certification," when it comes to professional psychics, but it is by no means a guarantee. I was referred by such a service to a very highly-credited tarot card reader whose standard fee is $100 an hour. That reading turned out to be the worst I have ever had. (For better or worse, it didn't even last the full hour.) So, buyer beware! If you use a referral service, ask all the same questions you would if you were doing your own screening. After all, you may be paying a premium for this service, so it's a good opportunity to dig for information. Look for psychic referral services in the same places you would look for individual psychics: through word-of-mouth, on bookstore bulletin boards, in classified ads, and in the Yellow Pages.

Psychic Fairs

The next place you can go to find a psychic who has already been screened is a psychic fair. These events are held in various locations—usually in hotels or shopping malls—on a regular basis, and if you keep checking advertisements (more on that later), you will see them listed quite frequently. Psychic fairs vary in purpose and scope. On the grandest scale, they include not just psychics doing readings, but lectures on a host of metaphysical topics, demonstrations of various spiritual development techniques, sometimes nutritional and natural foods information, and, of course, a host of things for sale—from quartz crystals to herbal cures.

Other psychic fairs consist simply of ten or 15 psychics in a large room doing brief readings. In this case, you will pay a nominal fee at the door—anywhere from $2 to $5—and then an additional $15 or so, which will entitle you to a brief, 15- or 30-minute psychic reading with a psychic of your choice. The advantage of these fairs is that the organizations running them will have presumably chosen only those psychics they consider to be of high quality, so you are guaranteed at least a minimal level of competence.

Craig Steele and Kevin Dormeyer are co-owners of Together Bookstore, in Denver, Colorado, which has been running psychic fairs for several years. Dormeyer explains some of the things he looks for in a good psychic:

> I prefer the term "intuitive arts" to "psychic." The term intuitive is more responsible to me. Interviewing the psychics for the fairs allows us to interface a little bit. We look for insight, compassion, and nourishment. We want them to be good counselors.
>
> We want our psychics to be qualified therapists, too, so that they can handle dependent people. They aren't really selling their wares, they're selling themselves as facilitators. . . . Everyone I respect as a psychic, I respect as a therapist. We let them do their number on us in order to evaluate who we will accept. We want integrity, skill in facilitating, insight.
>
> What I ask [a psychic for] is to give me a reading on what's most appropriate for me *now*—physically, emotionally, spiritually. I look to see if they reveal something new [about myself] or if they give me added insight about something I already know.

Dormeyer stresses the responsibility professional psychics take on when they choose to give readings. His advice to the consumer: "Pick your psychic like you would pick your doctor."

Similarly, Steele says he looks at two aspects of a psychic's ability: 1) How do they access the information? and 2) How do they process it and relate it to you? "I watch the process," he says. "Is this person going to a place where he can experience that reality and bring it back?" Steele also cautions against confusing spiritual enlightenment with psychic ability:

Channelers, for instance, are not spiritual teachers, they are psychic teachers. It's not [spiritual] evolution, it's just experience. It's like a card trick done on the spiritual-psychic level. If I needed a guy to go catch passes, I would hire a guy to catch passes. If I needed a psychic, I would hire a psychic—it's just an ability.

Unfortunately, not all psychic fair organizers are as exacting as Dormeyer and Steele. Just because there is a sponsoring organization listed on a poster is no guarantee that you will get a quality reading. And, because of the time constraints, the noisy atmosphere, and the relatively low fees that are charged, not all psychics want to do psychic fairs. Others feel that psychic fairs are "beneath" them.

Tarot card reader Ron Havern was originally skeptical about doing psychic fairs. But, as he explains, there is a positive side to doing short readings:

I kind of like the format. Let's face it, most people who aren't really tuned into all this really can't absorb that much information. So I think it's more useful to give them 15 minutes—sort of the news of the day, a news summary. I think that's more helpful for a lot of people. And I don't get so involved with them. So it's kind of a nice, energizing thing.

Remember that a 15-minute reading can only give you a taste of what psychic readings are all about. In addition, because of the nature of a psychic fair, only certain kinds of psychics tend to participate. You won't find any channelers, mediums, or psychic healers at a fair. And although you'll see some people billing themselves as astrologers, a true astrological chart takes hours to prepare and at least another hour to explain. A good astrologer may be able to tell you a great deal about yourself in 15 minutes, but you'd be better off booking a regular appointment if you want a horoscope done. Tarot card readers seem to be the best represented at psychic fairs, maybe because it makes for better visual presentation than a person just sitting there and staring at you while reading. In any case, it does tend to be well suited to the brief format.

The reason these psychics are there, of course, is to drum up repeat business after they have whetted your appetite. In this way, a psychic fair can be a useful tool in screening a variety of different readers without investing too much time or money. In my own case, I found quite an excellent tarot card reader at a fair one Sunday afternoon. I was so impressed by how much he did in 15 minutes—and with his manner of reading—that I took his business card in order to book a full hour-long reading. It was only later, when we met for my appointment, that I found out he was also a practicing psychologist with very impressive academic credentials.

The other nice thing about a psychic fair is that it's a golden opportunity to meet other "psychic junkies." Here is your chance to pull aside almost anyone you see and ask him for the name of a good psychic without fear of ridicule. You'll also have a chance to find out what other people consider to be the mark of a good reader, as well as what they personally get out of psychic readings. Of course, you'll also meet your share of flakes, but that's part of the fun as well.

Classes, Lectures, and Group Meetings

If you're interested in investing a little more time and effort in your investigation of the paranormal, you might consider putting yourself into other situations where you'll be surrounded by like-minded people. The simplest is to take a class. It doesn't have to be a class with a psychic, but any lecture on metaphysics, philosophy, or religion. Today, there are countless lectures and classes being offered through New Age learning centers and adult-education programs that cover everything from parapsychology to Buddhism. Through these learning opportunities, you won't just meet like-minded people, but also find new resources for locating good psychics and spiritual counselors.

If you want to go a little deeper, you can attend a meeting of a spiritual support group. These groups are generally run by people who are professional psychics, and they include formats as diverse as simple lectures and experiential workshops. Most groups are open to anyone and range anywhere from intimate discussion groups of five to ten people to group channeling sessions of 50 or more. Since you pay on a one-time basis (anywhere from $5 to $35, depending upon the reputation of the teacher), you can attend one meeting to get the flavor or to meet some other psychic searchers. Although most of these groups are made known by word of mouth, you will often see announcements for them in metaphysical bookstores, New Age learning centers, and spiritual newsletters and magazines.

Andrea Hinda, who works as an assistant facilitator with a number of psychics and channelers in Boulder, Colorado, and who is a psychic in her own right, explains that when she was booking appointments for Barbara Rollinson, she encouraged those who were curious to attend a group channeling session before booking a private appointment. That way, she says, people have an opportunity to see what Rollinson is like and what the whole process of channeling is like. It also encourages people to trust their own sense of what is right for them. As she puts it:

> A lot of times, if people haven't known Barbara and there's a group channeling coming up, I suggest they attend that first, because it gives them an experience of who she is, in an indirect type of way, and an experience of her [spirit] guides. They can feel her out and they can decide if that works for them. I always try to leave it open for people to make their own choice—to come out of their own free will, their own feeling, their own intuition. The question you have to ask is: "Does this feel right to you?"

These group meetings are not only an excellent opportunity to see what channeling is all about, but they can expose you to a number of different psychics and a wide variety of personal styles. Very often, two or more channelers may run a group together, creating a psychic experience that transcends what either psychic does alone and affording the curious psychic seeker an inexpensive opportunity to "window-shop."

In addition to group channeling sessions, there are weekly spiritual support groups that are generally more experiential. In these groups you may be guided by an experienced psychic in everything from contacting your own spirit guide to past-life regressions. Although such groups are generally ongoing, they are usually open to anyone who wishes to sample a single meeting. Many people have found these evenings to be instrumental in unlocking their own intuitive powers, an experience which in turn reinforces for them the validity of psychic ability in general. Cindy, an executive at a multinational bank, described what attending a group workshop has meant to her:

> It's a need that I have to believe in something [spiritual]. I want to believe in psychics, I want to believe in God, I want to believe that there's a reason for my existence. I was brought up Jewish, but I've always shied away from organized anything, which is why even with this group stuff, it's so difficult, but also why it's so rewarding for me. It allows me to share with other people, while still having that sense of individuality that I need.
>
> Also, I'm afraid of being sucked in, or duped, or being told what to do. So I really need to feel I'm in control. And this way, I feel like I'm in control, but I also

feel like I'm supported, and that there's a lot of power, a lot of energy, and a lot of things out there that are mine to use.

Spiritual Communities and Retreat Centers

If you are really adventurous, you might consider looking into more intensive spiritual workshops. These are generally held over the course of a weekend, but may run as long as three to five days. In them, you may confront deeper emotional or psychological issues with the aid of a psychically skilled facilitator, remove spiritual blocks, discover past-life issues with the help of a channeler, or develop your own meditation and visualization skills so that you can work through specific issues even after the workshop is over.

Many of these intensives are held at spiritual communities or retreat centers. These communities, which are usually located in remote, pastoral settings, range from New Age learning centers to self-contained villages that grew up as hideaways for those involved in the Spiritualism movement. Others consist of people who follow the teachings of a particular spiritual leader, who may or may not still be alive. These communities offer classes, workshops, and psychic readings, as well as a place to go to simply relax and pursue some quiet introspection.

The beauty of a spiritual community is that the setting is more conducive to the inward search that many people undertake when they go for a psychic reading.

The flip side is that you won't find anyone practicing fortune-telling at any of these places. There is usually a strong spiritual component underlying the work, although nobody will try to convert you to a specific way of thought. Again, the message is to simply follow your own inner guidance.

Restaurants and Nightclubs

A more "neutral" atmosphere in which to get a psychic reading is in a restaurant or nightclub. As psychic readings have gained in popularity, many restaurants, at least in large metropolitan areas, have made a table available to either one or several psychics. Generally there will be a card on the table offering you the chance for a psychic reading with your coffee and dessert. The prices are usually good for such readings ($10 to $20), and the psychics have at least been screened by the restaurant management, so again, you are assured of some minimal level of competence.

A bit more far out are psychic readings that are done in nightclubs—a relatively new phenomenon. Some promoters have experimented with "psychic nights" at major nightclubs and discos, where some channeling may be done for the audience followed by individual readings off to the side. Although it may seem unlikely, some reputable psychics do participate in these events, if only for the publicity. Others may be involved if the proceeds are going to a worthy cause. The loud music, alcohol, and smoke may not strike you as the optimum place for deep introspection, but as one psychic told me, "Since I'm in a trance when I'm channeling, all that really doesn't bother me." The clients, of course, aren't so lucky.

Other Psychics

Yet another way to get a word-of-mouth recommendation for a psychic is simply to ask another psychic. That isn't to say you should just call up someone you've never met and ask her for a bunch of names, but if you've visited a psychic who you felt was not exectly right for you, you might make use of the opportunity to ask for a referral. This is especially easy to do if you are looking for a different type of psychic. For instance, say you went to a tarot card reader simply out of curiosity and liked what you saw and heard—so much so, that now you think you might be ready to visit a channeler. Simply explain to the card reader how much you enjoyed the reading, adding that you were skeptical when you came in but now feel much better about the idea of psychic work, and ask her if she can recommend a good channeler.

Another way of handling this would be to say that you are asking for a friend who is looking for a specific type of psychic. Likewise, if you know someone who is going for a specific type of reading, ask him to get a couple of names for you in the same way before he leaves his reading. Most psychics don't operate in a vacuum, and they'll know at least a few people doing similar work. A psychic who is reputable and who believes in the process should have no problem in recommending someone else in the field. Anyone who finds such a request threatening should probably take a closer look at her own motives for doing psychic readings.

Television and Radio

If you have exhausted all the other possibilities, or simply want to "see what's out there," you can continue your search for a psychic through the media. Television and radio are not slow in picking up on the latest craze, so there is no dearth of video and radio psychics these days. Simply turn on your local public-access cable station and you'll see quite a range of people doing psychic readings over the air. (Of course, if you're a regular viewer of Oprah Winfrey or Phil Donahue, you are already an expert on everything from past-life regression to faith healers.) The cable stations and radio shows give you the opportunity to have a brief but free reading right in the comfort of your own home.

As in the case of the psychic fairs, the people doing these shows are hoping to drum up repeat business, and you'll see two telephone numbers flashed on the screen. One is the number to call to ask a question on the air; the other is to find out about booking a regular appointment. The drawback is that unless you manage to get your question asked during the course of the show, you won't have any clue to how accurate the psychic is, but you will most definitely be able to form a judgment about her style and manner of reading. (Personally, I find some of these television psychics to be so off-putting that I wonder why they even bother to show themselves on the air.)

Remember that the quality of the air-wave psychics is as varied as any other group of readers. The fact that they are on the air is by no means a guarantee of how good they are. There are some serious people who have chosen to go on the air, not so much as a way of drumming up business as to add some variety to their work and to reach a wider audience. As more and more reputable psychics decide to expand the scope of their work, we will probably see more quality work being done through the use of electronic media. This will make it easier to discern between those who are doing good work and those who are modern-day snake oil salesmen.

In addition to the broadcast media, metaphysical bookstores stock a full range of video and audio cassettes of psychics, faith healers, and channelers. Some of them serve simply as good introductions to what these phenomena actually are, others carry more inspirational messages or are guides for channeling or healing yourself. Ask the people in the store to help you sort out the different types and what you can hope to get from each.

Publications and Mail Orders

Newspapers, spiritual newsletters, and New Age magazines are all good places to look for psychic listings. The problem is that you don't have much to go on in trying to decide how reputable they are. If you do decide to go this route, you should either write or telephone the psychic in advance, asking for some information as to what he does, what his fees are, and what his background is. As with any method of referral, try to get as much information in advance before deciding to invest.

Many of these magazines contain classified ads for mail-order psychic readings. The best that can be said about these is that they are generally cheap. They range in quality from those that offer full readings by phone to those that offer to answer "two questions for $10, five questions for $20, and a full life-reading for $50." If you like the idea of buying your psychic information by weight, these ads will appeal to you.

That's not to say that psychic readings done by mail always have to be frauds. Some of the greatest psychics the world has known have been able to tell a lot about a person just from a signature or a letter that was once in someone's possession. And many psychics who do in-person readings will willingly read photographs of other people. It is simply that trying to discriminate between the legitimate ones and the questionable ones on the basis of a three-line advertisement is difficult at best.

If you decide to try these services just out of curiosity, use common sense. It is unlikely that a reading based solely on your writing a letter with three questions in it will be as accurate as one which is at least based upon a photograph you have sent. If you opt for a telephone reading, at least you will be able to have a dialogue with the person on the other end, whether she is psychic or not.

As far as mail order goes, an astrology or numerology reading promises to yield the best results, since these methods are based upon numbers and charts and require no special psychic powers to operate through the mail. If you choose one of these methods, though, do so carefully. Many services that advertise astrological or numerological charts mean just that: a chart of numbers or calculations with no explanations. If you want more information, you are then asked to send for a book—which you'll have to shell out more money for—or for a full "life" reading, which will also cost you. These kinds of astrology and numerology readings can be offered cheaply because people use computers to print out the charts, requiring little time and no effort. That's not to say that these charts are inaccurate; they will simply make little sense to someone who lacks a full working knowledge of these methods of divination.

If you still want to try a mail-order reading, pick out the ones that look the most promising and write to them—*before* sending any money—asking for as much information as they can furnish: what services they offer, what their fees are, how they receive their information, etc. Interestingly, I've found that even mail-order psychics who are inaccurate are only too happy to write to you about what they do, in some cases writing long explanations by hand about their services and the significance of their work. At least if you have more to go on than a few lines in a classified ad, you'll be able to make a more informed choice about which ones seem the most reputable.

Specialty Bookstores

Bookstores that specialize in metaphysics or occult subjects are also a good place to hunt for the names of psychics. Generally these stores have bulletin boards that are plastered with cards and flyers, advertising a smorgasbord of New Age and self-developmental techniques and services. As with any printed ad, the best you can expect is to come away with a bunch of names and numbers to contact for further information. These are good places, however, to look for announcements about psychic fairs, spiritual workshops, and group channeling sessions. You might also ask some of the people who work in the store if they can recommend anyone or any group that they feel is reputable.

The Yellow Pages

Finally, there are the good old Yellow Pages. Yes, you too can "let your fingers do the walking" in your search for a psychic. Look under such listings as "Psychic Life Readings," "Astrologers," or "Occult Research," and you may turn up everything from your local astrologer to a psychic referral service. As with any advertisement, call first, ask questions, then decide.

Storefront Readers

All of which brings us to that traditional stronghold of the psychic profession—the storefront fortune-teller. If you know someone who has been to a tea room or "reader/advisor" and loved the results, by all means invest a few bucks and go for a reading. If, however, you want to simply walk in off the street and have your fortune told, be advised that you are really taking a shot in the dark. It is possible that you will connect with someone who is very accurate, very reasonably priced, and very helpful (as has happened to me), but it is also possible that you will end up being the victim of a shady—and scary—sham (as has also happened to me).

The fact that there is absolutely no regulation of people who call themselves psychics makes trying to find one off the street a dubious endeavor. Considering that fortune-telling is illegal in many states, it's particularly ironic that you can't walk down the street of any major city without being bathed in the pink light of neon palms, crystal balls, and "tea rooms." If the legal position were changed from proscription to prescription, there might be more protection for those seeking psychic services. As it is, though, you are advised to tread cautiously.

Lately there have been some tea rooms that have opened up near major urban business districts that cater to a primarily young, white-collar clientele. (One midtown Manhattan tea room was even written up in *The New York Times* under the title "White-Collar

Psychics.") These are a notch above the "one flight up" school of crystal-ball readers and usually consist of half a dozen or so card readers doing 15-minute readings much in the manner of the psychic fairs. They can be entertaining, perhaps informative, and can provide a quick fix for those people who feel a need for frequent consultations.

But when it comes to the average storefront psychic, the service is far from reliable. Of course, the price is much more reasonable, but what many of these readers miss in legitimate receipts they make up in more dubious ways. We will discuss some of the more obvious scams that are used further on. Suffice it to say that if you decide to walk in off the street, be sure you are acquainted with every possible trick to separate you from your money, and be prepared to walk out the minute something doesn't seem right to you.

III: What To Watch Out For in a Psychic

What Makes a Good Psychic?

Frauds are not confined to storefront operations, of course. Often, the bigger the reputation of the psychic, the bigger the fraud. It is an unfortunate fact that many people see price as a measure of quality. As a result, the more they are willing to pay, the more they are willing to believe. Psychic reading, like any other profession, is beleaguered by people willing to exploit this gullibility.

It is not the purpose of this book to rate the accuracy or legitimacy of different psychics or to expose individual frauds. Its purpose is rather to educate you, the consumer, to the point where you will be able to make informed choices about the people and services that are available. But because the psychic profession is unregulated in any way, unlike other healing professions, and because the array of services that come under the umbrella of "psychic" is so varied, the incidence of fraud is regrettably very high among those who profess psychic ability. (Alan Vaughan, the former editor of *Psychic* magazine and himself a psychic channeler, has suggested that professional psychics take a "Psychic Hippocratic Oath," or at least be educated about ethics.) It is therefore necessary to isolate a few specific examples of fraud, some more blatant than others, so that you will be able to recognize warning signs when you see them.

It should first be pointed out that what makes a psychic good or bad is not how accurate the predictions are, but rather how helpful the information and the presentation of that information is. Someone can be dead-on accurate, but if that accuracy consists of telling you that a safe is going to fall on you tomorrow and there is nothing you can do about it, the reading would not exactly be considered "good." If, however, a less accurate psychic told you that you have a tendency to walk under open windows where safes are being moved, and that if you want to get ahead in your life, you should walk on the other side of the street, you would at least be leaving your reading with some constructive, helpful advice.

As in any professional transaction or business relationship, you have to rely on your own sense of character. Do you think this person is a good person? Do you feel she cares about her clients? And finally, do you feel she has developed her ability to the point where she can use it in a helpful, constructive way? Although you have to be open to new experiences when you go for a psychic reading, there is no reason to check your mind at the door. A little skepticism is a healthy thing, and it can go far in enabling you to evaluate what you see and experience.

Frauds

If a psychic acts in a particularly mysterious way— as though you couldn't possibly understand what is going on—or tries to impress you with a lot of psychic mumbo jumbo, such as foreign words or cryptic messages, you can pretty much figure you're in the wrong place. Unless, of course, you simply want to be entertained in the same way a magician would entertain you. If a psychic seems to be hiding behind his ability in any way, a little warning bell should go off in your head.

Some psychics—particularly channelers—may be a little flashier than others and may invoke certain prayers or rituals before beginning, but these should be simply for the purpose of preparing either themselves or you to receive the information that is about to be given. If you are puzzled or put off by something, ask what it's for. Any psychic who employs such invocations should be prepared to explain them—and most will without being asked. If *anything* is done that makes you uncomfortable, and the reader refuses to explain it to your satisfaction, *get up and leave.*

One woman I spoke with went for a "soul-clearing," which in most cases is a simple, affirming meditation that some healers use to remove blocks to someone's creative energy. This woman was in such an emotionally vulnerable state, however, that by the time she realized that she was to be the subject of an exorcism, she had already been given cocaine and told that she was possessed.

If anyone ever mentions the Devil, or Satan, or anything about evil spirits, leave and don't look back. *All* reputable psychic work, whether it is simple card reading or channeling spirits of the dead, is *always* devoted solely to working with positive energies and achieving the highest good for all involved. If any other reason is given to you for what is about to be done, bow out gracefully and refuse to participate.

Unfortunately, most questionable psychic work is not as blatant as giving someone cocaine. Subtle means can be employed either to exercise power over someone or to extract money from an unsuspecting victim. We have already mentioned the problem of people who do possess psychic ability but who allow their own prejudices to get in the way, sometimes causing their clients a great deal of pain. But in other cases the desire to inflict harm is much more calculated, and because many people visit a psychic when they are in an emotionally vulnerable state, the opportunities for such power displays are all too frequent.

If any psychic seems to be trying to convince you of something that doesn't make any sense to you, don't stay to get into a discussion over the matter. Nothing you hear should sound threatening or ominous or be phrased as a warning ("Either you do this or that will happen.") Both you and the psychic should recognize the fact (if not drive it home) that you have free will and that your destiny is ultimately in your own hands.

Similarly, if anyone tries to get you to do anything, don't listen to her. No psychic should ever tell you what to do, except in cases where you specifically ask for advice. And if that advice is given, it should be put in the context of the whole situation and presented as only one of your alternatives. If someone tries to persuade you to do something that you normally would not do or that doesn't make sense to you, you can assume you are being manipulated.

Fortunately, most frauds do not involve psychological manipulation and are merely devoted to financial gain. These are the typical phonies, who rely mostly upon people's gullibility and their own knowledge of human nature, but who also employ certain standard tricks to make you think they are psychic.

Financial scams range from simple hustling, to get as much money from you as possible before you leave, to more elaborate plots that set you up for more serious crimes. A storefront psychic typically will advertise a ridiculously low price, such as "Special Reading, $2." When you get inside, you will be told—among other things—that someone is threatening your life, but that "the crystal ball is getting cloudy," and if you want to know the name of that person, it will cost you another $5. If you are confronted with such a situation, tell the reader you haven't got any more money and get up and walk out.

Other setups are more intricate. One woman was convinced by a fortune-teller that all her money was in danger. She was told that if she took her money out of the bank and put it in a brown paper bag under her pillow, not only would it be safe, but that it would multiply. The woman followed these instructions, and when she looked in the paper bag several days later, her money was gone. So was the psychic.

Other scams play on people's fears. A typical scenario involves the reader who tells you that she sees that someone has put a horrible curse on you and that if you give her X amount of money, she will remove it for you. This may require a one-time lump sum or long-term installment payments. Anne, although a mature professional woman, found that she was susceptible to such a scam, particularly because she was recently divorced, and therefore in an emotionally vulnerable state:

Everybody talked about this psychic—my cousins had all gone, she had ads in the paper, and it was like 15 bucks, so you go, why not? When I walked in, she looked at me and she said, "Who's the J?" And I was there because of someone with a "J." And she made some other observations that were accurate.

It was only after I went back the second time that she told me I had a curse on me, only after she had really impressed me. She said that the curse had been put on my grandmother, that it came down to me through my mother, and that it had something to do with children. (I don't remember if I told her that I had lost a child.) The curse was that I should never find happiness, that I would always have difficulty with relationships. She said it was put on my grandmother by someone who couldn't have children. My grandmother had 15 children, so it was a question of jealousy—it made sense to me.

She was going to take the curse off. I had to bring a piece of fruit—three fruits, I think it was. I had to bring it there, and I had to keep money in my shoe, which I then had to give to her. I think I had to give her $100 or something. And she was going to take more money to light candles. I think I probably gave her a total of $200. And then I stopped going—she wanted me to come back, but she didn't bug me, because she must have figured I got wise.

Another trick to watch out for is the psychic who tells you not to tell anyone else about your reading— that it will affect the outcome in some way. One woman who visited a storefront psychic with her friend did compare notes, after being warned not to, only to discover that they had both received identical readings!

Although many of these tactics seem so obvious as to be totally ineffective, people who use them are professionals—not professional psychics, but professional observers of human nature and expert manipulators of people's fears and feelings. They have learned to make quick, on-the-spot assessments of people based not only on your appearance but on your mannerisms, your reactions, and the type of questions you ask. They have learned to hook you with some seemingly psychic bit of information in order to induce you to go along with whatever comes next. It's hard for any of us to resist believing what someone says—no matter how preposterous it sounds—if that person has just revealed something about ourselves that we consider to be hidden.

These techniques vary in degree of skill and subtlety. A storefront psychic who charges $10 a reading will be less adept than, say, a television psychic who does private readings for $100 an hour. The latter may be a master of manipulation. On his show, he may have phony calls set up to show how accurate he is (and many do, if only to screen out the "crazies" who invariably call in on such programs). His accuracy demonstrated on TV, you will invariably be more apt to believe him during a private reading. (The fee alone may be enough to convince you that he is genuine.)

During the reading, he might employ certain techniques to reinforce your belief in his ability. For example, it's a fact that there are certain psychological characteristics that seem to apply universally. An experienced charlatan will be well versed in what these are and how to use them skillfully. One psychic I spoke to, who is also a practicing psychologist, recalled a class in which the professor handed out individual "character analysis" sheets to each member of the class, who were then asked to rate them for accuracy. After the majority had agreed that they were exceedingly accurate, the professor revealed that everyone had received the same exact list.

An abundance of generalizations is a good indication that the person you are with may not be psychic. It's true that many of us face similar problems during the course of our lives and that the phrases used to describe them often sound trite and stereotypical, but a good psychic will relate anything she says directly to the specifics in your life. You will certainly know when you haven't been told anything special to your situation, and you will most probably come away feeling that you didn't get your money's worth.

A similar type of whitewash is the psychic who spends an entire reading talking about your past lives. This is generally a safe thing to do, since you have no way of verifying how accurate the information is or whether you even had any past lives at all. It may be couched in complex language, or sprinkled with references to "the Akashic records" or "the lost continent of Atlantis," and it will most probably take place in some exotic locale, like ancient Egypt or the Middle East at the time of Christ. (I have yet to meet anyone who remembered a past life in Iowa circa 1889.)

You are more apt to encounter references to past lives and karma with channelers, since we seem to expect that spirit guides will say mysterious and otherworldly things. Also, by going into a trance, a channeler can avoid taking responsibility for anything she says, especially since many don't even recall what took place while they were "gone."

Treat past-life information like anything else you hear from a psychic. If it makes sense to you, if it seems to apply to a situation you are in now, then listen to what is being said and how it can help you. If a psychic tells you that you were a priest in ancient Egypt and were stoned for violating religious laws, you should also be told what significance that has for you now, beyond the fact that you are afraid of going into ancient Egyptian tombs. Similarly, if you are told you lived an important life in China, and that it had great significance for you, you should think twice about accepting this information as useful if you have never had even a remote interest in China or Chinese things. One man shelled out his $100 and was given quite an array of "historical" facts:

This psychic told me that I was a troubadour in the Middle Ages, that I wrote wonderful ballads, lyrics, and political satire, that I was respected for the stories I told, and that at the same time I was also a spy for the king. It sounded great—like I was Errol

Flynn. She also told me that I had been a child sold into sexual slavery in Babylon, not to mention a monk in the Middle Ages who was stuck with a vow of silence—that I couldn't talk, couldn't listen to music, and wasn't even allowed to illuminate the manuscripts, which I would have enjoyed. Instead, I was out tilling the potatoes. Now, I'll admit that I've always loved Gregorian chants, but beyond that, what am I supposed to do with this information? I would love a bell to ring and say, yes that's the truth, and that unclocks some problems I'm having, but it just didn't happen.

Just as you should be wary about past-life information, beware of psychics who are heavily into predictions. Unfortunately, foretelling the future is what most people expect from a psychic, and if they don't get a long list of predictions, they don't feel that they got their money's worth. The problem with predictions is that there is no way to verify them until much later. So it is easy for a psychic to simply bombard you with tales of things to come, knowing that you'll probably never be back.

Your reading should be an even blend of observations about who you are now and about how those aspects of your personality may affect you in the future. Also, as with past-life readings, the information about your future should make sense to you. If you are told you will be taking a trip to a western city to attend a funeral or some kind of "sad occasion," you ought to think about whether you even know anyone who lives in a western city. Or if someone tells you you'll be getting a new job within a month and you're not even looking for a new job, it should give you reason to wonder.

Not all phony psychic readings are made up of past lives or future predictions. Those practitioners of this deceptive art who are really good will actually rely upon you to supply the information. For instance, when you arrive for your reading, there may be some light chitchat about the weather or the trip over. All the while, judgments are being made about you. You may be carrying a briefcase, you may be dressed a certain way, you may have booked an appointment at a time when most people are at work. And, you may drop little bits of information about yourself without even realizing it during the course of the conversation.

But a really good operator will not only rely on piecemeal "slips" on your part. He will actually get you to tell him what he wants you to tell him and feed it back to you during the course of the reading. For instance, he may know, from your last name, that you are Italian. He will then say he is "getting a name. It sounds like Maria or Marietta or something with an M," at which point you may chime in, "Mariella?" At the instant you say the name, the psychic will also be saying it, making you think you both arrived at it at the same time. (The fact is, most psychics do not get specific names of people. "Name dropping" seems more often to be a technique used to sucker you in to believing in the accuracy of the reading as a whole. If you are sitting with someone who seems to have this amazing ability, you should be sure that *you* aren't the one who is supplying the names.)

Gordon, an investment banker in New York, recalls a reading he had with a psychic who had greatly impressed a friend of his, but who, upon further examination, wasn't so impressive:

> I went to a psychic—the first one I ever went to—and I was very impressed. I came home and I thought, wow! Then I went back and listened to the tape and it turned out I told her more stuff than she told me. I didn't even really listen to the content, because I was just sort of running a little tab in my head, trying to see who spoke more often, and I realized she asked me more questions than I asked her. At one point, she said to me, "You really have a poker face, don't you?" Because I wasn't giving her any feedback. And then, when she said that, I felt bad. I thought: Oh, maybe I shouldn't be so hard; work with her, give her a little stuff, after all, this isn't magic . . . and from then on, *I* was telling *her*. She didn't say one thing to me that was definite. It was always, "You know someone with blond hair, don't you?" Not like, "You do, and this is who it is." Everything was like, "Right?" "Correct?" It turns out I was supplying her with the answers all along!

All this isn't to say that you should never tell a psychic anything about yourself or refuse to verify some information. Clearly the process is a two-way street, and a psychic's interpretations of impressions she is getting will depend upon you to a great extent. But most reputable psychics will want to do most of the talking, usually first, and only after the bulk of the reading will they fine-tune it according to your questions or need for clarifications.

Intuition vs. Professionalism

This also does not mean that any psychic who tells you something wrong is a fraud. I have met people who studied long and hard to "become" psychic, but who I felt were fulfilling their own wishful desires. I didn't doubt their sincerity, but felt that they perhaps *wanted* to be psychic more than they actually *were* psychic. They may, in fact, have been very intuitive people—and very sensitive at that. But intuition alone is not enough of a basis for going into a professional service where you will be giving people emotional and spiritual counseling.

Also, psychics, like anyone else, do have "off" days. And psychic ability, being somewhat fickle itself, may prove difficult to turn on and off at will. But if you make sure that the person you are visiting is experienced, there is a much greater chance that she will have learned to harness her ability and achieve a greater level of consistency.

A psychic's ability is constantly changing as she grows, both experientially and spiritually. Thus the nature of her ability may change, and the type of reading she relied upon one year may not work as well next year. Or a new dimension to that ability may manifest itself, and it may take time for her to learn the various nuances of that new insight and to be able to use it professionally. This is particularly the case with channelers, who almost never channel just one spirit entity. Often they are able to channel not just different spirit guides, but different levels of spiritual beings, and those who "come through" may depend as much upon who the client is as who the psychic is.

Thus every session is unique, and a psychic is always on the edge, not knowing exactly what is going to come through or necessarily how to work with it. That's not to say that you should be paying for a professional psychic's education, but only that you shouldn't be ready to dismiss a person's ability completely on the basis of one visit. If a psychic is honest and trying her best, she won't hesitate to admit that she is being blocked in some way or that she's having an off day. In that case, she shouldn't charge you and should offer to reschedule a new appointment or to recommend someone else.

If she does not offer to make up the session, you shouldn't be afraid to say that you are not satisfied and don't feel comfortable giving her full payment. Many psychics feel that if they don't take money from you, you'll assume they aren't legitimate. So even if they themselves are dissatisfied with a reading, they will accept payment almost in an effort to prove to you that the session was good. But if they are honest, and you voice your dissatisfaction, you should be able to arrive at some equitable arrangement.

Fees

The question of money is a tricky one. Most people will assume that, as with anything in this life, you get what you pay for; that the more a psychic charges, the better she must be. Although it is generally the case that a more *experienced* psychic will charge more, it doesn't follow that those on the lower end of the fee scale are not as good. In some cases they may be better, because they may be more concerned with the work itself than with making money.

Fees range quite a bit, not just among different kinds of psychics, but within each category as well. Generally, psychics who practice on a word-of-mouth basis—that is, not storefront readers—range in price from $30 up to $300. (One psychic healer I was told about charges $1,000 a visit and "guarantees" to cure you of absolutely anything that ails you.) In the larger metropolitan areas, where most of the work is being done, $40 to $60 is considered low, $70 to $85 is mid-range, and $100 or more is top dollar. Be advised, however, that the length of each reading varies, so a psychic who is only charging $50 a session, but whose readings are 30 minutes, is actually charging $100 an hour. Be sure to ask how long a reading lasts and whether they ever run over. Most psychics will not book appointments so close together that they have to shove you out the door the minute your hour is up.

Astrologers tend to charge more because in addition to spending an hour or so with you during the reading, they put in preliminary time researching the positions of your planets and drawing up the chart for your reading. Storefront readers get anywhere from $5 up, depending upon the type of reading, most of which range anywhere from five to 15 minutes.

Some psychics are more concerned with the work itself than with making a living off it, and although they may not advertise the fact, they will often reduce their standard fee, accept something in barter, or even waive the fee entirely in the event someone in need of help simply can't afford a reading. Others will ask you to pay what you feel the reading was worth. Many feel that at least something should be exchanged for the reading, because it implies that you have received something of value, and chances are that you will take the reading more seriously if you have given something in return. For example, Judy Damron, a channeler and psychotherapist, sees her psychic work as a chance to free herself up from the standard fee structure of conventional psychotherapy:

> I don't have a fee. I ask people to pay what they feel is in truth. And that came to me in a very clear way. It seems as though for me, on a rational level, there's no way to assign a figure to this. I could assign a figure based on my time, which is how therapists work, but because I feel this is coming from the spiritual realm, I thought I would turn the whole thing right back over to that realm. I'm interested in my life in living as much as possible within spiritual law, particular on the economic level—that the universe will take care of me. I really believe that. So the channeling is a place for me to directly experiment with that and use it.
>
> Sometimes people get very upset and say, "What do you mean? Give me a guideline," or "Give me a fee." Then I'll give them a range. But what I say, and what I feel strongly about is, "Go to your inner knowing,

and you'll know what's right for you, you'll get a figure." And sometimes people do that and they're surprised. I feel like that is a little lesson for them in trusting. That they can go to their inner voice and get a very specific answer.

Some psychics come from a traditional therapy background and have simply extended that fee structure to what they do now. Although this may make them less flexible in terms of reducing their fees, it can also work to your advantage. For instance, if you visit a psychospiritual counselor who was trained in transpersonal work or psychosynthesis, or you find a licensed psychologist who utilizes psychic perception in his work, you'll be able to use your health insurance (assuming it covers psychotherapy) to cover the cost of your reading! I have even met a traditional Mexican *curandera,* or healer, who works in the Denver mental health system and is therefore covered by Medicare and Medicaid.

Beware of any psychic reader or especially psychic healer who already knows before a session has begun how many repeat visits you'll have to make and at what cost. Treatment should be individually tailored to your own needs and be determined on the basis of the progress you make in healing yourself. If a healer tells you that the success of the treatment depends entirely upon her ability and that it will require a minimum number of sessions, look for someone else. No one—not even a psychic—can forecast the rate at which you will make progress in healing yourself or achieving significant spiritual growth.

In addition, don't be afraid of looking for a lower-priced psychic. Just because a reader charges "only" $40 doesn't mean he is inexperienced. He may have been studying or apprenticing with a more experienced reader or healer for several years before beginning now to go out on his own. If that is the case, he will begin by charging less. In fact, if you hear about a particular psychic with a good reputation, but whose fee is beyond your means, you might call him and ask for a recommendation for someone more reasonable. Many teachers break in their students by referring clients and, in cases such as psychic healers, those students will often have the option of consulting their teachers on specific problems, so you might in fact end up benefiting from the more expensive psychic's experience after all.

No good psychic should bristle at being asked for a recommendation, especially if you make it clear that you just can't afford her rates. Most have found that as their professional obligations increase and the scope of their work broadens, they have to make more and more referrals to other people whose work they know and trust. If a psychic is booked up eight months in advance, there is no reason to make you wait for an appointment when you could be going to someone else. And it certainly is no loss for someone who is that popular.

The only role money should play in your choice of a psychic is in deciding how much you can afford. It may be important enough to you that you don't want to limit your choices and are therefore willing to pay top dollar. On the other hand, you may feel that if you can find someone who comes highly recommended for $50 instead of $75, then there is no reason to pay more. Whatever you decide, be sure that you are not basing your opinion purely on reputation or the fee.

Because psychic work has become such a big business in recent years, the media has given rise to certain psychic "stars." Books such as those of Shirley MacLaine have catapulted individual psychics to stratospheric heights, and their fees reflect that fact. Other psychics have written books of their own, produced videotapes, and recorded cassettes for sale both in bookstores and through mail order. Bear in mind that in these situations you are not only supporting a psychic's work but an entire business as well.

Although it would not be fair to condemn anyone who has utilized the media for "spreading the word," when it comes to psychic stars or local people with big reputations, be attuned to the reality that the work itself may have taken a backseat to the business of selling. As with anything you buy, decide for yourself if the quality of the product is worth the increase in cost.

Now that you have all the information you need to make an informed choice about the type of psychic you want to see and the kind of person you think could best meet your needs, we will take a closer look at just what these people do, how they do it, and what a typical psychic reading is like. We will also get an idea of how these people see their own ability, what *they* feel is the mark of a good psychic, and how they view the field of psychic reading as a whole.

CHAPTER FOUR

The Psychic Reading

Clairvoyance, Precognition, and Psychometry

Psi—psychic ability—can take a variety of forms and may require that the psychic use some kind of external device or tool in order to focus or express her inner sense of awareness. On its most fundamental level, however, psi implies the ability to access information about another person, place, or thing directly—without the use of some form of intermediary apparatus such as tarot cards, without going into a trance, and without some form of elaborate ritual, such as a séance.

Probably the simplest form of psychic ability is intuition. Although we are all intuitive to some extent and may therefore get flashes of psychic insight from time to time, a professional psychic usually possesses a greater degree of psi, which manifests itself in one or more of a number of ways. These include: telepathy; clairvoyance, clairaudience, or clairsentience; precognition and retrocognition; or psychometry. Because many psychics with these types of abilities are "on" all the time, or at least can turn on their ability with a minimum of fuss, they have long been the subjects of parapsychology experiments that seek to examine psi either in the laboratory or under controlled circumstances.

Telepathy is one of the simplest forms of psychic ability because it reveals only information that is present in someone's mind. Although it might be called mind reading, some researchers insist that telepathy, in the truest sense of the term, only involves the deliberate transmission of a thought from a sender to a receiver. Many experiments, both formal and informal, have been set up to prove the existence of telepathy. Although it may one day prove to be a useful means of transmitting information instantaneously, it has little use for the person seeking a psychic reading. After all, why would you want to pay someone else to find out what you yourself are thinking? There are very few psychics who can actually "read minds," and most instances of telepathy seem to be spontaneous events, in which someone suddenly knows what another person—very often a person at a distance—is thinking or dreaming.

It's more likely that a psychic reader who works professionally will be either clairvoyant, clairaudient, or clairsentient. Clairvoyance is a French term meaning "clear seeing"—that is, the ability to see things that aren't immediately present. Similarly, clairaudience involves the sense of hearing, and clairsentience the sense of feeling. Some psychics even speak of clairguscience, which involves the sense of smell. In these cases, a psychic will either see, hear, feel, or smell something that reveals information about you or someone important in your life. Beatrice Rich receives information in all these ways:

> Sometimes it is like a narrative, like reading a very short novel. It is as if it were written down and I would be reading it. Occasionally, I do hear it. It is as though a source outside of myself were telling me something—giving me information. I will sometimes feel like it is being spoken inside my head or someone is standing there telling it to me. There are occasionally visions: I can see the people and events I am describing . . . floating as if on a movie screen. I will also apprehend sensations: if somebody is ill, if they are sick or are in pain, it is transferred to me physically. I frequently know what part of the body is afflicted. The sensation only lasts about 30 seconds, but that is how I know where the problem is located.
>
> I remember having an experience when I first started doing this. I was doing a reading for a woman, and I knew her husband was sick. I knew he was very sick, but I could not get what was wrong with him. I was struggling with it, in my way, and suddenly it was as if somebody was standing next to me, and they said, "It is a heart attack," just totally exasperated with me. "Why can't you see that? It is so evident." I knew that was not from within me. It was from my unseen friends or teachers or whomever.

It may not always be a literal vision or voice that appears to the psychic, but rather something symbolic. For instance, the psychic may get the image of a rose. Rather than meaning that you are interested in flowers, it may be that your memories of your grandmother include a rose garden she used to take special pride in and that the information that is to follow relates to your grandmother. Or the psychic may suddenly get the smell of fresh-baked bread, another image that may be reminiscent of childhood visits to your grandmother's house. Because psychic information rarely comes in the form of rational discourse (channeling is an exception to this rule), these impressions are all ways in which our inner selves seek to communicate with us, whether through psychic readings, memories, or dreams.

When these impressions reveal information that pertains to the past or future, it means that in addition to being clairvoyant, the psychic is precognitive or retrocognitive. Precognition is what we all think of when we imagine a psychic reading—the ability to predict the future. Retrocognition, the ability to see events that happened in the past, is rarely talked about but is actually much more common among psychics and certainly just as impressive. A psychic may be able to reveal not only events that happened in your past that affect who you are now and why you behave a certain way, but many even claim to have the ability to tap into your past lives, thereby offering an explanation for a recurring emotional problem, perhaps, or even a chronic physical ailment.

Another form of clairvoyant psychic ability is

psychometry, the ability to access information from an object. Many psychics will use psychometry as an adjunct to their other skills as a way of cross-checking information or gaining greater clarity. Or it may simply be a way for them to focus their psychic attention on you, the subject. Psychometry takes many forms. On one level, it simply involves a psychic holding an object that belongs to you. Some psychics insist on holding something metal, others stipulate that it should be something that you bought for yourself and that has been in your possession for at least three months. In other cases, a psychic will be able to "read" a photograph of a person you seek information about. Some will simply look at the picture, others will hold it or rub their finger over the surface. Generally, if there are other people in the photograph, it will obscure the reading.

Psychometry has been used not only to gather information about living people but to access information about the past. In some situations, antique objects have revealed intricate details about a person who is no longer living, and who may not even be known to the sitter (the person having the reading). In still more startling experiments, archeological artifacts have been read, enabling a psychic to paint a detailed portrait of life in another era, even as far back as prehistoric times. Although the mechanism by which this is accomplished is not understood, almost all psychics agree that objects seem to be encoded with detailed information about those who owned them and the way in which they were used and that that information can be accessed by human beings.

Before leaving the different types of psychic ability, the subject of dreams should be mentioned. Although dream interpretation does not involve psychic ability per se, many psychics will offer this service as part of their "repertoire." This "ability" should be looked upon with a strong measure of doubt. Dreams are themselves the language of the subconscious—*your* subconscious—and are encoded in symbolic language that is personal to you. In the same way that a psychic receives information from her intuitive self in the form of symbols or images, so do your dreams represent the language of your own inner self. This "language" is not open to interpretation by another person. Some schools of thought hold that dream symbology is universal, much like Jung's archetypes, and indeed, dream interpretation is an integral part of many forms of psychotherapy. However, such interpretation does not involve psychic ability and therefore is more the province of a skilled psychotherapist rather than a professional psychic. This is not to say that a psychic cannot offer this valuable service if she is functioning in a therapeutic role and is familiar with the literature on dream imagery. But be advised that if you choose to avail yourself of this service, you will not be benefiting from someone's psychic ability but perhaps merely good therapeutic skills and possibly psychological training.

Most people who go for psychic readings with a

clairvoyant are merely curious or are seeking help with a specific problem in their lives. Whatever your reason for choosing to visit this type of psychic, rest assured that the hocus-pocus and the mumbo jumbo will be kept to a minimum. Most psychic readers operate quite professionally: many work out of offices or homes, require advance bookings for readings, tape-record the sessions, and accept personal checks for payment. Many even have agents to handle the heavy flow of readings they do.

Once you have arrived for your reading, the method and the tenor of the experience will vary depending upon the particular psychic. Some will launch right in, telling you intimate facts about your personality and life. Others will ask you if there is anything specific that you want to know about or ask you to choose a particular type of reading: i.e., business and career, personal life and romance, health, or other people in your life. You may also be asked if there is anything you don't want to know about, or whether you want to hear the negative aspects of your reading in addition to the positive ones. Whatever you decide, no reputable psychic will tell you anything that isn't for your own benefit. If you hear bad news, it's usually so you can do something about it, make significant changes in your life, or be better prepared to handle adversity.

To reinforce that everything you hear is purely for your own highest good, many psychics will ask you to join in a brief prayer or meditation designed to open both of you up to only the most positive energies. Some psychics will also use this meditation to prepare themselves for the reading, for instance by putting themselves into a state of deep relaxation or an alpha state. Pat Einstein is a New York psychometrist who uses a brief meditation to prepare both herself and the client:

> It's a focusing, a centering. You let go of the state you're in and allow yourself to enter a higher one. When I say higher I mean more aware. And it's also a way of telling a person, "You're an equal partner in this. You're as much involved as I am."
>
> The beginning of [the meditation] is a breathing, because breathing will immediately bring you to a deeper, higher awareness. And breathing in a rhythmical, aware way brings the person into another space. You get the person to go on this little trip with you. And it's a trip into themselves really.
>
> Then I let them know that we're open only to the highest knowledge. So that's a way of letting them know, "Don't worry, we're not going to get any negativity here." I also affirm that the person getting the knowledge is going to use it, or I might say, "We know that the information will be used in the most loving, constructive, and positive way." Using the expression "we know" gets into the difference between knowing and believing. Knowing is accepting. You're accepting Truth, with a capital T. At this moment, you're accepting. And the idea is that at some point you will integrate that into the rest of your life.

Most psychics will begin the actual reading with a general analysis of who you are—your chief personality traits, your particular talents and skills, and your most significant desires and goals. This brief analysis seems to be a way not only for the psychic to tune into you as a person, but also to be able to double-check that he is on the right path—that the information he is receiving does pertain to you. If all this information seems wrong, or it sounds like he's talking about someone else, speak up and tell him. You are either in the presence of a fraud or the psychic is tapping into someone else who is close to you or who may be on your mind a lot. If you voice your concerns right away, you'll know soon enough which it is.

In the case of psychometry, if you've brought an item that once belonged to someone else or one that has been handled extensively by another person, the information coming through may pertain to that other person. Beatrice Rich, who uses psychometry in her readings, recalls many cases where the information she was getting related to a previous owner of the object she was holding:

> I am so sensitive to these objects that I start giving people information about the giver. That means, if somebody got divorced five years ago, and their ex-husband gave them a watch, without knowing it I will start telling them all about that situation and the ex-husband and what happened then. Sometimes an emotion— like a divorce—is so strongly connected to an object, that it comes out, even though it has been years.
>
> I remember an incident with a girl when I was telling her all about her grandmother without realizing

it. I also mentioned the grandmother's name in the course of the reading. Then she realized that she had given me something that had belonged to her grandmother—her grandmother's ring.

Chances are, if you've done your homework and located a reputable psychic who came highly recommended, you'll be hearing things about yourself that immediately ring true. This accuracy should dispel whatever doubts you have had up until now and enable you to relax and concentrate on the reading itself. Most psychics prefer not to be interrupted at this point in the reading. They feel that if an issue is particularly important in your life right now, it will show up soon enough during the course of the reading. If it doesn't, it's possible that you may be putting too much emphasis on minor things and what you think is worthy of worry is simply sidetracking you from more important areas of your life.

In any case, a psychic will only want to know if she is totally off the track with what she is saying. If she keeps asking for confirmation for every piece of information she turns up, it's likely she is either not very psychic or is having a bad day. Most good psychics prefer not to be interrupted, wanting to see for themselves how accurate they can be without being coaxed along by the sitter. Others claim that frequent interruptions break their concentration and interfere with the flow of images.

The following excerpt, taken from a psychic reading with a reader who is clairvoyant, is an example of the kind of general, free-flowing information a psychic might begin a reading with:

I see that you have a very busy year coming in. I see that you're going to put in a lot of hard work and energy. But I see something that is going to be a major success for you that you may not see or even conceive of right now. I see something that you already have in the background as being much more important than what you're presently doing. I see it as being something that you will be very proud of after it's done. And it will come together easier than what you're working on now.

I also pick up that you're going to be traveling in about six and a half months—a pleasure trip, but a business trip also. I see a lot of discussion going on. I see you meeting someone that you do not presently know for the first time on this trip. This is someone you will come to know and respect. It is the beginning of a long-term friendship-partnership.

I also pick up that you're going to have a family member going into the hospital, needing some kind of minor surgery within the next five months. I see them being in a week to ten days, then they're going to be out again, a very fast recovery. It's a woman.

I also see that your work area is going to be a complete mess for at least four months. At the end of that time, I see you putting things in order, sitting back and almost sighing. I see that your financial situation is going to be okay this year, but I see it as okay, not great. But I see you as steadily building, and I see you as doing exceedingly well—*exceedingly* so—next year. I also see some sort of legal papers being signed: Read the fine print. I see something very important being there that you will need to change. And I see that as coming up between now and June. It's worded where it could have a dual meaning and unless you get it changed, you could become caught in some red tape later on. I also see here that you will be doing something to earn money, but only as a vehicle to earn money. I don't see it as something you're going to have a great passion for, but I see you as doing it on and off this year.

I see you meeting a lot of new people this year, but I see them as moving in and out of your life. It's funny, you meet friends, you have them for a while, they're important to you at the time, and then you move on. I don't see you as losing the friends you have, they just move to the background. You're a collector of people. . . .

After a short period of this kind of free association, the psychic will pause in the reading and ask you if you have any questions about what you heard. This is your chance to clarify anything that didn't sound exactly right or about which you would like to know more (perhaps a more specific time frame for a prediction, or the exact nature of a health problem that might have been alluded to). Or if you've understood everything you heard, you can go on to other questions on your list (for more information about preparing a list of questions, see Chapter Five).

The degree to which you enter into a dialogue with the psychic will depend upon both you and the reader.

You will know soon enough whether your psychic likes to "discuss" the information he is giving you or whether he is the type who works best at a distance. (You may already know this, as a result of the research you did before booking your appointment.) During the course of your reading you will get a sense of the best way to interact with your psychic and to what degree you are both comfortable with a dialogue as opposed to a monologue.

Above all, avoid the temptation to sit back and make the psychic "prove" herself. This attitude too often breeds hostility and will make it difficult for the psychic to establish a connection to your own subconscious self, especially if she is aware of the fact that she is "on trial." Remember: a good rapport is an integral part of the psychic reading. If you feel awkward, or are turned off by the psychic, make sure it isn't the result of your own attitude. If it isn't, then this particular psychic simply is not for you.

Assuming you are at ease with your psychic and feel comfortable enough to speak freely, you should turn your attention during the course of the reading to the quality of the information you're getting. What you hear should make sense to you. Answers in response to your questions should be clear and specific. Trust your own common sense. If something doesn't feel right, it probably isn't right. Don't be afraid to voice your doubts at any point in the reading. You're paying good money, and you don't want to leave feeling that you haven't clarified what you have been told.

Most psychics will not kick you out when your time is up (although many use the length of the cassette tape as an indicator that the session is over). They will usually give you the opportunity to ask a last question or two or at least to clarify anything you're still not clear about. A psychic reading is a process, and it should feel like it has a beginning, a middle, and an end. If you feel that you've been cut off abruptly and ushered out the door, you may have chosen a psychic who is more interested in running a business than in helping people with their lives. Again, it's up to you to trust your own feelings about the experience. Does it feel complete? Do you feel that you've gotten your money's worth? Was it uplifting? If you are unable to answer such questions affirmatively, try to figure out what is missing and, if possible, clear it up with the psychic before you leave. If it's obvious to you that he is more interested in getting paid than in answering your questions and addressing the issues that are important to you, then you may have to take your reading with more than a grain of salt.

Tarot Cards, Rune Stones, and the *I Ching*

In this section, we will deal with the practice of casting lots—using a special divinatory object or group of objects to access psychic information about someone or something. Such objects can include almost anything. Traditionally, divination has been practiced using everything from tea leaves to the entrails of slaughtered animals. Storefront readers are notorious for' reading tea leaves and tarot cards, perhaps because to many of us these are the expected trappings that indicate someone is psychic. For our purposes, we will deal with the methods of divination that are used by reputable, legitimate psychics. These include: tarot cards, regular playing cards, rune stones, and the *I Ching*.

Before discussing each of these methods, we have to draw some distinctions in the way these devices function. On one level, they are considered to have inherently psychic qualities— that is, they possess some kind of power of their own that can enable anyone— psychic or not—to do a reading, provided that they have studied the symbolism and understand the methodology thoroughly. On another level, however, such equipment functions merely as a focusing point for a person who is already psychic. According to this way of understanding, there is nothing inherently special about these items; they are devoid of any kind of power of their own and depend entirely upon the psychic ability of the reader to yield information. Thus anything could be used as a point of focus for divination by someone who is psychic—a pile of rocks, a light bulb, even a blank wall.

Each psychic has her own approach to the question of divination and the way in which she uses such apparatus will depend upon that view. Some psychics combine elements of both, using the inherent symbology of the particular item as a starting point and then embellishing the reading with their own psychic input. It's a good idea to determine what approach your particular psychic uses before going for a reading. You will want to know if the person you are seeing is truly psychic or simply a very skilled and experienced card reader, for instance. The nature of the information you can expect to hear will vary depending upon that approach, and you will want your expectations to be in line with what is available.

Probably the most ubiquitous type of fortune-telling device—at least in the West—is the tarot deck. Emblazoned with colorful and cryptic symbols and figures, these cards have long been considered very powerful forecasters of the future in their own right. Ironically, however, tarot cards first appeared in Italy in the fifteenth century as a means of gambling in a game called "tarocchi." They were the precursors of the modern deck of playing cards. Like playing cards, they are organized into four suits of ten cards each, with four additional court cards for each suit (page, knight, queen, and king). These are referred to as the minor trumps, or minor arcana. In addition, the tarot deck includes 22 major trumps, ranging from The Fool, number 0, to The World, number 21. The Fool has been incorporated into the modern playing deck as the joker.

Although no one knows why, it wasn't long before the tarot was being used as a means of divination, especially by those who saw in it mystical allusions to the great religions, with Jewish, Christian, and Egyptian symbols. The major trumps in particular were seen as a secret book of knowledge that had been passed down from ancient times. Perhaps the main reason for this development was the uncanny correspondence between the tarot and the Jewish mystical tradition known as Kabbalah. In particular, there are 22 letters in the Hebrew alphabet, just as there are 22 major trumps, and the numbers four (four court cards), ten (ten remaining cards in each suit), and seven (a multiple of 21 major trumps minus The Fool) are all highly significant numbers in Jewish mystical thought.

Whatever the original intentions of the cards' designers, today the tarot is considered to be a good deal more than a simple method of divination. Much has been written about the correspondence between the tarot symbols and Jung's universal archetypes, and most psychics and metaphysical psychologists consider the major trumps to be a powerful psychological tool, if not a complete system of mystical knowledge. They see the tarot as a metaphor for the self's journey through various stages of growth—physical, emotional, and spiritual. Others see The Fool's journey through the major arcana as the path taken by the individual soul as it makes its way through the various stages of birth and death leading to ultimate reunion with the God Force.

Although there are one or two "standard" decks of tarot cards, today there has been a proliferation of new designs and new interpretations, some of them based upon a particular psychic's own insight into the meaning and significance of the cards. Nor is there any one standard way of reading the cards. Some readers use traditional spreads, placing the cards in a precise pattern, while others simply draw cards from the deck one by one, interpreting the significance of each as it appears. Some psychics employ Jung's theory of universal archetypes, looking for standard meanings, while others meditate upon the images, allowing themselves to be open to whatever meaning seems appropriate at the time. All that seems certain is that the tarot does indeed possess a universality that speaks to each person in a very individual and intimate way.

Tarot readers are perhaps the easiest of psychics to find. They generally work the psychic fairs, perhaps because tarot lends itself to short but precise readings, and you will see advertisements abounding in metaphysical bookstores and New Age learning centers for tarot readers utilizing everything from transpersonal psychology to Jewish mysticism. Even though the ways of reading the cards vary, the format of your reading as a whole will follow certain standard patterns.

Generally, the tarot reader will begin by selecting a card that represents either you or the person you are asking about (known as the querent). This is generally a court card and the selection is based simply on hair color, eye color, sex, and age. You will then be asked to shuffle the cards, and in some cases to concentrate on a specific question you have or a particular person you want to know about. This is so that your own inner self will have a chance to affect the order of the cards and the way in which they fall. In other cases, the psychic will simply be looking for your "vibrations" to enter the cards, much like a psychometrist will read an object that has been in your possession. Many psychics feel that what affects the way the cards fall in a reading depends upon the higher faculties of both the reader and the querent working together to produce a single end result.

You may then be asked to cut the cards into three piles (sometimes with your left hand, which is controlled by the right hemisphere of your brain). The psychic will then pick up the cards and begin to deal them out. Some psychics use a standard spread, in which each card occupies a position that corresponds to some aspect of your question (i.e., past influences, immediate future outcome, hopes and fears, environmental factors, etc.). Others start by simply placing the cards down in a line and talking.

What happens at this point depends entirely upon the psychic. Some interpret specific symbols they see on the cards. Others merely use them as a way of focusing on you and your intuitive self. At some point in the reading you may want to ask the psychic what particular symbol or aspect of the cards led him to certain conclusions. This will at least give you an indication of what type of interpretation, if any, is being done. Ron Havern, who uses tarot cards but is psychic as well, explains the way in which the cards speak to him:

> An experienced reader can enter into each of the cards in a spread, just as an ordinary person might enter into a room in his or her house. The psychic looks around inside the client's card, just as you might look around your living room. The psychic hears the conversations between the client's cards and sees them interact with one another, just as the realities which they represent interact within the client's life. The true psychic sees the battle plan of the client's life —the client's position on the cosmic chessboard. The cards provide a road map for the client's life, the map to his or her hidden treasure.

A reader such as Havern gets very graphic images pertaining to the querent's life. As a result, this type of reading would be very concrete, almost like a narrative of events that have happened in the recent past and are about to happen in the near future. If you were interested in concrete facts and precise predictions, this would therefore be the kind of tarot reader you would want to visit. The following is an excerpt from one of Ron Havern's readings, which demonstrates the specificity that his psychic ability yields:

> Coming from outside you, you have the seven of swords, which is making good connections, both work and friendship. It also means that other people help

you in making a place for yourself. And there's something like luck in making these attachments right now; you meet people and make good connections out of the blue, without trying. The card crossing you could be a person about your own age, maybe a little older. He would have a very fair complexion, light blond hair, sort of green or blue eyes. This is someone who seems to somehow block your plans, who creates obstacles for you. Someone to watch out for . . . The person might cross your path by confusing you and by disrupting your relationship with other people—influential people. They would get misinformation or misinterpret things that were said. This person could undo a lot of good that's been done, like undermining your relationships with people.

It seems like you've just come out of a sort of wretched period. The past is The Wheel of Fortune upside down, so that means that you have been pretty much on the bottom of it. So the indication is that things aren't going to get any worse. It's as though you had to bottom out. This happens because things often work in a way that you have to be brought to the lowest point in order to really receive something good, in order to really appreciate something good that's coming to you. The Wheel of Fortune is a wheel—as soon as it goes down, it comes back up again.

You're entering into creative conflicts with the people around you. It's a time when you're forced to defend what you believe in or find out what you believe in by having to define it. . . . There seems to be a pattern where in conversation with other people there is a way in which you misrepresent yourself, by twisting what you want to say around so it's no longer what you want to say. You can improve that, but it's something to watch out for. It seems like there could be a lot of little setbacks by people getting the wrong idea from what you say. So I think it's safer for you to have something written to refer to and talk on the basis of that. It seems like that happens more with authority figures than with anyone else—that you get tongue-tied when you have to deal with people in position of authority, so it's better to deal with them in writing and save the arguments and creative conflict more for peers and family . . . .

Other tarot readers get more general impressions from the cards and then allow their psychic sense to interpret what they are seeing. These readings usually deal more with inner growth or spiritual development than concrete facts and predictions. Often the subject of the reading will be the ways in which your life experiences are manifesting deeper psychological or emotional growth patterns as symbolized by the figures on the tarot cards. For example, Stephen Calia, a tarot reader who is also a numerologist and astrologer, reads the cards in a much deeper, more spiritual manner. This excerpt from one of his readings has a tone and style that is unique to his work:

This is the card of inner unity. I feel that what you're working on is a process of internal growth and that that growth is reaching a good place for you—a place of finding more sense of balance and peace within yourself. The outer world may be in disarray, but the inner world may be reaching a place where you're feeling more balanced, more unified. Where that leads to is that in the unconscious the way will be shown to you. I feel like you're moving into a whole new world, like you're moving from the person you were to the person you're becoming. You're in a transition time. You're going through a death right now. As the inner world gets more form, the outer world will reflect that. But the way will be shown to you. Because you've found out a lot about yourself, you've been given some understanding by touching the core of yourself. And you're now willing to show what's really inside of you—of tapping in. Consciously, what you need to do is not worry about the future, but simply deal with where you are today. You can't really see where this new dawn is. It happens day by day. Don't get ahead of yourself. You need to have hopefulness for the future, but take care of business and have trust and faith in the future. As long as you have that, you'll be able to do what you need to do today and you'll feel good about it.

Whatever kind of psychic reading you decide is best for you, be sure you know what to expect from your particular reader. You don't want to find yourself trying to decipher what is being told to you while you are at your reading. If you've prepared and thought about what issues you want addressed, your questions will make more sense in the context of that particular reader's style. As with all psychic readings, don't be afraid to ask questions. If something doesn't make sense to you, speak up. Be sure to clarify anything that is hazy or that you don't see as relating directly to your life at this moment in time.

Standard playing cards are similar to tarot cards in that they can be read either symbolically—based on which cards fall where—or they can be read intuitively—purely as a focusing device for a reader's psychic insight. Although there are some people who still read playing cards symbolically (and these are generally people who learned it as a part of a cultural heritage or ethnic tradition), the overwhelming majority of professional psychics who use playing cards do not actually read the cards per se. Rather they either use them as a way of focusing their psychic attention or as psychometric vehicle by which your own energies are encoded upon the cards while you shuffle them. Beatrice Rich explains that although she uses a deck of playing cards in her readings, there is nothing inherently psychic about the cards themselves:

I could probably do this with chicken bones. This is the way that I am comfortable. There is a process going on here: you are concentrating, and your manipulation of the cards means something in a way that I am not even sure of. It is not as if the seven of clubs matters or the two of diamonds matters; it is like the pages of a book. I can't read the book by just holding onto it. It is easier to open up the book and read one page after another. It is my means of transmitting information.

Another psychic who is extremely clairvoyant confessed that for her the cards function more or less as a prop:

I use [the cards] as an escape: If you don't like what I tell you, you can always walk out and say, "It's just cards." So it leaves an opening. This way [people] feel if they just shuffle the cards again, it will come up differently. . . . I also use the cards because once you shuffle them and I turn them over, I rub them, and I can pick up your vibration a lot easier. There is a way of reading them, but I never learned it. That's being 100 percent honest. But it's a vehicle for me. Some people use water, other people use psychometry, I use cards. Sometimes if I get caught up, I'll forget, and I'll start doing a reading before I actually have the person shuffle the cards. Usually I don't do it on my first or second reading, but by the time I'm involved during the day, I forget. And I have a few people I read for now who will sit down and say, "I know you don't need them, so let's just talk." When I first started out I really didn't want to do [psychic readings]. I realized that I needed something to do with my hands and my eyes, instead of just looking at the person. I felt very strange. The cards makes [the clients] more comfortable, too.

If you do encounter a psychic who reads playing cards symbolically, the method will be the same as for a deck of tarot cards: you will be asked to shuffle the deck and perhaps to cut the cards; the reader will then place them in a spread or in a specific order so that each card occupies a symbolic position. The playing cards, too, have standard meanings, depending upon the system the reader is using. Since the modern deck of playing cards evolved from the tarot deck, it isn't surprising that they can be read in a similar manner.

Another method of divination that is similar to tarot cards is that of rune stones. Although runes are more ancient than tarot cards, they have only recently been rediscovered, mainly by those who are interested in the shamanic traditions of northern Europe. Dating back to the time of the Vikings in Scandanavia, the runes found their way into Germanic and Anglo-Saxon magical practices. Last used commonly toward the end of the Middle Ages in Iceland, the runes ultimately went underground in response to a Church edict banning their use in 1639.

The earliest runes were simply stones or twigs that had certain symbols etched into them, which were cast upon the ground in order to foretell the future or to evoke the powers of the Norse gods. Eventually these symbols evolved into a primitive alphabet, known as a *futhark* (after the first six letters in the series). Today, a typical set of runes consists of 24 flat pieces of clay, stone, or wood, each of which has been carved, etched, or painted with one letter of the futhark, and an additional piece that has been left blank. Since the 24 runes are divided up into three sets of eight, some psychics prefer to work with one group—eight runes—feeling that the smaller group is more workable for most readings.

The runes are similar to the tarot in that they can be read very specifically with regard to the symbolic meanings of letters but can also function as a bridge to the subconscious of the reader, unlocking her psychic insight on a particular problem or question. Because the rune symbols are much simpler than those of the tarot, they lend themselves to shorter readings and simpler interpretations. In fact, there are rune casts for the sole purpose of divining a yes or no answer. The possibilities for interpretation grow in complexity as the reader's skill and insight also grow, so the runes are indeed a vital, evolving tool for spiritual growth.

Because they are usually made of some natural material, such as clay or wood, runes also furnish a link to the natural world as expressed in the pagan traditions of the West, which many psychics find speak to them vividly. Many rune enthusiasts will either fashion their own set of rune stones or have a set made for them, in an effort to forge a more personal connection with what they consider to be a powerful vehicle for magic and divination.

As with tarot reading, rune casting takes many different forms, but in each the querent will pose a question or subject that forms the basis of the reading. The rune caster then takes a small pouch that contains her runes and either casts them directly upon a plain piece of cloth laid out on a flat surface or has the querent shake them while concentrating on the question and then cast them onto the cloth. Depending upon the method, the runes will either be read immediately, with only those whose symbols face upward used in the reading, or they will all be turned facedown and "shuffled" using a circular, swirling motion with one hand. The caster then selects a number of the runes—how many depends upon the type of reading—and places them, still face down, in a line or a particular pattern (known as a rune cast). As with a tarot spread, each position in the rune cast deals with a particular aspect of the question. The runes are then turned over, one by one, and their meaning interpreted.

Most professional psychics who cast runes also read tarot cards, and it is more usual for them to consult the runes only as an adjunct to a tarot reading. Rolla Nordic is a 90-year-old tarot reader who also reads runes. In addition to designing her own tarot deck, she claims to have brought the runes to the United States when she emigrated from England in the early 1950s. Nordic's feeling is that the runes function in the same way that the tarot does but are a quicker way of revealing information. Here is an excerpt from a very brief rune casting she did as a follow- up to a more lengthy tarot reading:

> Well, things are going slowly for you. There's a lot of research and study for you to do. You've got some very good relationships with the people you are working with, and you do have money in the offing. But there are delays. I think you're going to do deeper study than you think you are right now. . . . You might travel a bit. You might find that at the moment you feel very

tired, but you're going to be creative, very creative, and when you find things have to be finished, you will certainly have the energy to do them. This is really a reading of creativity and self-expression, so I think I would work on that. You're going to be a very hard worker. It looks to me as if you are building up a foundation for the future—that it's not just for now. You're getting your feet on the ground, you're getting known, you're making the contacts that are important to you. And so when the future comes, you'll have something to fall back on.

The third method of divination that is enjoying a resurgence of interest here in the West is the Chinese classic known as the *I Ching,* or *Book of Changes.* The *I Ching* is probably the earliest of all standardized methods of divination, dating back perhaps as far as 3000 B.C.E. In addition to affording the preliterate Chinese peasantry a quick and easy means of consulting an oracle, the *I Ching* evolved into a work that not only embodied the essence of Chinese folk wisdom but came to be commented upon and utilized by China's greatest sages, including Confucius and Lao-tse.

The practice goes back to a time when Chinese soothsayers would heat the carapace of a tortoise or the shoulder bone of an ox and read the cracks that appeared in various patterns. Certain patterns came to have standard meanings that were eventually codified into a system of 64 hexagrams, known as *kua.* The *kua* are made up of a block of six horizontal lines, either solid or broken. Traditionally yarrow stalks were thrown to determine the hexagram, probably because, as a form of plant life, they were considered to be connected to the source of all life. Although the yarrow stalk method of reading is still extant, it has mostly been abandoned here in the West in favor of a simpler method of tossing three coins, usually made of bronze and with a hole in the middle and a Chinese inscription on one side.

What separates the *I Ching* from other methods of divination is that it doesn't simply predict the outcome of a series of events, but recommends a course of action. Ethical meanings came to be attached to each of the interpretations, and the book became a blueprint for righteous conduct and spiritual development as well as a means of fortune-telling. The essence of Chinese philosophy is bound up in the *I Ching*, especially that of Taoism, the system of thought that holds that all of reality is constantly changing through the interplay of yin and yang—negative and positive forces. It is only by understanding the relationship of an individual action to the whole of life that the right decisions can be made and the proper conduct undertaken.

This relationship between the whole and the parts is at the root of Eastern thought, and the Chinese sages were masters of incorporating this truth into the world of the mundane. The *I Ching* contains the prescriptions for how to work toward the goal of unifying all levels of reality. In interpreting the hexagrams, various meanings are also given for individual lines in particular positions, as well as for each line in relation to the whole. The diagram itself is seen as being in a state of transition and is therefore considered not just a symbolic representation of the situation but an embodiment of reality itself.

Like the runes, the *I Ching* can be read on a very simple level and can also form the basis of much deeper spiritual insights. With names like "Difficulty at the Beginning," "Peace," and "Preponderance of the Great," the hexagrams are direct enough to give the spiritual novice concrete advice yet fluid enough to grow with the experienced diviner. Paul Gallagher is a scholar of Chinese culture and philosophy, a teacher of T'ai Chi Chu'an, and a practitioner of the Taoist healing arts who has been studying the *I Ching* for 20 years. In his view, the *I Ching* functions more as a living master than as a book of wisdom:

> I found that the *I Ching* is very much like a human teacher in many ways. It's not like a book. It actually will deal with you on different levels as you evolve. So what I've found with a lot of beginners is when you do beginning divinations, the *I Ching* gives you something so direct that there's no way you can "head-trip" it or make believe it's not what it is. As you advance with the *I Ching* over the years, it starts getting a little more subtle—often the *I Ching* in the later divinations will address your inner state, just as a master might.

In the same way that the tarot is capable of opening up pathways of psychic insight in the practitioner, so, too, does the *I Ching* offer a vehicle for the reader to access right-brain, intuitive knowledge. As Paul Gallagher explains, there is a steady evolution of the psychic faculty through the use of the *I Ching:*

> I think the *kua*, the diagrams, when you know how to read them, can resonate in your mind to bring out other levels of the right brain, rather than the left brain. I think that does definitely happen. So my experience is—and this is borne out by one of my teachers—when you first start using the *I Ching*, you're using the words: "The Prince is given horses three times in a single day"—what does that mean? But later on, you learn to just look at the images by themselves, and they can resonate in your mind on their own level. And then finally there's the level of divination where you do see something, and that's like an immediate omen; you don't even need recourse to the *I Ching*.

Part of the difficulty in interpreting the *I Ching* stems from the fact that the images used today originated in China around the time of the Shang dynasty (1150 B.C.E.). Besides the fact that most Western readers will be working with translations, these references are part of a culture that does not speak directly to the modern Western mind. Consider, for example, the image given for *kua* number 8, "Holding Together":

> On the earth is water:
> The image of Holding Together.
> Thus the kings of antiquity

> Bestowed the different states as fiefs
> And cultivated friendly relations
> With the feudal lords.

Perhaps it is for this reason that very few Western psychics actually use the *I Ching* for professional readings. However, many tarot readers and rune casters frequently consult the book for their own personal guidance. The value of the *I Ching* in terms of fortune-telling lies in the depth of its approach to divination in general and the lessons it affords to all psychics, whatever method they use. If you find a psychic who has been studying the *I Ching*, even if it doesn't make up part of his professional services, chances are you have located a skilled reader who truly understands the spiritual value of divination and who will be able to help you with your own personal growth.

Before leaving the subject of casting lots, we should briefly mention throwing dice, since this form of psychic consultation is thought to be one of the oldest (some sources say it may date back some 40,000 years). There is some evidence that the first "dice" were the knuckle bones of sheep or goats, which were four-sided and different on each face. The Greeks and Romans were known to paint figures on these bones to facilitate casting lots.

There is no one standard way of throwing dice, since the meaning that is assigned to each number depends heavily upon the psychic's own intuitive sense and the particular tradition she may identify most strongly with. For example, in one such method three dice are thrown, each of a different color so as to be ranked in order. The numbers that come up may be added together for a quick answer or they may be ranked in three positions, each representing a different aspect of the question posed. Or each die will supply one digit for a three-digit number, which is then read as a general description of the situation.

Although casting dice may be the most obvious example of the degree to which a reader's own intuition or psychic ability figures heavily in divination, to a great extent all the methods described here rely upon such ability. The standard meanings of tarot symbols, rune stones, and the *I Ching* hexagrams are meant only as guidelines for the beginning reader. Presumably a skilled psychic will utilize these devices only as means of accessing her inherent inner knowledge, and eventually will find deeper shades of meaning and more personal levels of understanding in these systems of thought.

These methods of divination have often resulted in the initial appearance or greater development of someone's psychic ability. As such, they do possess a significant level of power. Whether that power is simply the effectiveness of a good textbook or the indication of some profound mystical efficacy, divination represents a level of knowing that is rooted in the deepest levels of the human psyche, reaching back to a time when human beings felt connected to the forces that ruled the universe and sought to bring themselves into harmony with the laws of nature. The way in which we utilize these tools will determine to what extent we wish to reestablish those connections that our ancestors took for granted.

No discussion of psychic apparatus would be complete without mentioning that icon of the psychic reading—the crystal ball. In an effort to throw some clarity on a generally murky subject, it should be noted that the word "crystal" may be misleading, especially in light of the recent penchant for crystal healing and crystal-aided meditation. We will discuss quartz crystals at greater length in another section, but suffice it to say that these naturally occurring minerals have been credited with having certain energy-focusing properties, which, when properly harnessed, can aid the psychic in her work. Quartz crystal balls—which have been cut, shaped, and polished—are available, but owing to the rarity of completely clear quartz, these are expensive. They generally range in size from marble-size to a couple of inches in diameter.

Crystal balls of the type made famous by such luminaries as the Wicked Witch of the West—those large enough to see a detailed image—are made of glass. Now, even if we assume that there are some psychics who are able to see images in clear quartz crystal, it does not follow that glass shares the same properties. At best we can say that a so-called crystal ball of "traditional" size might only function as a focal point for someone who is extremely clairvoyant and already apt to see visions. Although I am not aware of any reputable psychics who use crystal balls (quartz or otherwise) for seeing visions and forecasting the future, if you encounter such a practitioner, be aware of the differences in material and the limitations these impose. As we mentioned earlier, if someone is psychic enough to see things in a crystal ball, then a blank wall might do just as nicely, as might a tortoise shell, an ox bone, or, yes, even tea leaves.

Astrology, Numerology, and Palmistry

The word "psychic" is actually a misnomer when it comes to astrology, numerology, and palmistry. These systems of divination can, in some ways, actually be considered "sciences," since they represent well-ordered systems of calculation that can be learned by anyone and then applied using objective criteria, requiring no psychic ability. They are based on the idea of "correspondences"—that all phenomena in the universe, whether physical or spiritual, are inter-related on some fundamental level, and that the patterns found in the physical universe—for instance, the movement of the planets—are reflected in the realm of human endeavor. By first taking a close look at astrology we will get a better understanding of the mechanism by which these practices work.

Astrology dates back about 4,000 years to the Chaldean and Babylonian civilizations. We can be sure that human beings were observing the motions of the heavens from the time they first gazed upward, but the actual mapping of the movements of planets and stars evolved along with civilization as a way of charting the change of the seasons to facilitate agriculture. Very early on, however, stargazers also began to use the planetary cycles to mark human and cultural events—what later became known as "mundane astrology." We can speculate that at this early point in human history the connection between humanity and nature was still strong, and that on some level people were still very much aware of the intertwining of the cycles of the natural world and the human organism.

From the region of the Fertile Crescent (Babylonia), astrology, which was still synonymous with astronomy, was passed along to the Egyptians, Greeks, Romans, and, some say, the Chinese. (We know, however, that the Chinese had already formulated a working calendar by the thirteenth century B.C.E. and that by the year 350 C.E. had charted some 800 individual stars, as well as a number of celestial events.) The Greeks adopted the Babylonian practice of naming the planets after their gods and from the stars formulated the zodiac, which means "the zone of the animals," because it contains constellations with names such as "the Crab," "the Scorpion," and "the Lion." By the second century C.E., astrology was firmly ensconced in Western (and Eastern) civilization, and the Greek astronomer Ptolemy published his *Tetrabiblos*, a thorough treatise on astrology that is used to this day. In fact, words such as "disaster" (from the Greek "aster" for stars), as well as "consider" (from the Latin "sidus" for star), and "lunacy" (from the Latin "luna" for moon) all reflect the degree to which astrology was once a part of our culture.

The ancient astrologers believed that the planets actually had a direct influence on human events, and although modern astronomers dismiss this idea, there is at least some evidence that a connection exists. Take, for example, the fact that the length of a woman's menstrual cycle corresponds to the phases of the moon, or that the gravitational fields of the sun and moon are strong enough to cause the rising and falling of tides on the Earth (and that the human body is 70 percent water!). Current theories of cosmology posit that at the moment before the "big bang" that created the visible universe, all matter and energy existed at a single point in space and time. This means that on a profoundly real level, everything that exists in the universe is fundamentally related. Physicists now also tell us that all matter is bound up in fields of energy, so much so that the explosion of a supernova in a distant galaxy impacts on our solar system in some way.

In spite of all these indicators that there might be some grain of truth in the ancient view of astrology, most modern astrologers believe that the mechanism by which astrology works is much more subtle. They reject the idea that celestial events assert a direct physical force on earthly occurrences and instead take a more holistic view of the process. This thinking is based upon the metaphysical axiom, "As above, so below." This means that there are larger patterns of energy that govern all interactions in the universe and that these patterns or cycles are reflected in the movements of stars and planets in the same way they are reflected in the movements of people and cultures. Thus it is not that planetary motions *cause* events on earth, but simply that those motions are *indicators* of universal patterns. Linda Hill, a New York astrological consultant of 14 years' experience, explains this relationship:

I don't think anyone knows exactly why it works; it just works. Carl Jung used the term synchronicity. It's simply a synchronization. Ecologically, why does every microscopic protozoa affect everything else? Well, there's a chain that links it back—some kind of a relationship between the microcosm and the macrocosm. We are a part of everything *and* we are individuals. We are part of this whole solar system, and somehow we are uniquely imprinted at birth. We are somehow synchronized to the celestial patterns that were present at our birth. It's not that the planets are doing it *to* us, it's that we're synchronized *with* them. It's not a causal relationship.

Science is starting to catch on. Quantum physics has changed everything. The truth is that what is looked on as magic today is anything science hasn't figured out yet, and the truth is that astrology works. It works because it's holistic—it's about looking at your whole life holistically, from standing way outside it and looking down at it, and going deep inside it, exploring the internal landscape and moving things around. Bringing the external and the internal into balance.

The holistic patterns that astrology deals with are chiefly manifested in the dynamics of relationships. The relationships between planets reflect the relationship of the individual to the world at large. Although this relationship takes many forms, it essentially involves the ways in which a person sees the events that take place in his life. The point of astrology is not so much to try to alter or avoid those events as to put them into a context that enables an individual to use them as opportunities for growth. The astrologer does this by preparing a horoscope.

A horoscope is basically a map of where all the planets and zodiac constellations are at a specific time. A natal horoscope charts the positions of the planets at the time of your birth. Mundane horoscopes chart the planetary positions at the time of particular world events, such as the establishment of nations or of political groups. A business or financial horoscope would fix the positions of the planets at the time a new business is launched or contract is signed. A horary ("of the hour") horoscope is designed to answer a specific question a person might have—the chart is drawn up for the moment at which the astrologer is asked the question. Synastry is the process of comparing two individual natal charts to determine the compatibility of two people. Sometimes a third chart will also be drawn up for the relationship itself, which is considered an entity in its own right.

The astrologer begins preparing your horoscope from the moment you call for your appointment. You will be asked for the *exact* time and place of your birth. (For myself, it wasn't enough to say that I was born in New York City; the astrologer wanted to know what borough the hospital was in!) Your time of birth should be given down to the minute since the positions of the planets are constantly changing and the entire chart changes every four minutes. (An astrologer can determine, for instance, that the sun entered the zodiac sign of Aquarius on January 20, 1959, at precisely 7:19 P.M.) Your birth time is first converted into Greenwich mean time and then into sidereal time, which is a universal time measurement based upon the stars rather than the rotation of the earth.

At this point the astrologer will look up your sidereal birth time in a book called an ephemeris, to determine what the exact positions of the sun, moon, and planets were then. Your sun sign, which is the one used in magazine and daily newspaper horoscopes, is determined by the position of the sun at your time of birth. In the same way the 12 signs of the zodiac mark the path of the sun during the course of a year, they are said to embody the evolution of the individual throughout the course of his life. As Ronald Davison puts it in his book *Astrology:*

> The twelve signs of the zodiac may therefore be said to constitute a blueprint of the Universe, containing in essence the totality of all possible experience. In another sense the zodiac may be regarded as a

representation of the Cosmic Man—the Macrocosm, compared to which individual man is the Microcosm, embodying the same principle on a smaller scale.[1]

The planets, which move through the signs, represent distinct archetypal energies or functions in relation to the whole person. A planet manifests its function within the context of the sign that it is in, much in the way that a person's wishes and desires are expressed through the mediation of his personality and psychological makeup. Thus planets in Aries express their energy assertively and forcefully, for example, while planets in Gemini are manifested logically and verbally.

In addition to the zodiac signs, the astrologer also charts the planets with regard to the 12 houses, which, unlike the signs and planets, are purely artificial divisions. There are different ways of dividing up a horoscope into houses, and each astrologer has his own preferred method. The houses indicate the area of your life in which a planet will manifest its energy, whereas the sign is the "style" in which that energy is asserted. The second house, for example, is the house of personal values and money; the seventh house is the house of one-on-one relationships, such as professional partnerships, marriage, or even patient-therapist.

To understand how all this comes together, take the example of someone with Venus in Aries in the second house: such a person would have a great love of personal values and money, which would be expressed forcefully and with great impulsiveness, and he would tend to attract money, since Venus is the planet of attraction. Similarly, a person with Venus in Gemini in the seventh house would have a strong desire for marriage or partnership, especially with someone who is logical and intellectual, but would find it difficult to remain with just one partner.

In addition to these elements of your chart, an astrologer will also determine your ascendant, or rising sign, the transits of the planets (their movement through the zodiac), and the aspects of the planets (the angles formed by their relationship to each other). There are also a number of other celestial movements and astronomical relationships that can be factored into the horoscope for a more precise reading.

The degree of research and calculation necessary just to prepare a horoscope is extensive, which is one of the reasons why astrologers are generally more expensive than other types of psychic readers. (It is also the reason why magazine and newspaper horoscopes, based purely upon the 12 sun signs, are at best hopelessly general and at worst, outright frauds.) The advent of personal computers, however, has enabled the skilled astrologer to cut her calculation time drastically, and there are many programs now available that will handle all the mathematics for the reader, freeing her up to devote her time to interpretation rather than calculation. These programs also make up the basis of most astrology readings by mail. Although these mail-order services can be valuable to the person who simply wants to know the various locations of the planets and stars in order to draw up his own horoscope, their interpretations tend to be as general and simpleminded as newspaper forecasts. If you are interested in such a service, choose one that supplies you with only the calculations (the rates are exceptionally reasonable) and do the interpretation yourself.[2]

When all the research and calculations are done, it is still the ability of the astrologer to synthesize all the information in a coherent manner that finally determines the accuracy of the reading. This requires much more than simply looking everything up in a book, as this excerpt from a typical astrological reading illustrates:

> The first thing I notice about your chart is that it is very concentrated on one side of the chart. This indicates that you're very much a team player—you have a tribal mentality when you're with other people. At the same time you don't share very much of who you are. . . . You are a very emotional person. You have Taurus rising and moon in Pisces. So you tend to pick up other frequencies, emotional frequencies, vibrational frequencies that other people can't sense. You can walk into a room and pick up what's going on and tend to feel that other people are being insensitive. . . . But I don't think people know how emotional you are, how sensitive. I think you mask it very well. And with Scorpio in Taurus, you appear "solid as a rock"—that's the way you present yourself to the world. But the truth is, under there there's a lot of sen-

sitivity, a lot of wateriness, your own kind of inner storm going, that most of the time other people don't see. . . . And it's good because you attract people to you, and also you appear more conventional than you are. . . . But under it, you're very radical, you have radical motivations. You want to change things. . . . And you're very ambitious.

There are only two cardinal signs, six fixed, and five mutable. Now what that tells me is that, although there are other things in your chart to compensate for it, it's sometimes hard for you to get things started. But once you've got things rolling, it's easy for you to stay with it—you have a very strong sense of completion. So you may need support in that area. You may need to dovetail projects to get new energy started on things. You actually need an intermediary or some sort of support system to help you with that. Because it's always going to be there. . . . You're a very hard worker, very serious. You probably have to be careful not to overwork things. There's a strong sense of perfection here. And you need to work at being light about things.

As is evident from this reading, most astrological work involves psychological analysis—using the natal horoscope to help a person understand who he is, what his inner composition is made up of, and what patterns of behavior tend to manifest themselves most strongly, so he can work with them in dealing with life's twists and turns. Pinpointing those twists and turns is the job of predictive astrology, which relies heavily upon the transits and aspects of planets. The transits don't necessarily predict that a specific event that will occur as much as they indicate a tendency for something to happen at that point in time. In this way they trigger the potentialities that are present in the natal chart. As Linda Hill explains:

Transits are like cosmic weather conditions: which forces are impacting us at any given time; why sometimes we feel terrible and sometimes we feel great and sometimes we feel powerful and sometimes like we want a change. They begin at certain times, they end at certain times. We tend to remember, when bad things are happening, that they're going to pass, but we forget that when good things are happening, they're also going to pass. So you have to maximize the good times by knowing how long you have to get things handled before they pass and you have to know, if you're in a difficult period, when there's going to be a letup and how it can be used positively, as opposed to just sort of caving in and going to bed with it. Because it can always be transmuted and transformed into something useful for your own growth.

Although a full natal chart requires detailed preparation, a skilled astrologer who looks at the transits and aspects of the planets can glean quite a bit of information about the cycles of energy a person will be experiencing during a certain period. The following excerpt is taken from a brief reading done by Christine Rakela, a New York astrologer, using only an ephemeris to determine the various transits and aspects for the coming year. Although no horoscope was prepared, it is nevertheless a compelling example of the kind of information that can be deduced purely from the movement of the planets.

This next year will be a pretty good year as far as work is concerned. I mentioned new opportunities. I know that January and February should be pretty good months for you because of the way Jupiter is going to be hitting some of your planets. Saturn's going to be affecting your Venus. So Saturn's going to make you look at things realistically, with your talents, your self-worth, and everything that you feel is worthy of yourself. And Jupiter, on the other hand, is going to bring you a touch of luck in these areas. So I think the combination is favorable. It's as though you have one coming in from one end and one from the other. One without the other could cause problems. Because with Jupiter you can get over-optimistic, thinking that everything's going to work out, and it doesn't. Or with Saturn, you can just hibernate and work, work, work, work, and accomplish nothing, because you're not out there looking for the open doors. You're going to find a lot of your opportunity around January, February, March, and April. Those are key months for you, when you really want to be pushing for things. Those four months in particular are when Jupiter is really zapping your planets, and it's good, because Jupiter just adds a touch of support and encouragement, all those nice things that we need. . . .

Although these readings sound very cut-and-dried, a skilled astrologer relies as much upon his intuitive skills as upon his objective knowledge. So although we might not consider astrology a function of psychic ability, neither is it a pure science. Astrology at its best is an art. Linda Hill describes her work in this way:

> The thing about astrology is it's very intellectual; there's a lot of concrete data that needs to be synthesized. There's a lot of information that needs to be learned—symbolism, correspondences, mathematics. It is a language with a complex vocabulary structure. At the same time, it involves interpretation and art, too, in terms of what meaning is assigned to this data. These meanings are constantly evolving and changing—they are tested and revised. And then at another point, you just sort of have to let go of it all and it becomes a set of symbols that trigger certain understandings. So depending upon who the person is in front of me, I don't have any control over it— some of it is channeled, some of it isn't. I'm open to whatever happens.

In a way, we've come full circle: although there are astrologers who approach their work in a purely scientific way, at some point, every skilled reader is going to have to rely upon less tangible methods of interpretation. Whether those intuitions are purely the product of extensive study and experience or the manifestation of psychic ability depends upon the astrologer and upon how you view psychic ability as a whole. But like other methods of divination, astrology clearly integrates us with a level of knowing that lies deeper than the rational mind. Perhaps if we concern ourselves less with the mechanics of that insight and more with its content, we will come to appreciate astrology as yet one more valuable tool in the search for self-knowledge.

Numerology, the use of numbers to divine spiritual truths, is closely related to astrology, and many psychic readers use both techniques, sometimes in combination. It is obvious from the degree to which mathematics is involved in astrology that it is as much the study of numbers and the relationships they represent as it is the study of the stars and planets. In numerology, numbers are thought to represent not just quantities but qualities as well. By examining a person's "numbers," a numerologist can discern the same patterns of energy an astrologer would deduce from the movement of the celestial bodies.

Like its sister science, astrology, numerology dates back to ancient Babylon, where it was in use as far back as 700 B.C.E. Its roots, however, lie in the earliest periods of the Jewish rabbinic tradition, when scholars sought to interpret the Torah, or Five Books of Moses, using a system called *gematria,* in which the Hebrew letters were converted into numerological equivalents and plied with esoteric formulas to reveal hidden truths. It was thought that Moses was given such formulas directly from God at the same time he received the Torah at Mount Sinai, as a way of preserving the oral tradition. In time, this system of analysis came to be quite complex; Gershom Scholem, an expert on Jewish mysticism, cites one historical manuscript that lists 72 separate methods of gematria.

The ancients were apparently well aware of the way in which numbers represent both quantities and qualities, and just as the science of mathematics was evolving, so, too, was the more esoteric discipline of numerology. By the sixth century B.C.E., the Greek scholar Pythagoras had set up a school of mathematics in Alexandria that taught both the basic principles of geometry as well as the more esoteric aspects of numerology. To him, both sciences were intertwined, since the world seemed to be ordered according to very exacting mathematical principles. According to one occult axiom, "God geometrizes," and Pythagoras saw in geometry the physical expression of more subtle spiritual truths. These truths were measurable as progressive cycles, which in turn were expressed in numbers. Indeed, such examples of ancient architecture as the Egyptian pyramids and Solomon's temple in Jerusalem were based upon very precise measurements intended to express mystical relationships in physical form. (The Freemasons of today, who still practice a form of mystic ritual, claim as their heritage the ancient stonemasons who built the original temple in Jerusalem.)

Although most numerologists today still base their work on the teachings of Pythagoras, there are as many different methods of divining by numbers as there are spiritual traditions. But they are all based upon interpreting the numerical values of your full name at birth and your birthdate. In calculating these values, all sums are reduced to the numbers one to nine, which are thought to embody one full cycle of evolution, both on a universal and an individual level. Thus if you count back in your life nine years, you will supposedly recognize similar drives, motivations, and concerns active in your life, even though the way in which those patterns were manifested may differ. For example, 1987 becomes 1978, both of which have the same numerological value; by comparing those two years you should be able to see similarities in the issues that were key in your life at both times.

Most numerologists believe—as do most astrologers—that the particular time we each choose to incarnate is based on a series of past lives. In order to work out our accumulated karma, we each enter the world at a time when the energy fields are such as to set the conditions for the karmic lessons we have to learn in this lifetime. By analyzing the numbers in the date of your birth and the name you "chose," the numerologist can reveal the specific lessons that you seek to master this time around. Stephen Calia, a reader who uses numerology, astrology, and tarot, describes this relationship:

My main orientation for these readings is to give people a focus, to keep them on track. . . . The birthday gives me an idea of what you're here to do in this lifetime. The name at birth is the essential mask that you take on in order to accomplish that. In astrology, the nodes [of the moon] give you a line of evolution and the natal chart shows you how to go about accomplishing that. The astrology gives more details; the numerology is more of a shorthand—more to the point.

In the same way that the different signs and houses in astrology correspond with different aspects of the self, so do the different numbers that numerologists calculate signify particular areas of an individual's life. In Stephen Calia's system, for instance, one primary number is deduced from your birthdate and three primary numbers are deduced from your name. Your "life lesson number" indicates the lesson you were incarnated to learn—basically, your reason for being. Your "soul number" is your "inner life," in other words, your deepest urges and desires. It reveals aspects of yourself that you have accumulated over the course of past lives. The "personality number" is the "mask" that you take on in this lifetime; it deals with the ways in which you see the world and the world sees you. Finally, the "integrated-self number" constitutes your mental and emotional self; it represents the highest goal that you seek to achieve in this incarnation.

A numerologist will take your birthdate and full name (as it appears on your birth certificate) at the time you call for an appointment. When you appear for your reading, he will already have prepared an interpretation and, in some cases, have it written out. He might begin like this:

Your full birthdate works out to a 44, which is an 8. Forty-four is the number of learning about the creative process. Essentially, it's having your concrete plan in mind and then working to manifest it on a material plane. The 8 is the number of power, authority, responsibility. So it says to me that you're here in a generic sense to be a teacher, to be a leader in whatever way that manifests. . . . To get to that place will take a lot of hard work and discipline. The tendency with a 44 is to sort of stay up in your dream world. Because inherently there's the knowledge that it will take a lot of hard work to make any of those fantasies real. And there can be a lot of avoidance before you actually get around to doing that. So the challenge is to learn the creative process. Take one of those wishes and work on it creatively. . . . One of the most interesting things with regard to your name is that each one of these numbers has a zero in it, which is very unusual. Zero is the number of wholeness, of spirituality, of God. . . . The top number is the soul number—the number 50 is the number of emotional opening—your desire to experience things, to get your hands on things. And the 50 is the number of struggle. So one of the things that you have to accept . . . is that there's a part of you that really wants to get out there and experience things and also the struggling aspect means it's okay to fight [for it]. The personality number is a 7, which is very private and very quiet, and it's the number of spiritual studies. So on a personality level, you're like a people-watcher; sort of like a specialist. . . . But inside there's someone who's very emotional, who wants to get out there and expand and explore and see more of the whole world. . . . And the difference between those two is 20, or 2, so it's opening up partnerships and relationships; how to communicate, how to deal with the two sides of your personality. . . . There's a real wild side to you that most people never see. You're a specialist. If you're to succeed in the world, you need to specialize. In a way that's good—it'll slow you down. Otherwise, you'd probably dissipate yourself because you're interested in so many things.

You can see from this excerpt that a numerology reading is not quite as cut-and-dried as perhaps an astrology reading. One of the reasons for this is that the reader has less data to work with—there are just so many permutations of numbers that can be worked out of your birthdate and name. An astrologer is dealing with a much greater amount of data. Consequently, a numerologist may have to rely a little more on her own intuition in applying the interpretations to your particular life experience. The system may give her a framework in which to put her insights, and may even spark her psychic perception, as we have seen with other types of readers.

Unlike astrology, with its heavy emphasis on psychology and personality, numerology focuses on predicting upcoming patterns. This is done by breaking up the year (known as your "personal year," because it begins on your birthday) into three sections of four months each. The numerologist uses these intervals to map out larger patterns that you can expect to experience as you live out the year. For instance, the following excerpt, taken from one of Stephen Calia's readings, characterizes one individual's experience for the period of March through June:

> This is a decision time. You need to expand in home/career/relationships by taking on more responsibility. You need to look at all these areas and see if it is possible to expand. Are you given more responsibility? Recognition? Do you want to have more say in how things are run? If the answer is yes, are you able to expand? If not, you want to leave.
>
> On the other hand, this can be a culmination in your work—a reaching a fruition of your goals. As a result, opportunity for advancement may occur, recognition and rewards for the work you have done can come your way. This is a karmic return time and is a time for the positive and the negative to come back. Take responsibility for it all and take the credit and the blame.
>
> In the home, you may be looking to put more energy into decorating and generally creating more space. You do need the feeling of more room, and if you feel cramped, you will feel angry and frustrated. You might also be looking at the possibility of a move. What you want is to have more responsibility and to feel more in charge. This could lead you to want to buy a home.
>
> All of this takes money. You need to sit down now and work out your finances. Set a financial plan that will help you achieve your goals. Just be careful you don't overindulge. This is a test of your sense of pro-

portion. Don't try to do too much at once. Be patient. You will have what you want in time.

In addition to these seasonal forecasts, the numerologist will prepare a month-by-month guide to the upcoming energy patterns you will be dealing with. These will include certain days that are "peak points," which, according to Calia, are points at which "what you have been working on all year comes to the surface." Your month-by-month forecast is your "road map" for working out your karmic patterns through your behavior and desires. Here is an example of a peak point that occurred in the month of May:

For you, it is a month of introspection and study. There is a need to pull in and study your situation. What you will be looking at now are the people in your life to see who your friends are. You will be feeling very vulnerable right now and need to see who you feel *safe* to share this vulnerability with. You want to and need to express your feelings and your passions with another and now is the time to see if there is anyone in your life with whom you feel safe to do that. This may be a time when a significant romance starts or the point of reaching a decision to make a deeper commitment in an existing relationship.

On the other side of the coin, you will need to notice who the people are that you don't feel safe with—who are needing you, but you know can't meet your needs. You need to filter these people out of your life. You may have to learn this lesson of whom to trust by being involved with someone who is not trustworthy. Try to listen to your instincts so that you don't get too involved before you are willing to see the truth about this person.

Whether you decide to visit an astrologer, a numerologist, or someone who combines both techniques, will depend upon your needs and your own sense of the metaphysical. If you prefer a more detailed approach, then astrology, with its wealth of data and clearly observable relationships between planets, signs, and houses, may appeal to you more. On the other hand, numerology, with its simplicity and clearer, more orderly cycles, may be easier for you to apply to your everyday life. If neither of these approaches appeals to your sense of truth, then you might consider a third divinatory science—one that is as close as the hand in front of your face: palmistry.

Palmistry—the process of reading someone's palm, or more precisely, entire hand—is a particularly rare form of divination in today's psychic world. This is because most people who claim to practice palmistry do not really read the physical characteristics of the palm, but merely use it as a focal point for their psychic abilities. Even more than astrology and numerology, which still contain some element of intuitive or psychic interpretation, palmistry has evolved into a true occult science. A good palm reader need not have any psychic ability, but can rely purely upon diligent study, good powers of observation, and solid experience.

It must be pointed out, however, that true palmistry does not endeavor to predict specific events in someone's life. Perhaps more than any other of the divinatory arts, palm reading deals with the psychological, emotional, and mental composition of an individual. It may indicate certain trends that can be expected to occur or tendencies for events or changes to take place, but this is not its true value. If you desire hard-and-fast predictions, you may want to restrict your search to those readers who are truly psychic.

Palmistry breaks down into two aspects: "chirognomy" (also called "chirology"), which deals with a reader's ability to interpret the hand as a reflection of an individual's personality, character, and potential; and "chiromancy," which encompasses a reader's ability to divine the past, present, or future from what she sees in the hand. Both words are derived from the Greek word for hand, *cheir* (which is also the root of the words "chiropodist" and "chiropractor").

Practical use of palmistry originated in the Middle East, although Stone Age handprints made with red ocher and black pigment have been found in European caves. The Greeks, Romans, and Egyptians all made use of palm reading, and such ancient thinkers as Pythagoras, Hippocrates, and even Aristotle were acquainted with this means of "reading" a person. The ancient East seems to have evolved its own method of palmistry, completely unrelated to our own, with the practice going back at least 5,000 years in India and China, where observing the hands is still an integral part of both Ayurvedic and Chinese medicine. The Chinese system of palmistry as a divinatory practice may have been derived from the *I Ching*.

Despite the fact that there are references in the Old Testament to indicate that hand reading was widely practiced, shortly after the Middle Ages the Church banned its use as the Devil's work. This may be part of the reason why palm reading has long been considered the province of charlatans. Today most people are still unaware of the fact that a great deal of scientific research has been done on the correlation between the appearance of the hands and the inner emotional, psychological, and physical state of the individual. Nathaniel Altman, who has been reading palms since 1969 and who is the author of three books on palmistry, explains the purpose of palmistry today:

From my point of view, palmistry mainly gives a very objective view of where a person is in his life, what his talents are, his general health level; it talks about relationships, possible career directions, and areas of personal expression. What I like about it is that it gives an objective view about where your life is, where it's probably going, and what experiences you've had that helped bring you to the point you are at now.

A lot of people in palmistry see it as a fortune-telling tool. I see it more as what a doctor does; you go to the doctor, he takes your blood level, cholesterol, etc., and he says, "I feel you could have a heart attack in three years unless you start controlling your cholesterol level." So, by giving you a warning, a signpost, you can change the tendency for later. So you ask, is he predicting the future or is he giving you probable or possible trends? And that's what palmistry can do.

Because every line, ridge, or protrusion on your hand has some significance, and because each of your hands is different, a good palm reader should take full note of all these details. For this reason it is a good idea to avoid anyone who claims to be able to read your future by looking at one hand, or a psychic who offers palm reading as an "extra" service. Serious readers will often draw outlines and make ink prints of your hands, as well as take notes on their size, shape, texture, and color. This affords a record of the reading as well as a basis for comparison with later readings.

Such a record is important because the lines in your hands do change over time, sometimes in a matter of weeks. Nat Altman recalls a particularly dramatic case in which a subject's hands changed completely in six weeks:

> This person became a vegetarian, changed his major in college, told his father [who was an army colonel] that he wasn't joining the army reserves, and got into theosophy. He made major, major changes suddenly, and [as a result] the lines changed. They have not changed a lot since then, but that was like a quantum leap in his life. And all in six weeks' time.

In another case, someone he read for had a major break in his lifeline, indicating a problem at around age 49 (at the time, he was 30):

This shows a major problem with health, it could be a cause of death. Now this person stopped smoking and became a vegetarian, and in two years the line mended. So a lot of things can change. It's also interesting that his marriage line . . . was broken in the middle. At that time he wasn't married and had very bad feelings about [relationships]. Then he fell in love and got married, and the line just grew tremendously, even in that two-year period.

Some palmists attribute the ability of the lines to change to the fact that the palms are the sight of thousands of nerve endings— more than any other part of the body. Others point out that these nerves are connected to the frontal lobes of the brain, the seat of human consciousness. Perhaps in some way we cannot yet fully understand, our thoughts, feelings, and desires are transmitted through nervous impulses to the various tissues of the body, affecting changes in its physical structure.

A detailed analysis of your hand can reveal a wealth of information. A palmist's evaluation of a client actually begins even before looking at the palms themselves. The way a person holds his hands and uses them to gesture is a primary indicator of what that person is like. A skilled reader will take note of such details and use them in constructing a coherent, comprehensive picture of the client as a whole. Other aspects of your hand that are considered include its size and shape; skin color, texture, and temperature; degree of resiliency (tense or relaxed); position of the fingers at rest; amount of space between the fingers;

length of the fingers; shape of the fingertips; and length, shape, and color of the fingernails.

These preliminary observations will enable the reader to construct a framework in which to put the rest of your reading. Like astrology and numerology, the "standard" meanings attributed to particular lines and formations on your hand can only be interpreted in the context of who you are as a whole person. And although a palm reader may not be psychic per se, he will invariably draw upon his intuition in determining the correct meaning for some aspect of your hand. As Nat Altman explains:

> You put [all the elements] together and you get a gestalt or a synthesis of the hand and then you proceed that way. I see the lines, the mounts, the flexibility, the shape, the color, the way the fingers are. These all have a bearing. So you take the general areas and then you intertwine them. I get very skeptical when a person who has been reading for three months calls himself a palmist, because it takes an awful lot of study and understanding of all the elements and how they work together.
>
> Having short fingers and no knots, I like to work more out of my instinct and have a feel for [the process]. I don't like to say I'm a psychic, but I'm intuitive—it's kind of an intuitive feeling. Some hand readers are more psychic—maybe 80 percent psychic and 20 percent reading, like the woman who taught me. I'm more like 75 percent reading and 25 percent intuition. And again, it depends upon whom I read for. With some people I would be more psychic or intuitive, with other people less.

There are certain general categories for the hands themselves that a palmist may use, although many prefer a synthesis of several. For example, Nat Altman uses a system that divides the hands into five types: the square hand, which denotes an "organizer and planner"; the spatulate hand, which indicates an "energetic, tenacious, innovative, and self-confident" person; the conic or artistic hand, belonging to people who are "sentimental, intuitive, impulsive, capricious, and romantic"; the psychic or intuitive hand, which reveals a person who is highly creative and who possesses a strong imagination; and the mixed hand, since most people don't fall into one single category.

Such divisions give the palm reader a place to begin his analysis and a basis for further observation. A hand with good basic proportions implies that the person will be able to harmonize the various forces that make up her life, both internally and externally. Conversely, a hand that lacks a certain degree of balance or symmetry indicates a person who may have a more difficult task in attaining harmony in life.

Some readers feel that because each hand is linked to a different hemisphere of the brain, it will reveal information that is unique to that half. For instance, if you are right-handed, your left hand, which is related to the right brain, will reveal the more esoteric aspects of your nature: your intuition, your genetic makeup, your spiritual orientation, and, some believe, knowledge that you brought with you from past lives. Your right hand, however, will indicate those aspects of your personality that have been learned during the course of your life, as well as the way you tend to express the "essential you" in the context of your life's experiences. Thus, by comparing your two hands, the palm reader will be able to determine the way in which you are using your innate capacities to deal with life's challenges. This is similar to the way in which an astrologer would compare the transits and aspects of certain planets with your natal chart, to see how you would handle certain life events against the backdrop of who you are.

It is interesting to note that the fingers on the hand are named for particular planets. There are also eight "mounts," or localized areas of the hand, that also correspond to the planets and represent the same personal attributes that they represent in astrology. For instance, the index finger and corresponding mount beneath it are named for Jupiter and indicate ambition, pride, leadership, and honor. Similarly, the pinky and its mount are named for Mercury and deal with sexuality, quickness, and business acumen. The degress to which each of these areas is developed indicates the extend to which that quality is inherent in the person.

In addition to fingers and mounts, the palm reader will pay a great deal of attention to the lines of the hand. (Many people mistakenly believe that this is all a palm reader looks at.) The three major lines are the life line, the head line, and the heart line. In contrast to popular belief, the life line does not necessarily indicate the length of your life. Rather, it reflects the quality of that life, and the degree to which you may have to undergo major life changes, whether in philosophy or lifestyle. Similarly, the head line is not a barometer of intelligence, but rather indicates the manner in which you process information—creatively and intuitively or analytically and linearly. The heart line may indicate both your sexual and emotional disposition as well as the physical health of your heart.

In addition to these three major lines, there are a host of smaller lines, forming patterns of their own as well as linking together the more pronounced formations on the hand. Because every hand is unique, it will contain only some of these lines, which will in turn have to be interpreted relative to the rest of the hand. Each reader has his own way of looking at these lines, based upon his own study and experience. The following excerpt from one of Nat Altman's readings indicates the degree of detail that the hand can reveal to an experienced reader:

You have an interesting formation, called a simian line. It's the joining of the head and heart line. Now what that means is that it intensifies your personality a lot. . . . You could be yelling and screaming at someone one minute and then have your arm around them and be joking the next. . . . People with this hand are often very creative; there's a lot of energy—and a desire to do a lot of things. . . .

This is the life line here. This generally indicates the basic constitution, and particularly now, it's stronger than it was earlier—which means your life is probably more focused than it was earlier, and your health is better as well. Later on, you have some cross-hatchings and islands, which indicates that you would need to take better care of your health in general. . . .

The life line is not separate here from the simian line, which would tend to make you cautious and careful and also a little bit curious about what people are thinking about you. It takes you a while to make decisions. It could also mean you tend to hold back on your feelings. . . .

Now the career line is coming up on the mount of luna, which could mean a variety of careers in your life. You may very well be doing two careers at once. It could also indicate being known by the public, and working with the public—speaking, lecturing, teaching. . . . The Jupiter finger is fairly strong, which is this leadership quality—needing to be in charge, liking to be the boss. You don't like to be working for other people. You would like to be self-employed or running the show. . . .

With the type of heart line you have, you need to find someone who is very compatible with you—someone who is sensitive and also tough when necessary. You have to have that balance between the two things. And these little pads on your fingers also indicate sensitivity.

It's a good hand. It's a complicated hand. Your life isn't easy, but it's very rewarding. But it's also rough. People with this hand, unless they really move their energy out and really say, "I want to have a creative life, and I can do this," are very frustrated. I don't know if you do art or any other kind of creative work, but maybe you should give it to yourself; it could expand a dimension and make your life a lot happier.

Don't be afraid to ask a palm reader which aspects of your hand he is drawing his conclusions from. I've asked that question many times—of both frauds and legitimate readers—and more often than not they have admitted to not reading my palm at all, but to using pure psychic ability. (In the case of one storefront reader, she admitted that she wasn't actually reading the lines on my hand, but then assured me that the lines change every three months, so I should be sure to come back for another reading! Another street corner "palm reader" responded to my question by insisting that these are "very mysterious" methods, known only to people who are psychic, and that, in fact, there were lines on my hand that were only visible to her.)

There is absolutely nothing wrong with a psychic using a palm as a focal point. But it is essential to know whether the information you are being given is the result of subjective insight or objective observation of your hand based upon traditional methods and experience. No psychic reader who is using clairvoyance should bill himself as a palm reader unless he is trained in that discipline. The same distinction applies to astrology and numerology as well. You should be fully aware how much of the information you are receiving is the result of psychic intuition and how much has been deduced using "scientific" methods. Any reader who refuses to answer that question openly and honestly should be viewed with a great deal of skepticism.

As with all types of psychic readings, there is nothing to be gained by trying to keep it "mysterious" or "spooky." One of the integral elements of astrology, numerology, and palmistry is the opportunity you have to share in the process and to know how the method that is being used functions, where the information is coming from, and how it is being interpreted. This aspect of these disciplines is one of their biggest selling points, and if you have chosen to pay for such a skill, you have every right to know exactly what you are paying for and the level of experience that the reader brings to his craft. So pay careful attention, ask plenty of questions, and above all, enjoy it.

Channeling and Mediumship

In the last couple of years, channeling has become practically a national craze. Ever since the publication of Shirley MacLaine's *Out on a Limb*, it seems as though every person who ever had a paranormal experience is channeling everything from Aunt Tessie to Jesus Christ. Although the term is new and the popular interest fairly recent, channeling has been around a long time. Unfortunately, because many people think of it as a recent phenomenon and don't fully understand its implications and applications, the true value of contacting the spirit world is widely misunderstood, and abuse is rampant.

Consequently, when you decide to visit a channeler you are entering dark waters indeed, and you will need to know what to look for and what criteria to use to evaluate both the person doing the channeling and the message being channeled. Probably more with this area of psychic work than any other, you will need to learn to trust your own instincts and to rely on your own sense of truth. Just because someone claims to speak for a spiritual entity does not make that experience valid, and even where genuine contact is made, it does not necessarily follow that the spirit that is contacted is wise, loving, or even good.

The channeling of spiritual entities was known historically as mediumship. But the practice of consulting nonphysical entities either for philosophical wisdom or in an effort to predict the future dates back long before the advent of the Spiritualist movement of the last century. In China and India, where the idea of astral beings goes back at least 5,000 years, spirits were regularly consulted for advice or given offerings in an effort to appease them. In the West, the Bible records several examples of specific communications with the dead, as well as numerous instances of prophets receiving messages from other planes of reality.[3] The Greek oracles, the conjurers and witches of the Middle Ages, and the shamanic traditions of Asia, Africa, and the pre-Columbian Americas, were all efforts to establish contact with nonphysical forces at work in the world.

The modern fascination with spirits began in 1848 in Hydesville, New York, when three young girls known as the Fox sisters began to get communications from a spirit who claimed to be the ghost of a traveling salesman who had been murdered in their house many years earlier. This episode kicked off the Spiritualism movement, which took America and Europe by storm, and which continued well into this century with all manner of séances, spirit communications, and scientific investigations. The psychic explosion peaked in the 1920s and '30s, when such luminaries as Arthur Conan Doyle and Harry Houdini would face off in public debates over the veracity of communicating with the dead. During this period, most mediumship took the form of contacting the spirits of dead friends or relatives, so it isn't surprising that many frauds capitalized on the public's desire to talk to "dear, departed Grandpa" one last time. As a result, Spiritualism took on a notorious image and, perhaps for that reason, kept a low profile for the next 40 years or so.

This poor image may also be the reason why the word "medium" is generally shunned these days in favor of the new expression, "channeler." As we shall see, however, channeling today encompasses a lot more than the Spiritualism of the past. The idea of contacting spiritual entities resurfaced in the early 1970s with the publication of Jane Roberts's "Seth" material, which led to the more recent explosion of channeling sparked by Shirley MacLaine's books. Today, such disembodied luminaries as "Lazaris," "Ramtha," "Jonah," and "Emmanuel" work the spiritual lecture circuit, holding forth on a variety of metaphysical topics, running weekend workshops in self-development, and gaining notoriety for both themselves and their human mouthpieces. Whole books have been channeled (rather than written), videotapes produced, and audio cassettes distributed with messages from the spirit realms. Unfortunately, as happened 50 years ago, a profusion of charlatans and frauds abounds, and many unscrupulous people are now capitalizing on the public's hunger for spiritual knowledge and the resulting psychic craze.

Channeling lends itself very well to those who pretend to have psychic ability because most channelers go into a trance in order to contact spirit entities. As a result, most do not have to take responsibility for what they say, attributing it to various and sundry "spirit guides" or "ancient masters." In addition, we in the West tend to assume that anything that comes from the realm of spirit is inherently wise—even if it makes absolutely no sense to us. As one writer put it, "It is a curiosity that many of us who never took Aunt Sally's advice when she was living find her eminently wiser now that she's dead and wants to deliver a message as a spirit guide!"[4] The theatrics associated with going into a trance and being taken over bodily by a spirit entity also offer the unscrupulous an excellent setting for putting on a convincing show.

Some channelers do go into a full trance, while others do not. In fact, the verb "to channel" has come to be used to refer to anything that implies an accessing of one's inner knowledge. This could include anything from writing a novel to preparing a gourmet meal, if the process involves a profound creative state through which one's "higher self" finds expression. (I had many psychics tell me, during the course of my research, that this book would be channeled.) Many people also use the term to describe the process of utilizing the right brain, which, as we have seen, is linked to the intuitive, psychic self.

A full trance is characterized by the individual leaving his body and being replaced by another entity or intelligence. The process has been described as being similar to dying (or at least to the descriptions brought back by those who have suffered near-death experiences), except that the "silver cord" that attaches the soul to the body remains intact (when it is severed, we die). Whatever entity desires to come through takes over the channeler's body, using the larynx to speak and sometimes using the rest of the body to gesture, walk around, or even drink liquids. The channeler, who is quite literally a "medium" or "channel" of communication, either remembers nothing of the experience or reports traveling freely in astral realms "doing other work." When the medium returns to his body, the session is over and he regains full consciousness.

Elwood Babbitt, "the Medium of Massachusetts," has been going into full trance since he was a small child (he is now in his sixties). While he is out of his body, his "control," Dr. Frederick Fisher, takes over. Babbitt describes the process of relinquishing control of his body:

> Well, I sit like I am now, and I turn my awareness to things [like] a tree, a beautiful sky, flowers. It's like changing the biorhythms of my energy. And gradually I begin to expand. The only way I can describe it is somebody turns on a huge cosmic vacuum cleaner, and I start feeling being sucked out of my body. As I begin to leave, I see the other energy move in over me, take over, and continue [to use] my body while I'm out of it. And once the transference is completed, I've reversed roles, where you would say I was dead and the spirit sustaining my body was very much alive. I'm not here; I'm just competing with Ma Bell. I go out into the energy, and I do my work there, and Dr. Fisher does it here.

Babbitt is very much aware of the spiritual dimensions while he is out of his body. He speaks about a "light, airy feeling of euphoria" and describes himself as "zooming" around, checking in on some of the people he has worked with to note the progress of their spiritual growth.

Other trance channelers don't recall anything of the experience of vacating their body. For instance, Hossca Harrison, a Boulder, Colorado channeler who is used by the spiritual entity "Jonah," describes the trance process in this way:

> When Jonah gets ready to come through, I feel an intense vibration in my forehead, in my third eye. Then

it rapidly takes over my entire body and I can feel myself being propelled out of my body. It's like there's this large tube or tunnel in front of me and the tunnel is made out of white light, and there's a brilliant gold light at the end of it. As soon as I reach the gold light, I'm back in my body and the entire session is over. So when I channel Jonah, for me, the period of time that it took is 30 or 60 seconds, whether he talked for a half hour or four hours. There's no perception of time; my consciousness is completely gone.

Still other channelers experience the trance state in ways that are perhaps more subtle. For instance, some may hear an inner voice or see a spiritual being in front of them, even though their eyes are closed. Unlike Hossca Harrison, some channelers remain partially present during the trance state: they are aware of what is being said, even though they may not be able to recall the conversation afterwards. Barbara Rollinson, also a channeler in Colorado, describes what this is like:

I kind of sit [off] to one side. What I had to learn to do, because I can hear what goes on, was to quiet that [part of my consciousness that sits off to one side], so that it wasn't making comments like, "You can't say that," or "That's not what needs to happen," or whatever. Because I know in my own personality I don't want to go anyplace; I don't want to miss out on anything. I know other channels go different places or whatever. I don't have any recall of the conversation; that's not there. I can just hear the voices that come through. I can feel myself just move to one side.

One of the debates surrounding channeling or mediumship is whether it is better for the channeler to go into a full trance, thereby removing her ego completely from the process, or remain present so that she is aware of what is being said and can clarify the reading. Part of the difficulty in channeling is making sure that the psychic's own spiritual issues and personal biases don't color the reading. Because such colorings are not always intentional, it is difficult for the channeler to be sure that the message that gets through is purely the result of spirit. This is generally referred to as the "clarity" of the channel. In those cases where the channeler doesn't use a trance at all, but simply interprets what she sees or hears from the spirit realm, the danger of personal bias is even greater. As Elwood Babbitt explains:

> A lot of mediums color their work. I don't criticize it, because they're doing it unconsciously. You see, clairvoyantly they'll see a symbol, the same as you would in a dream. But then they enlarge upon what they see. It's like passing a word around a circle, and by the time the last person gets the word, it's a whole sentence. This is what happens with . . . someone who isn't objective in his work. Clarity [means] simply widening to a whole deeper awareness so you see it beyond this dimension, rather than the vague starry pictures you get. It should be someone who can get out of the way through the trance condition. And then

you don't have to be afraid that untruth or color will seep into the work. Unless they've been well trained to stand aside. . . . But many of these sensitives—and I don't call them psychics, because everyone is psychic—they get into these extemporaneous messages. They're mixing their own consciousness with the flashes they're getting, so they lose that visual clarity that would come in a continuity if they could hold their brain completely still, which is a talent in itself.

Barbara Rollinson explains the role that the ego plays in doing spiritual work:

One of the things that I first thought is that the ego had to just leave entirely. But what I recognize [now] is that that's not where it is either. Because the ego has some value on our earth plane. So what I do is just silently ask it to move to one side, thank it very much for the all the work it does, but [tell it] I don't need it right now. . . .

Still, like Elwood Babbitt, she sees the need to keep the ego out of the channeling process itself:

I see the ego as helping to put things together on the earth plane, but not involved in the channeling process. Because I think it can be more of a hindrance than a help. And I have listened to different channels at different times, and I can tell when their ego is involved. It usually comes when they're tired, or if they're working a lot, or if they're having a lot of stress in their lives and they haven't cleared that out. They don't recognize it, because you don't when it's you.

The structure of the spiritual self is what enables a medium to leave his physical body and travel freely throughout the astral plane. This structure is intimately bound up with the nature of reality, which, as we have seen, is nothing more than a great conflux of energy taking a variety of forms. Most psychics— and mystical traditions—characterize the human being as being made up of three "vibrational" levels or frequencies. The "lowest," or most "dense," frequency is the physical body, which occupies a place on the material plane of reality.

That aspect of the self which is freed during a trance state and is liberated from the body upon death is the soul, which is of a higher frequency, or lighter density, than the physical body. The soul is the repository of character and personality as well as of spiritual knowledge. Because the soul survives bodily death, it carries the accumulation of experiences amassed over the course of past lives. With each reincarnation into a physical form, it acquires new insights into spiritual truth and moves toward a more subtle vibrational level.

When the soul has completed its cycle of death and rebirth on the physical plane, it is no longer needed. Having evolved to a level of profound knowledge about the nature of all things (and its own selfhood), the soul becomes pure spirit, which is that aspect of each of us that is the primary Creative Force, or, as some call it, the God Consciousness. Spirit is the level of awareness that all mystics seek to attain and that not only animates the entire cosmos, but links all being in Oneness.

If all this sounds very mystical, that's because it is. Channeling is simply the latest form of spiritual striving that humans have been bound up with for thousands of years. The Hindu tradition in particular (as well as the Buddhist) possesses a thorough and graphic description of the realms of spiritual experience and their corresponding planes of reality. According to Hindu scriptures, there are three levels of reality: the physical, the astral, and the causal. Whereas the body exists on the physical plane, the soul resides, between incarnations, on the astral plane. There, the soul possesses an astral body, which has form and character just as a physical body does. The Hindus speak of a karma of the astral plane, which must be worked through before attaining the final level of Oneness with the universe, the causal plane, or Godhead. As this system makes clear, simply because an entity exists on the astral plane does not imply a higher degree of wisdom or immediate enlightenment.

Although most psychics accept the reality of the astral plane, many reject this tripartite division as too simplistic. Most prefer the idea of a continuum of energy that changes form along with vibrational frequency. They are quick to correct the notion of "higher" or "lower" levels of reality, pointing out that all these levels exist simultaneously in the same space-time continuum. As Elwood Babbitt explains, the notion of expansion and contraction is a more accurate conception of the energy field:

Everything vibrates—everything's in a state of vibration. Like if you toss a pebble in a still pond, the ripples that go out. This is the life form we're talking about—it moves out to the outer periphery at the banks of that pond. And so this vibrational force keeps expanding outward. Then you reach the ultimate goal . . . and suddenly begin to realize it's all within yourself. You're going to see from past lives what you need to complete. And after a while you'll come back in another body. But probably it won't be for another 10,000 years. Who cares? But that is the way the force works. . . . The law of life demands growth. You might take 20 lives to grow an inch, but the growth is there, and you'll go from one progression to the next until you finally see the essence of who you were before you even decided to get into the outer density of life.

Babbitt claims that there are seven "progressions" of energy, each at an expanded level or frequency. He compares them to television or radio signals, each of which can broadcast through the same space without interfering with one another because they are on different frequencies. Within each progression there are degrees, each degree representing a kind of increase in voltage, so to speak, until the next progression is reached.

The nature of the spiritual entities that a channeler contacts depends upon the level of spiritual vibration that is reached. And herein lies the problem. If a channeler opens herself up to any energy that comes along, she could be the conduit for spirits from the lowest reaches of the astral plane. These spirits may not be "evil," but chances are that they will not have any great wisdom to impart. In some cases they may even impersonate other energies, claiming to be spirits from a much more evolved level. Or they could simply be wayward spirits who have been wondering around the astral plane, waiting for an opportunity to express themselves. In order to avoid this, a channeler or medium must set the conditions for the session, asking that only the highest levels of wisdom come through. If a psychic is inexperienced or hasn't cultivated herself spiritually, she will be unable to recognize the different degrees of spiritual evolution and may end up inviting in some unwanted guests. Elwood Babbitt calls this "obsession and possession"—the problem of unsuspecting channelers attracting lower forms of psychic energy:

> They [these entities] are impersonators. Like you could have one come in and say that it was Louis Pasteur, when it could be some nut who died in a nuthouse about two months ago, who was traveling in the energies and saw a light—somebody sitting in meditation—and said, "Hey, I'm going to look into that light." [So the entity] dives into it and begins to channel stuff to this person who thinks, "Hey, here's Louis Pasteur." No questions asked. They don't test the spirit; they're just anxious that they can be

called "channeler." But the person is led to believe that it is someone great. And it's a tragedy.

Similarly, a channeler may not actually be accessing the outer levels of energy, but may only be tapping into his own subconscious. There have been cases of mediumship where tests indicated the possibility of a split personality, in which the deeper realms of the repressed subconscious used the vehicle of a separate personality to overcome the fear of expressing itself.

Aside from the channeler's own subconscious, there are several general categories of spiritual entities that may become manifest during a channeling session. The first is the channeler's "higher self." This usually means nothing more than the psychic is expressing his own intuitive, right-brain knowledge. We all have a source of wisdom deep down inside us, which is what gives us our gut feelings about things.

During channeling, this higher level of knowing may take the form of a vision, such as a wise old man or a figure made up of golden light. Such visions may be easier for us to understand than pure spiritual energy.

In these cases the channeler may speak of a "spirit guide." Some people believe that these guides are merely the manifestations of our own higher selves; others believe in the existence of separate entities who aided us in choosing a body before we incarnated into this life and who now watch over us. A channeler might contact her own spirit guide for information about you, since all spirits supposedly have access to the "Akashic records," the sum total of all knowledge that we spoke about in Chapter One. Or you might be privileged to meet your spirit guide, who will have some advice to give you concerning your spiritual growth. These guides may have names and may recall a past life during which you were both incarnated at the same time.

In full-trance mediumship the psychic may vacate her body to make room for a "control." The control is the spiritual entity who acts as the "gatekeeper" or guide to the other planes of existence. Controls are spirits who lived on earth previously and who now reside in the astral plane, locating specific people you might want to contact and overseeing the channeling process as a whole. If you have specific questions about your life on the physical plane, the control will generally be able to answer them. If, however, you desire more philosophical knowledge or information about your past lives, the control may locate another entity who can better help you. Similarly, if you desire to speak to a particular person (perhaps a deceased relative, or even a famous personage), the control will either locate that person and turn over the body to him or simply relay messages back and forth.

One of the reasons for the control is that many spirits lack the ability to enter into a medium's body, a process that is dependent upon harmonizing the energies and sychronizing the differences in vibration. A control has usually learned to manipulate these forces effectively and knows his way around the astral plane, so to speak. A control will also watch over the medium's body and, in the event a session becomes too tiring, will call the session to a halt. Also, a control will know whether a particularly evolved spiritual energy, such as the Christ Force or the Buddha, is simply too strong for a medium's physical body and whether to avoid trying to bring it into harmonization.

Theoretically, anyone who ever lived (and who has not since reincarnated) can be called upon in the astral plane. As a result, there have been channeling sessions that brought forth everyone from Einstein to Elvis. Whether or not you truly believe these are the actual spirits of those people or simply the subconscious constructs of the medium's mind is a matter you will have to decide for yourself. In several cases, however, rigorous testing has revealed an intimate knowledge of the deceased person's life that could not have been known to the medium. In some instances, brain-wave measurements (EEGs) have revealed patterns that are entirely dissimilar from those of the conscious medium.[5]

Whatever your opinion of such contacts, spirits that exist on the astral plane possess no greater wisdom than they did in life. So if you desire to speak to Buddy Holly, and do get through, bear in mind that your channeling session should be looked upon as interdimensional fan mail, and nothing more.

In addition to the spirits of those who once lived on the physical plane, there are energies that come through who profess to never having been incarnated in a physical body. They represent forces or intelligences from other planes of existence who usually have a message they wish to pass on to those of us who dwell on the material plane. Even when a spiritual entity adopts a familiar name, however, it doesn't necessarily mean that it is the spirit of that deceased person. When Elwood Babbitt channeled Jesus Christ, for instance, the entity that came through explained that he was not the spirit of the man, Jesus Christ, but rather pure spiritual energy:

> I am the Christ Spirit, God-Force, the expression of all humanity, the expression of all nature. Christ Force is the flow of energies that vibrate through all of nature, and if you but harken in your humility you will see and hear the full expression of those creative waves that prove the Force to be the Spirit. . . .
>
> I am not the saviour. I am not the Star in the East. I am not the second coming to this planet. I am here, and have always been so, in Energy. You see me not, but you shall see me, for to see me remember I am the Light of your eye, I am that hand that rocks the cradle of the newborn understanding; I am the Force that pervades your being, I am your fullness, your expression.[6]

In addition to entities that may never have walked the earth by virtue of never having been incarnated, there are entities who have never walked the earth because they are from other planets. Many channelers hold regular dialogues with extraterrestrial beings known as "space brothers." Because interstellar space travel would require a mastery of time itself in order to overcome the astronomical distances, it follows that space beings that have visited Earth exist in a different dimension—namely, the astral plane.

These visitors from other worlds say that they are here because at this point in human history we are threatening the very existence of our planet. Some channelers claim that the explosion of the first atomic bomb in 1945 sent a shock wave throughout the galaxy and that by continuing to explode nuclear devices we are tampering with the very fabric of the cosmic energy field itself. As a result, our interstellar neighbors have taken it upon themselves to see that we don't destroy ourselves and take the entire galaxy with us. Although the cosmic law of karma does not allow them to intervene directly, they are here to aid us in our search for a new awareness and the coming of the New Age. The following excerpt is a message from "Ashtar," a fourth-dimensional space being who was channeled by Suzanne Kluss, a trance channeler:

We sometimes feel extrememly saddened by the fact that [laughs] "aliens" are so misunderstood on your planet. There has been much fear surrounding the awareness that you have all had—again, it is an example of our energies being felt and misunderstood—and they have been manifest in fear. But we are here solely for the purpose of exchanging lessons. Lessons that we need to learn from you; specifically, we are here to learn your linear conception of time. We know it not in our dimension. In our dimension, time is a space. It is simply a beingness. We all flow continually, constantly as One. . . . This energy exchange is what will help to bring about this new awareness which will lead to your New Age. . . . We have asked for your partnership. You have—on some level—consented to it, and we are supremely grateful. We embrace you in true, loving partnership. And we have really *always* been partners. We just send out love to you. And together, we *will* accomplish this Ascension. . . . It is truly a very exciting, dynamic time on the earth plane now. It is because you all chose to be partners that you are all living on your earth right now as you are.

The last category of channeled entity we have yet to mention is the one that you should be looking most to contact if you go for a session. This is the level of the Master—the totally evolved spiritual being who has attained the outermost progression of spiritual development. Masters generally take the form of the great spiritual teachers of human history: Jesus, Moses, and Buddha, for example. But they may also manifest as entities we are unfamiliar with, such as Lazaris, who never lived on earth, or Jonah, who claims to have been a spiritual leader known as the Teacher of Righteousness at the time of Jesus. Finally, spiritual energy on the level of a Master may make itself known as the Universal Life Force itself, such as Vishnu, one of the Hindu deities, or the Christ Consciousness.

It follows that a Master will not make himself known through a channeler or medium who isn't sufficiently evolved spiritually, if for no other reason than the energy transfer involved is too great for someone who has not prepared herself through right action and spiritual discipline. Unfortunately there are a host of channelers working today who claim to be the means of communication for such spiritual masters as the Christ Force. In the event you encounter such claims, let your own common sense be your guide. If a spiritual Master on the level of Jesus had decided to become manifest on the physical plane, it is likely that his message would be a great deal more significant than much of what is being channeled. If you hear something that rings true to your own sense of truth, that you can apply in your own life on more than an abstract level, and that gives you new insight into the mystery of existence, then and only then should you consider yourself in the presence of genuine channeled wisdom.

One recent phenomena that has cropped up is the channeling of animal spirits, such as dolphins and whales, and even some inanimate objects like rocks and trees. In the case of such communications, it isn't energy from the astral or spiritual planes that is being manifested, but direct communication from living creatures. Because dolphins and whales have long been thought to be highly intelligent, it is not entirely surprising that telepathic communication could be possible. What their message is, however, constitutes more of a mystery. Barbara Rollinson began channeling dolphin energy a few years back. As she describes it:

> The dolphin energy . . . completely overlays my body. And once that happens, the body begins to move, and it undulates the whole time. Then there are sounds that come, like a high-pitched thing. Then there is like

a mind-to-mind connection. I speak the thoughts as they come to me. . . . I was told what I needed to do was to get in touch with them and that they would give me information and then I was to put that information out to the world. It's taken me about four years to really get it and to understand what I was to do with it. . . . The information that comes is very universal. It's specific to our earth—the things we are going through and so forth—but they are totally at ease with their environment, and we as humans are always fussing with our environment. So there are a lot of lessons that they want to give to us as to how they live, how they see things, and so forth. . . . They're here on a path of service; they're very spiritual beings; they're very happy. Whales also come every now and then through me. I look at whales kind of like the sages of the sea, and at the dolphins as kind of the spiritual playmates—the joyousness and so forth. If we can get that message to people—that there is an inner communication between species, everybody would treat them very differently. If people would realize that there is a way to communicate with animals, with plants, and with minerals, they would have a different respect for them and would treat them differently. And we would also treat each other differently. That's kind of my main thrust as to why I'm doing all this.

Communications from the various spiritual planes take different forms, and those will depend as much upon what you hope to achieve by visiting a channeler as upon the channeler's clarity and experience. Over the course of the last hundred years the chief motive people had in seeing mediums was to contact friends and relatives who had recently died. And even today, in the age of channeling purely spiritual entities, many people get solace from the opportunity to speak to someone they miss or who they intuitively feel has a message for them. If you decide to visit a channeler for this reason, be sure to test the spirit entity thoroughly to insure that this is the person you wish to speak to. One Florida medium, who preferred not to be identified and who does extensive work in con- tacting spirits of the deceased, explains that she is careful to ascertain that the right spirit has been contacted:

A lot of the information that [channelers] give can't be documented. As a scientist, I have to have proof. That's why I have to come up with concrete things when I talk to these dead people—that they actually are the people, not some figment of my imagination. Because if I'm talking to a deceased person, I'll give a description of the person, like I'm seeing him. I did a reading where I saw a man who was rather tall, receding hair line, mid-fifties; I asked what he died from, and he said he died from a stroke. He said that he didn't die immediately, but that eventually it killed him. But the [client] wasn't really sold. So I said [to the spirit], "Could you give me some kind of concrete stuff, so I can relay a message to the woman?" So he put his hand out, and there was this glass eye. So I said, "By any chance, does this man have a glass eye?" And she said, "Oh, that's Uncle Harry," or whoever. So it's those kinds of concrete things that you have to come up with if you're going to do this sort of thing.

A similar example is recalled by another psychic who, although she is clairvoyant, visited a medium in order to contact her dead grandmother. Because she had never known the grandmother, she asked for some form of indisputable proof of identity. As she recalls:

> The first thing I heard my grandmother say was, "What took you so long?" And I knew it was my grandmother. And I asked her, "Tell me one thing that I would know about you that nobody else would know." And she said, "Go home and ask your mother if she remembers when I painted the whole apartment green, including the piano." And that was true; she did, for a St. Patrick's Day party. Nobody else would have picked that up. And there were other things she told us that made it very accurate.

What makes this example very compelling is the fact that the client herself hadn't known that the grandmother had painted the apartment green—she had to go ask her mother in order to verify the story. This rules out the possibility that the medium was merely reading her mind or picking up on images the client had locked away in her subconscious and manifesting them in astral form.

Another reason people will visit channelers is to contact some famous person from the past who may hold a special interest for them. Charles Hapgood, who wrote *Voices of Spirit* and worked closely with Elwood Babbitt up until Hapgood's death in 1982, was a professor of history. He saw an opportunity with Elwood Babbitt to contact several significant figures from the past with whom he had always wished to speak. These included such diverse personalities as Queen Elizabeth I and Mark Twain. In order to increase the chance of validity, Hapgood would meditate upon those people he wished to contact for a week or two prior to the session. He would then write the name on a piece of paper that Babbitt would hold in his hand but not look at. Hapgood would invariably connect with the desired spirit. Through a process of questioning and checking, the veracity of the spirit would be confirmed.

Unlike much of the mediumship of the past, many people who visit channelers today are concerned about getting spiritual advice that will aid them in their personal growth. This advice often takes the form of information about past lives. It may come from a spirit control or from the client's own spirit guide. Such messages generally include specific references to situations in the person's life, which is a good indicator that the contact is genuine. In my own case, a spirit guide came through and made reference to this book, which he then linked to one of my past lives:

> Your past-life issue seems to do with communication. Which is why it is imperative for you to write this book now. It seems that in a past life you gained knowledge that was in some way highly important and should have been disseminated.... The

knowledge that you gained was of a spiritual nature. However, you lived in a society, a culture, in which spiritual pursuits were feared, misunderstood, taboo. And rather than adhering to what you felt inside to be true, you bowed to the judgments of the day in fear of being rejected. It feels as if this lifetime occurred in the late 1800s— 1876 was an important year—and this lifetime was in Europe, in the Slavic countries— in that area. Emotionally, you feared being an outcast very greatly, and this fear surpassed your conviction about the reality of your spiritual intuition. This is a balance you are seeking to correct in this lifetime. Your communications chakra, your throat chakra, may be affected. It may be blocked. But as you pursue your endeavor—this book—it will gradually become clearer, and as it clears, it will help the flow of the book even more. So this is a growth process for you.

The highest form of spirit communication, that of the spiritual Masters, generally takes the form of philosophical discourses on a variety of metaphysical topics. These are the basis for the abundance of audio and video tapes that are available from channeled sources, and they deal with everything from the concept of love to the nature of God. If you are lucky enough to come into contact with a genuine Master, you won't be able to get much specific information pertaining to your individual life, but you will be treated to some deep spiritual insight. Though there is nothing new in these messages, which have been passed along by all of the world's great religions, they will generally be expressed in a language and context that speaks more directly to us than the sacred texts of the past. This may be one of the reasons why psychic information in general—and channeled messages in particular—seem to form the basis of a new spirituality throughout the world.

Another reason for this mass appeal is that most channeled wisdom is based on the concept that we all possess the truth already and that we have simply to look within our own selves for the guidance that we have sought in vain from external sources. One of the marks of a true Master is that you will not be told to follow a specific teaching or dogma, but instead will be encouraged to develop yourself to the point of discerning your own truth. If any channeled entity claims to have a monopoly on the truth and tries to command your allegiance, it's a good indication that you are in the presence of someone who hasn't learned to separate ego from the channeling process; at worst, you may be under the influence of someone looking to build a cult following. Elwood Babbitt explains that there is a simple litmus test for energies that claim to be spiritual Masters:

> Well, we give acceptance to the higher forces, what you call the expansive forces—you can call it the Christos, or the Christ Force—all the powers that Moses displayed. And if you ask, "Are you from the forces of the Christos or the Moses Force?" that spirit cannot deceive you, because you're asking from the light of truth, which essentially is the term for God.

And that spirit will depart if it cannot answer you truthfully that it is who it professes to be.

We will have more to say about ascertaining the truth of your reading in Chapter Six. But for now we will simply mention again—and it cannot be over-emphasized—that, in the final analysis, the only test for spiritual truth is the degree to which it resonates within your own being. If something doesn't *sound* right, then it isn't right. Don't let anyone—whether in physical or spiritual form—tell you that you're not evolved enough to understand the information or that the message should be taken on faith.

A good example of the channeled messages that are flooding the psychic world are those of "Lazaris," an entity channeled by an ex-insurance salesman named Jach Pursel. Here are some of the main points of his philosophy, as they were channeled by Pursel:

> We've come to do four things. To remind you that you don't have to grow through suffering and hardship. Instead you can grow through love and joy and laughter. . . . We're also here to remind you that you do create your own reality, not just as a philosophy but as an experience. Ours is not just to say it, but to teach you how—with specific techniques and approaches detailing ways in which you, by yourself, can consciously create the reality you desire. . . . And we're here to remind you that there is a God, one we call God/Goddess/All That Is, a Force greater than you, not better, but greater. . . . Fourthly, we're here to let you know that you're capable of loving, that you are

not the barnacles of the universe, the scum of the cosmos. Rather, you are very beautiful, powerful, and highly evolved spirtual beings who love. . . . And so, we're here to help you begin to find your wap Home, to follow your own breadcrumbs.[7]

Much of what takes place during a channeling session is nonverbal. The true meaning of the word channel is to channel energy. That energy may take the form of words or actions, but it may also remain in a purely spiritual form. When words are used, they carry a psychic "charge" that imparts more than just the surface meaning of what is said.

Some channeling sessions may consist of sounds that are thought to have a healing effect on the listener. In some, these sounds may take the form of chanting. In others, true melodies will issue forth from the spiritual planes. Barbara Rollinson, for instance, only recently began channeling an entity known as "Windsong," who communicates entirely through song, even though Rollinson herself has never had any formal musical training.

Finally, at the far end of the channeling spectrum is the ability to channel pure spiritual energy which does not take the form of sound. Readings are not usually made up entirely of this type of work, but at some point in a reading a channeler may simply channel energy to a client, if that is what is needed. In this way every channeling session can be different, both for you and the channeler. If the person is sensitive to you and your needs—whether that insight is on an emotional or spiritual level—she will react to where you are now. Brooke McAdam, a channeler in New York, describes her own process of development and how that affected her channeling sessions:

When I first started channeling I had people come who were really miserable. They just wanted practical answers. . . . And I was channeling but not feeling that I was giving what I could give. And then one day I just realized that I didn't want to do [it] that [way]. I had always thought of myself as a helper—I was going to drag people up into the light—and I spent my whole life trying to do that, even though people didn't want that. And as soon as I asked for [a change], my clients changed completely. Now I have people who come for affirmation, who come for something else. And it's always changing. And the people who are channels, we're changing too. So I find that I'm always letting go of the form. For instance, with the last person who was here, I didn't talk for the last half of the session. So, how could that be channeling? And yet I know that there was this incredible force coming through to her, that she was welcoming, that she had longed for, and it's really exciting to me.

Mediumship has evolved from an attempt to hold onto life by bringing people back from the dead to the full acceptance of death as a progression that we all must go through—and have gone through many times before. But channeling isn't dogma; no one is asked to accept what cannot be proved. The experience of channeling is all that counts, and the reality that you perceive during that experience is the means to validating your innermost feelings. Whether you see the spirit world as an aspect of the channeler's personality, a mirror of yourself, or a combination of both, the message you receive should be truth by any other name.

There has been a recent rise in popularity of classes that purport to teach people how to channel. As we have seen, some people consider any creative endeavor, any type of artistic expression, to be a form of channeling whereby an individual learns to tap into an inner source of inspiration. Thus classes that are designed to help you remove creative blocks, to get in touch with your inner self, or to develop a sense of wholeness are potentially valuable learning opportunities. Classes, however, that advertise the chance to learn to become a medium—that is, to channel spirit entities—should be viewed with more caution.

The question is not whether or not someone can learn to channel in this way; the ancient civilizations have been training spiritual adepts to do it for centuries. The problem lies in learning how to control the process and in knowing what you hope to gain by doing it. Unfortunately, it has become chic to call yourself a channel and to brag about having been in touch with your spirit guides. But as many of those quoted in this chapter have pointed out, in attempting to channel spiritual beings you run the risk of opening yourself up to harmful entities as well as psychological aspects of your inner self that you may not fully understand. There is also the danger of getting lost in the sensationalism of the experience to the detriment of genuine spiritual development.

Before exploring the possibility of channeling, therefore, clarify the reasons in your mind why you want to channel, and how you think it will help you with your own emotional, psychological, or spiritual development. Next, be sure that you find a competent teacher—someone who has *years* of experience in channeling and whom you respect not just as a channel, but as a *spiritual teacher*—someone whom you feel can truly offer you wisdom and guidance, not just while channeling but while fully conscious as well. Third, whenever you attempt to channel, or even meditate, set very clear conditions as to what entity you seek to contact and for what reason. Dedicate everything you do for the good of yourself and everyone involved and determine to open yourself up to only the highest sources of wisdom and inspiration. Also, be sure you are channeling in the presence of someone who is experienced in the process and whom you can trust to guide the session along in a responsible manner—and to bring it to a close the minute something seems awry. Finally, avoid the temptation to channel for anyone else—including friends and family—no matter how successful you seem to be at it. Remember, it takes years of experience to learn not only how to control the process but especially how to use it for the betterment of others. Leave it to your teacher to decide when you might be ready to help other people and under what conditions.

Psychic Healing

Psychic healers, like most psychics, have their roots deep in traditional modes of thought—both Eastern and Western—that go back thousands of years. It is only in the last couple of decades that Western techno-medicine has rediscovered the profound connection between mind and body, and, consequently, the power of psychic energy to overcome physical disease. Therapies that just a few years ago would have been considered complete quackery—acupuncture, biofeedback, chiropractic, even basic nutrition—are now widely accepted modes of treatment. As Western medicine continues to gingerly test the waters of alternative healing, the lines between what is considered a physical ailment and one that is "psychosomatic" are becoming increasingly blurred. It is not altogether inconceivable that what now goes under the guise of "psychic healing" will one day be part of the mainstream medical lexicon. Indeed, as we shall see, this is already beginning to happen.

Before looking at psychic healing per se, we need to understand the concept of health upon which it is based. This idea of wellness is one that was common to almost every healing modality used around the world before the predominance of Western allopathic medicine in this century. Today it forms not only the basis for much of the world's traditional healing practices, such as Ayurvedic and Chinese medicine, but it has been taken up by the holistic health movement here in the West. Even the technologically oriented medicine of our own culture has resorted to exploring this more traditional concept of wellness as it grapples with such "incurable" diseases as cancer, Alzheimer's disease, and AIDS.

Whereas the Western definition of health is essentially the absence of disease, the word "health" actually comes from an Anglo-Saxon root meaning "whole." Interestingly, this is also the root of the word "holy." As physician and author Andrew Weil writes in his book, *Health and Healing:*

> Medicine, religion, and magic are rooted in common ideas, and each sheds light on the others, but the supremacy of scientific technology makes it fashionable to believe that medicine has nothing to do with such old-fashioned practices as religion and magic. Consequently, many modern doctors cannot grasp the true meaning of health and can only define it negatively as freedom from disease.[8]

Weil goes on to say that "Sickness and health are not simply physical states.... They are rooted in the deepest and most mysterious strata of Being."

Why this is so is something that we have seen with regard to all types of psychic phenomena. In the psychic model of reality, the energy field that makes up the human being consists of many levels, some of them exceedingly subtle and not subject to detection or measurement by Western scientific methods. It is only by taking into account the interplay of all these energetic levels—that is, the wholeness of the person—that true health can be maintained. Health thus becomes a function of keeping all the aspects of the self—physical, mental, emotional, and spiritual—in a harmonious balance.

The definition of health therefore shifts from the idea of curing a specific illness to maintaining a state of equilibrium in the human energetic system as a whole. As a result, the responsibility for well-being also shifts—from the healer, who was previously conceived of as a mechanic who could simply "fix" what was wrong, to the healee, who must bring himself back into a state of harmony and balance. The healer therefore becomes a facilitator who aids in the process of self-healing, while the organism itself seeks a state of equilibrium. Weil defines healing as "the universal tendency to seek equilibrium, a reaction to and compensation for any disturbance, using whatever mechanisms and materials are available."

The degree to which we can control our own healing has been exemplified in recent years by the development of biofeedback. As described in Chapter One, this is a process by which certain physical functions previously thought to be autonomic (that is, beyond the control of the conscious mind), such as heartbeat rate, skin temperature, and blood pressure, are monitored electronically in order to enable a person to learn to control them at will.

Even more startling, perhaps, is the work that is being done with visualization as a healing modality. Carl Simonton, an oncologist, and his wife, Stephanie, a psychotherapist, have experimented with a process by which cancer patients visualize a tumor or cancer and then invent a way of combating the diseased cells. Some patients have pictured an "army" of white blood cells attacking and destroying the cancer. Others have visualized a vacuum cleaner sucking the diseased cells out of the body. In an overwhelming number of cases, the Simontons have witnessed substantial improvement as a result of such mind-over-body techniques.

The Simontons have also found that a strong belief system and positive outlook directly influence the ability of an individual to overcome disease. According to Carl Simonton:

> A positive attitude toward treatment was a better predictor of response to treatment than was the severity of the disease. . . . Patients who had very serious prognoses but positive attitudes did better than patients who had relatively less serious prognoses but negative attitudes.[9]

The flip side of such discoveries is the degree to which we are capable of undermining our own physical health. Emotional trauma, for instance, has been shown to directly affect the body's immune system. Studies have revealed that a large number of the elderly often will not survive beyond a few months following the death of a spouse. Even AIDS patients will very often confess to experiencing a lack of will to live *before* contracting the virus. Yet many people can carry the virus without it ever affecting their health, because their immune system remains intact.

Whereas for the conventional Western doctor such links between emotional well-being and physical health are, at best, abstract correlations, for the psychic healer they are very real indicators of an imbalance in one or several of the various human energy fields. A psychic healer will therefore not just treat the physical manifestation of the disease, but will try to determine, by looking at the more subtle psychic levels, exactly what caused the illness to begin with. He will do this in a variety of ways, depending upon the type and degree of his specific psychic ability. Some healers are thus able to see the human aura that envelops a person. Others use clairsentience to detect an emotional upset that underlies a physical problem. Still others may access information about a past life that explains a chronic or incurable problem you may be suffering from in this life.

What all these techniques have in common is that they are attempts to isolate the spiritual or emotional cause of a disease, rather than just its symptoms. The idea is that by the time the illness has manifested itself physically, it has progressed to its final stage. By treating the physical problems associated with the disease, one is at best eliminating the pain associated with it (at least temporarily) and at worst masking much more serious imbalances that exist on the more subtle energetic planes. The optimum situation, of course, is to detect an emotional or spiritual imbalance *before* it reaches the point of a physical ailment. This conception of illness is similar to that of traditional Chinese medicine and Indian Ayurveda, two systems of health care that date back thousands of years and that are currently regaining popularity in their respective countries, as well as in the West.

These two systems of thought are also the basis for much of the treatment that goes under the term psychic healing. In Chapter One, we briefly described the Indian concept of the human energy field, or aura, which in turn is made up of chakras, or individual energy centers. In psychic healing, the chakras are examined (using either sight or touch) to determine whether there are any fundamental weaknesses in the energy field, and what areas may be affected by such imbalances. From the Chinese system, we get the idea of *chi* (known in the Indian system as *prana*), which is the life force that runs through the body, animating the physical tissues and maintaining a healthy state of equilibrium when the organism is functioning properly. The chi flows over specific pathways, called meridians, which can sometimes be blocked, leading to an imbalance in the total energy flow.

Chi is the basis for acupuncture, which is a technique for removing blocks in the energy flow by inserting needles at specific points along the meridians. A needle may also be inserted in order to *cause* a block (in order to induce anesthesia, for instance). Although Western science has been unable to detect the presence of the chi flow, the efficacy of acupuncture cannot be doubted, since in China it is used successfully even as an anesthetic for open-heart surgery, during which the patient is fully awake and alert.

Psychic healers generally utilize the concept of chi flow, although they dispense with needles. They attempt instead to channel their own vital energy directly into an individual by using their hands or simply by concentrating on healing. It is thought that by placing oneself into a meditative state, a healer can "recharge" another person's fundamental energy supply and sometimes direct the energy to a specific area of the body or particular organ.

This method of healing was known traditionally as the "laying on of hands" (at least where direct touch was involved). Today, as a result of some groundbreaking research in the area of human energy fields, the idea of the laying on of hands has crossed over from the realm of dubious psychic practice into the mainstream of medical America. The new term—therapeutic touch—was coined by Dolores Krieger, a professor of nursing at New York University, and by Dora Kunz, a gifted psychic healer and past president of the Theosophical Society in America. Krieger began teaching the technique to students at the New York University School of Nursing in the early 1970s, and it is now being widely taught and researched at number of institutions throughout the country.

Janet Macrae, Ph.D., R.N., who was a student of both Dolores Krieger and Dora Kunz, has been practicing therapeutic touch since 1975. In addition to teaching workshops in healing and meditation, she is the author of *Therapeutic Touch: A Practical Guide*. As she explains it, the therapeutic touch practitioner is merely a facilitator for a person's own innate healing mechanisms:

> I affirm the wholeness of the patient—the fact that all living organisms heal themselves essentially, that I'm not the healer. That's very, very important, to not think of ourselves as doing the healing, but [to realize] that healing momentum is [present] within all living organisms and that with the help of this universal energy we're going to quicken the healing momentum within the organism itself—we're helping out. . . .
>
> I think we're all made up of this energy—we're like little whirlpools in a universal river of energy—the life-sustaining force—you could call it the "organizing principle." You never use your own energy, because then you just get depleted and irritable. And so, if you establish the intent, you attune yourself to the universal energy, then you're always replenished, you're never tired, and you can treat several people one after the other. You feel better, in fact, because you've been helped—the energy helps the channel, too. It's really a very healthy thing to do.

Dolores Krieger's research revealed that therapeutic touch is not only capable of inducing a state of deep physiological relaxation in a patient, but it also raises the hemoglobin level of the blood. She found that it was particularly effective with stress-induced illnesses. Other research has revealed that therapeutic touch increases the rate of wound healing in mice and the rate of growth in plants, and that it is effective in treating a variety of human ailments, including headache, nausea, difficulty of breathing, irregularities in heartbeat, poor blood circulation, and postoperative pain. It even aids in the physiological development of premature babies and reduces the severity of colic in infants. Most startling, however, was Krieger's discovery that even victims of paralysis who had severed spinal cords were able to feel the effects of therapeutic touch in limbs that were atrophied. This made her conclude that such people were feeling energy in a way that was "other than three-dimensional," bypassing the nervous system, as it were.

Psychic healers also work in such a way as to bypass the normal, three-dimensional framework of the physical body. They begin by observing the condition of the auric field that surrounds the body. According to various sources, the aura extends anywhere from 18 inches to six feet out from the physical body and is in a constant state of flux that reflects the way a person is reacting to various stimuli from the environment. Each chakra, or energy center, in the auric field corresponds to a particular gland of the endocrine system, as well as an emotional/spiritual aspect of the self. A weak chakra point therefore indicates a problem with that aspect of a person's self. For example, the heart chakra corresponds to the thymus gland and embodies the idea of self-love and expressing emotional trauma; the throat chakra corresponds to the thyroid and deals with the idea of communication and truth; and the "third-eye" chakra, located in the center of the forehead, corresponds to the pituitary gland and relates to spiritual insight and divine wisdom.

Each chakra is also associated with a specific color, which corresponds to the vibrational frequency of that energy point. Just as the different colors of the spectrum are caused by different wavelengths of light, so, too, are the different chakras the manifestations of different wavelengths of spiritual energy. Psychics who can see the auric field see a specific color for each chakra: pink for the heart, blue for the throat, and violet for the third-eye, for example. These colors may change slightly or fade when a particular energy center is weak or blocked. A psychic healer who sees auras can read your state of health simply by observing your energy field. Barbara Brennan was a physicist with NASA before becoming a therapist and later a psychic healer. In addition to channeling, she is able to see the human aura and manipulate the energy field. She describes some examples of how the aura is affected by a person's emotions and behavior:

> One woman came in, sat down, and started telling me what a good week she had. She was moving her hands, like this, throwing off this pink cloud. At the

same time, I saw this black spot here, the pain in her heart, the confusion in her head, all this red energy being held here. So I said, "All right, this is what's happening in your [energy] field, so why don't you just stop making the pink cloud and denying everything?" So she did, and we worked on this. It turned out her mother was very ill in the hospital, and she was all upset about that.

Another woman was sort of sitting between anger and pain and she was working in a therapy group, and suddenly this red blob came out of her throat and went into her heart, and she started crying. Then I started observing this person who snorted coke a lot, and his aura would get this gray, mucousy junk all over it. He [usually] snorted on Saturday night, and I'd see him every week on Wednesday, and I'd tell him whether he was snorting, because I'd see this junk all over [his aura]. [Another] person, who smoked a lot of pot, always had these dark blobs in his field.

The effectiveness of Brennan's treatment lies in her being able to relate her observations on a physical level to emotional or spiritual factors. The aura therefore becomes an indicator for healing that must take place on a much deeper, psycho-spiritual level. The following is an excerpt from one of her healing sessions:

As I'm looking at your chakras, there's some blockage in the chest area. The pain in the back is related to the collapse in the chest area, and there's strain above the third chakra. One of the things that is happening with you right now is you're pulling your power back, especially in the second chakra. This is related to sexuality, where you pull your sexuality back, to the back of your body a bit. Usually that is kind of a defensive mechanism from some past experience. . . . The major thing that I'm seeing in terms of the psychodynamics is this protection of the heart chakra, and a bit of a collapse. It's just above the third chakra. This is the linear mind and the intellect, so we're talking about a block between the intellect and loving, about those kinds of issues—about thinking and loving. To solve those you have to go up to the sixth chakra, which is the higher mind, and right now you're blocking a little bit on the right side, and on this side of your body. So there's a real sensitive emotional quality about you, but there's a tendency to defend against it, so you won't be so vulnerable, by reasoning, intellect, and by will—by pulling yourself back, by a little bit of passivity and being more active with the mind in terms of the intellect.

Other healers may not be able to see your aura, but will be able to sense it using their hands. This is similar to the therapeutic touch technique, which adherents claim anyone can learn. Each area of the body is scanned by moving the hands slowly over the skin, without touching it, until disturbances are felt. Healers describe these sensations as heat, cold, tingling, pressure, electric shocks, pulsations, or a "ruffling" in the energy field. They are then smoothed out or balanced by running the hands over the affected area while focusing the attention on healing. Before actually administering treatment, however, a healer will generally put herself into a meditative state of mind, centering and balancing herself. Janet Macrae describes the process in this way:

> Before I treat somebody, I first quiet my mind, and then I quiet my emotions. I could focus on an image of peace, such as a tree, a mountain, and make sure that I'm very quiet and stilled—that my body is relaxed. And then, when my mind and body and emotions are in harmony and quiet, I visualize light coming through me, and my self attuned to that universal energy, which I visualize as light—light is a good metaphor. I think of myself as serving as an instrument for that healing light, and then I approach the patient, only then.
>
> There is certainly a shift in awareness, because I'm tuning out all the distractions around me and I'm just becoming sensitive to these subtle energies. So this is definitely a shift. . . . It isn't the brainwave frequency, it's more the synchronizing of the right and left hemispheres, so it's the unifying of the mind and the intuition. Because the healing energy, I feel, comes from that deeper, intuitive level. It comes down through, and unless the mind is synchronized, and you make the intent to attune to that, it's not going to come through. So I look at this method as unifying and integrating, not only the patient but also the practitioner.

Linda Chagnon is a psychic healer in Rhode Island with ten years of experience working with people's energy fields. She describes what it's like to be a human energy channel:

> When I'm doing laying on of hands, it's working with the electromagnetic fields. I have all this energy going through my hands all the time—it's like a faucet—it's healing energy. It feels like a current. And when I do healing, it's very strong. . . . When I'm not doing enough healing, I feel blah. I need an outlet—I need to channel a certain amount of energy a week. And if I'm not doing it, I feel kind of lousy. It's like a need now. That's when I feel like I'm really myself— when I'm doing it—working with all my circuits running.

That different chakras correspond to various wavelengths of energy explains why some psychic healers use crystals to aid in the channeling of energy. Quartz crystals have long been appreciated for their scientific properties, which include the ability to generate an electric current when squeezed. Similarly, if a current is applied to a crystal, it will expand and contract, vibrating with a natural frequency. Crystals have long been used in radio transmitters, television, radar, and, of course, watches.

Today crystals have taken on a new meaning, as New Age adherents attribute to them everything from healing properties to encoded information from ancient civilizations. Different color crystals are thought to have different energy frequencies and to correspond to different chakras in the human energy field. Rose quartz, which is pink, might be used to send energy into the heart chakra; amethyst, which is violet, would be used for the third-eye; and citrine, which is yellow, would be used to recharge the abdominal, or power, chakra.

Although many people have taken to wearing crystals on certain parts of their bodies and meditating with specific colors for desired ends, the most that can be claimed for such uses is that they function as totems—that is, the personal belief in their effectiveness may empower an individual to achieve certain results either in life or in the spiritual growth process. On an energetic level, it may be that crystals are perfectly capable of amplifying the human energy flow, much as they vibrate in fine Swiss watches. But be advised that such use depends primarily upon the power of the healer herself to channel energy to begin with—*with or without crystals*. Many people make the mistake of attributing magical powers to the crystals themselves, when, in essence, they are merely tools which, when used properly and in the right hands, can be effective adjuncts to psychic healing.

Barbara Brennan, who frequently uses crystals to channel energy into her clients, describes their function this way:

Crystals function on two levels. First, they have a lattice structure, and they have a dipole [and therefore] a field, and I believe that's measurable. Crystals attract positive ions. Positive ions are always related to low energy, or unhealthiness in the aura. So the crystals absorb that or collect that. And when you stick them in salt water, it sucks [the ions] off, and then you put them back on the body. So there's a physical phenomenon going on with crystals.

Then energetically, I can see the field of the crystal, and I can see what happens with the aura. When I'm teaching students, at a certain point they'll be working on the auric field and they'll be sensitized enough to use a crystal. They'll be in the middle of a healing, and suddenly I'll just put this crystal in their hand and everything will go "Pow!" It just increases the energy much more. They're tools, but again they are tools one shouldn't be dependent on.

I put them on the chakras to energize the chakras. I put them in the hands of the patient when I'm doing a certain kind of healing so that they absorb the energy. I also use one as a scalpel, because certain crystals have this long needle of white light, and I actually dig globs of dark energy out.

In addition to channeling energy by using their hands or crystals, many psychic healers use sound to energize various weakened parts of the auric field. Just as different colors are made up of variations in the wavelengths of light, so, too, are sounds made up of different frequencies. By making a sound that corresponds to the vibration of a particular chakra, a healer will try to channel energy into the affected area. Many healers will even record tapes of such healing sounds to be taken home and played during meditation or relaxation, thereby extending the treatment. Or they will teach the client how to make a particular sound in order that he might heal himself during the course of the next few weeks.

When you go for a psychic healing, the healer will not just treat a particular ailment, but will do a complete checkup on your auric field and individual chakras. You may be asked to fill out a questionnaire describing not just your physical ailments, but emotional or stressful events as well. This is because the psychic healer is looking for the root cause of your illness. She will be able to channel energy to a weakened part of your energy field, thereby reducing pain or temporarily correcting an imbalance you may have, but ultimately the job of healing will be yours. In order to aid you in this task, the healer will try to determine what emotional or spiritual factors were instrumental in causing your illness. The following excerpt, taken from the previously cited reading by Barbara Brennan, is an example of this kind of linkage:

> I did see something in terms of your relationship to your parents and how that relates to your third chakra area, and that is that there is a bit of a laxness or weakness in the liver that's related to your father. There's a certain passivity in the father figure in your life, and a bit of dominance from the mother side. But what I read in the pancreatic area was some sort of a false sugary sweetness from the mother that wasn't real, but that had the affect of weakening the upper half of your body. That's from a very early childhood connection.

Often a reader will go beyond the causes of disease found in this lifetime and access information about a previous lifetime that accounts for an ailment or disease you may be suffering from now. For example, Barbara Brennan recalls one woman who was suffering from several problems, all of which stemmed from a past life:

> This woman was afraid of water, and she was asking for help. That didn't turn around until I saw the past life where she fell off a boat and drowned; she was screaming for her shipmates, but they couldn't hear her. (She was a man at that time.) So she's been afraid of drowning all her life. But, primarily, she couldn't even talk loud, couldn't ask for what she wanted. It was stopping her work and stopping her from projecting who she was. She just couldn't do it. And when we did that past life thing, everything started changing. She's now a successful TV producer.

Many psychic healers are also channelers; they will gain information about someone through the use of a spirit guide, in much the same way that a trance channeler relies on a control to supply guidance to a client. Just as in channeling, psychic healing with a spirit guide can range from the healer being "told" what to do during the course of a session to a full trance, during which the spirit itself is responsible for the healing.

Probably the most famous examplar of this type of healing was Edgar Cayce, known as "The Sleeping Prophet." Cayce, who died in 1945, did some 9,000 health readings during the course of his life. He would regularly go into a full trance during which a spirit entity would come through, diagnose a particular illness, and prescribe treatment. What is more remarkable is that Cayce was usually given no more information about a person than a name and address; the subjects themselves were rarely present. Prescriptions ranged from esoteric herbal concoctions and major lifestyle changes to conventional medicines then unknown even to most doctors. Considering that Cayce himself was a sixth-grade dropout—as well as an intensely religious man—it is unlikely that any hoax was involved. Today there are clinics throughout the country that utilize the Cayce methods of healing, all of which were carefully documented.

Barbara Brennan also combines channeling with healing, and like Edgar Cayce she is also able to see auras and look into the human body to determine the cause of an illness or injury. Her spirit guide, "Heyoan," often prescribes modes of treatment for particular patients. In severe cases, he may assist someone suffering from a terminal illness in seeing beyond the "veil" that separates this reality from the spiritual realm, as he did with one patient who was dying from AIDS:

> When [this patient] first came to me, he knew nothing about the spirit world, or the higher consciousness, or the "melting of the veil." Many times I talk about dissolving the veil between the worlds—it's an illusion anyway. So the work I did for him was to dissolve that veil, so that [he would know] what was going to happen when he died: how it was going to feel, what

it was going to be like. And when I described it to him, he said, "You know, that has already happened. . . . Two weeks ago I was dehydrated, I was dying, and I had those experiences. . . ."

Heyoan finds very good ways to speak directly to that person and to that soul—to the deeper wisdom of the individual who is dying. That guy who was dying of AIDS spent his last several days lying in bed, and his consciousness had risen to the higher plane. He was watching the angels. He'd be looking around the room saying "They're so beautiful! They're so beautiful!" And then he'd close his eyes and come back to this level of awareness and say, "I hate it here!" Then he'd close his eyes and he'd be there, at that higher realm. He kept doing that back and forth. And one of the last things he did was he just opened his eyes, he looked at his mother and held her hand and said, "I love you, Mom." And he quit breathing. What a way to die.

Many psychic healers use a wide variety of healing modalities when treating a patient, ranging from nutritional recommendations to acupuncture. Because the aim is to cure the person on every level, an eclectic group of techniques is often employed including everything from traditional psychotherapy to deep massage therapy. Many healers maintain a substantial network of resources so they can refer a patient to the proper practitioner for specific treatment. Once a person is enrolled in a particular therapy, she can then check the patient's progress with periodic visits. Maria Tadd, a healer in Winchester, Massachusetts, describes the scope of her work:

> I look at health from a very holistic perspective. I do an evaluation of a person's case history—look to see if they've had a lot of bacterial infections, a lot of allergies, just to get a sense of the strength of the constitution. I ask them to describe themselves emotionally and assess themselves from one to ten in terms of love and contentment, in terms of their emotional status; and I ask them to do the same thing with their spiritual life and their lifestyle. That's phase one.
>
> Phase two is how foods do support them or don't support them energetically. Because if you're eating a lot of foods that don't support you energetically, you're going to be tired. I might test them for 50 foods, so that takes a while.
>
> In phase three I work with their chakras. With my hands I actually feel the activity level of each chakra—make a comparison, see which ones are overactive and which ones are underactive, give them an interpretation of what that means in terms of their physical health and perhaps their emotional health. Sometimes I pick up past-life information when I do that.
>
> And in the process of tuning into people's energy fields, I get affirmations for them to say to heal whatever it is that needs to be healed, and meditations. And then a person will leave here with a tape of meditation and affirmation, which is one tool with which they can work. Often I'll suggest nutritional supplements. And then if it looks like they need more work, I'll recommend homeopathy, acupuncture, a

Chinese herbalist, depending upon what their needs are. But first, I want to see them take responsibility for themselves and deal with the food, to see if they can make some changes just with food. And if the changes don't happen, then they can see someone else.

Up until now we've been looking at psychic healers who work primarily with the human energy field. There is another group of healers, however, who take a more ritualistic approach to healing. Instead of working specifically with prana or chi, these healers work on the emotional and spiritual levels of the human psyche. They do so through the use of dramatic ritual and vivid symbolism. Such healers are known as shamans and have traditionally included witch doctors, medicine men, and voodoo practitioners. In their native cultures, shamans played the role of medical doctor, psychologist, and spiritual counselor all wrapped up in one. Thus their understanding of the interrelatedness between physical disease and spiritual and emotional imbalance was integral to the success of their treatments.

Today the shamanic traditions—especially those of Native Americans—are being rediscovered by healers in the West, and many modern practitioners of these ancient arts are combining them with other traditional modes of healing as well as with modern psychological theory. Numerologist-astrologer Stephen Calia also runs a spiritual healing group, which he calls the Inner Relationship Workshop. As he describes it, much of the techniques he uses are shamanic in origin:

"Jack and the Beanstalk" is a typical shamanic journey. A lot of people do visualizations, but they don't know where they are. Well, what I do is to go in and say, "What's our question?" The clearer your question on a shamanic journey, the clearer the answer. A shaman in the old-fashioned way would do all the work. What I do is guide people through their own journeys, so *they're* doing the work. I'm a guide to the terrain.

There's a middle world, an upper world, and a lower world. And there are many levels of each. And so by having a terrain, you now can go in specific places to get specific kinds of answers. The lower world is home to the power animal—how you use your power on earth—and one place to go to heal physical illness. The middle world is parallel to this one, but in non-ordinary reality. It is entered through a cave behind a waterfall that leads to an inner garden. There you connect with a guide, and that's where you can work to balance the positive or negative energies that are creating upsets in your daily life. The upper world consists of spiritual levels.

The first time I did a journey to the upper world, I flipped into a past life—I was shown a passageway into the past lives. So I know how to get there, and I lead people through to get to past lives through a shamanic journey. You go up to the Akashic records, find the book that deals with that lifetime, and just go right into it. Very simple.

In addition to guided imagery, the shaman employs whatever devices or techniques are necessary in order to evoke a deep emotional response in the patient. Spirit guides, powerful drugs, healing herbs, oils, incense, candles, and chanting may all make up part of the shaman's "black bag." And the shaman will use these prescriptions on himself as much as upon the patient in order to facilitate his journey through the various levels of spiritual reality. Stephen Calia describes the way in which such ritualistic tools function:

> In one case, I used a brain coral, which we empowered to symbolize all our outmoded brain patterns—all the rigid structures in our life that we were now ready to let go. So we created a ritual: this room was dark, that room was light. As we put down the coral—our outmoded patterns—in the dark room, we told the group something lovable about ourselves, walked into a circle of light, and then got hugged.

The shaman can be seen as a guide through the intricate web of physical and spiritual forces that make up the world. But the shaman is master of these forces, manipulating them in such a way as to evoke a specific response. Unlike the trance channeler, who is "used" by a spirit entity, the shaman uses the spirit entity for his own ends, always cajoling, manipulating, invoking—but never surrendering.

One reason for the effectiveness of the shaman's treatment is that the categories that he works from are shared by the patient. Because he understands the cultural gestalt of the patient, he is able to utilize imagery and symbolism that are appropriate to that person. We might speculate that working within a particular cultural framework creates a type of collective unconscious through which the healer can better connect with the healee.

The degree to which traditional healing has crept into modern American society is typified by the work of Diana Velazquez, a Mexican-American *curandera*, or healer, who has been practicing healing for 42 years. What is unique about Velazquez is that she is employed by the Southwest Denver Community Mental Health system, where she works in a clinical setting, side by side with psychologists, psychiatrists, and conventional mental health counselors. Her clients include not only her fellow Chicanos, but people from every ethnic background and every walk of life.

Because of her diverse patient group, Velazquez tailors each specific treatment to the cultural context of that particular person. Thus if someone comes from a deeply religious background, she may rely more heavily on prayer, whereas if someone is more atheistic, she will utilize various "props," such as candles, oils, incense, and herbs. Much of her work involves psychodrama—bringing to the surface and physically acting out the hidden causes of neuroses. Guilt, for example, when kept suppressed, can be a major cause of disease, physical as well as emotional. As she explains:

If you've done something wrong and try to forgive yourself, or others say that they forgive you but you haven't paid for it, you find it very hard to forgive yourself. So, many times punishment is included in my therapy. . . . I usually try to match it with the "sin." A woman who has committed adultery will be "stoned" by her peers or her community with paper stones. . . . Calling her names and "stoning" her goes on until she feels that she has been punished. In this way, she is being punished and the community is doing the punishing, which they think should be done anyway. We're killing two birds with one stone.

She recalls a woman who was referred to her by a physician who could find no discernable cause for an incurable rash that covered one side of her face. After working with the woman for a while, Velazquez discovered that the woman was trying to punish herself for various shortcomings. She therefore acted out the woman's suppressed impulse by "punishing" her, "killing" her, and "rebirthing" her. The woman's self-destructive tendencies were therefore given expression, and the rash disappeared.

The power of ritual is central to the work of the shaman. As Velazquez puts it, "What you call behavior modification, I call ritual." She recommends that her clients practice daily, weekly, monthly, and annual rituals in order to maintain their own wholeness and sense of well-being. These can include everything from lighting candles to participating in a traditional sweat-lodge ceremony. In this way, the responsibility for self-healing is impressed upon the person seeking help. Patients often receive intricate prescriptions for curing a condition. These include herbs and tonics, oils, water, eggs, and colors. Although Velazquez studied for much of her life with her father-in-law, a Yaqui Indian medicine man, the specific formulas she uses are not the result of that training. Instead, she receives the prescriptions psychically:

> There was no training. I just know. I was born with it in my brain cells, and when the situation comes up, my intuition, my guiding spirits, will trigger the answer. Not only for me, but my grandmother and daughter. We never discuss anything and we prescribe exactly the same thing.

Ellen Hendrick, although not from a shamanic tradition, is a student of voodoo and a well-known psychic healer who gained national notoriety for the rituals she performed for the New Orleans Saints football team. (Yes, they won.) She believes that her power—and everyone's personal power—comes directly from God, but that using symbols and props is simply a way of expressing that power:

> If you tell a person something, they won't believe you, but if you give them something they can hold, something they can see, then they may believe in it, in what they're doing. But they have this [power] all the time inside of them. They need something that they can relate to and bring it out. It's planned out. Everything in life is a ritual. Putting on your clothes every day is a ritual. . . .

The idea of personal empowerment is central to all forms of psychic healing—indeed, to healing in general. No one can be cured who does not want to be cured and who doesn't believe that the ability to heal lies within the self. This is why psychic healing can be of value, even if it is nothing but the result of a placebo effect. Whatever empowers the individual to heal himself is good medicine. Peter Janney, the previously mentioned psychologist in Cambridge, Massachusetts, explains that the mark of a good healer is to enable a patient to accept himself:

Any good healer understands that to get to that special place means to be able to drop all pretension. What ultimately happens is that people heal themselves. That's always a choice, and there's always a level of will that has to be activated to make that happen. All a really good healer can do is understand that and help facilitate the process for that person. It may be simple things they end up doing. But they're so pure in what they do, it has a dramatic effect. The example I could give you is that if you're sitting with someone who is really disturbed or really upset, then the quieter you can be—the quieter the healer can be—in a sense, just exude a very loving, accepting presence, a sense of okay, a sense of complete and total safety to whomever he's working with, that in and of itself can radiate a very powerful kind of energy, which, when the person gets it—when he allows it to come into himself—can be quite remarkable in terms of what it starts to promote.

The other aspect of healing that Janney brings out is the relationship between the healer and the healee.

In every form of psychic healing a profound spiritual bond is created between the two people involved. The level of communication that takes place may go way beyond the mere transference of energy. In the shamanic tradition, this connection is given expression through the healer's attempt to emulate the spiritual/emotional mind set of the patient on a physical plane, and then leading the subject through the journey of self-healing. But even in a process as "mechanistic" as therapeutic touch, the connection between healer and healee is a profound one, as Janet Macrae explains:

> I think to really work with it, you do have [to have] a sense of compassion. You have to open up and start sending out in order to get the healing energy moving down through you. So it's this opening up and compassion to the person who's suffering that gets the ball rolling, so to speak, that gets the energy moving and flowing outward. Without this reaching out to help, I don't think the energy flow would come through you—or not as much. . . .
>
> It's also important to forget about yourself and just want the other person to get better in his own way. Because if you put strings on it, it hooks, and the energy doesn't flow out. Like personal expectations, and personal anxieties—the more all of those are in there, the less the energy will flow. . . . [Your main focus] becomes, "How is this person doing?" not, "How am I doing?"

All legitimate healers speak about the profound changes their lives underwent when they began the practice of healing. A certain level of spiritual development seems to be an integral part of effective psychic healing. As a result, if you come into contact with a healer who you feel is primarily concerned with running a business or making money from her ability, you should probably look elsewhere. The overriding motivation for working as a healer has to be the desire to help individuals in particular and humanity as a whole. This isn't any moral platitude—research into the phenomenon of psychic healing has taken into account the intention of the healer, and most such studies agree that this intention is central to the process of healing itself. Peter Janney points out that this process of self-development is integral to every form of healing, whether it is psychotherapy or the laying on of hands:

> A therapist can only take you as high as he or she is and no higher. If you were in therapy with Buddha, you would be enlightened. Any good healer, any good therapist, has had to have done a requisite amount of work on himself in terms of his own healing and wholeness process. If people who are in a healing profession are not taking care of themselves—not working on their own personal evolution, on their own personal healing and wholeness—then they're on the road to becoming a charlatan.
>
> It takes a lot of time and energy and investment to get good. Baryshnikov is good because he is totally committed, totally invested. And he also had the genetic material. Some people are born with higher quality genetic material for that particular purpose, but there are a lot of what I would call unmanifested

geniuses walking around on the planet. They've got incredible potential—great talent—but they don't have the discipline or commitment to use it. Having the talent is only a third of the battle. The other two-thirds is do you have the guts? Do you have the fortitude? Do you have the commitment to really take your talent and really mold it, shape it into godliness? That's what it takes.

An odd phenomenon that has captured the attention of researchers in recent years is also worth mentioning. At the farthest end of the shamanic spectrum is the practice of psychic surgery. This type of healing is practiced mainly in Central and South America and the Philippines, and although it is occasionally attacked by the established medical community, it continues to draw patients, especially in remote regions where Western medical assistance is not readily available.

The name psychic surgery is somewhat misleading, since this is supposedly surgery in a very real and graphic sense. What makes it "psychic" is that it is performed without any form of anesthesia, usually under extremely septic conditions, and without the use of conventional surgical instruments. Practitioners of this obscure art, who are generally uneducated in any form of medical treatment, attribute their special abilities to the intervention of spirits who either take over their body while in a full trance or direct them verbally as to what to do. Incisions are made using everything from rusty pen knives to old scissors. Sometimes the healer will simply choose a spot and plunge her hands through the skin directly into the body. Tumors may be removed, foreign objects extracted, organs replaced, and even bones patched up or repaired—all in a matter of seconds. The wound generally closes as quickly as it was opened, leaving little or no trace of a scar.

Evidence has been amassed on both sides of the debate, some defying rational explanation, some offering conclusive proof of quackery. Whatever the truth about psychic surgery, it seems to depend as much upon the belief system of the patient as on the surgeon. Interestingly, cases have been cited in which Western visitors who had been cured by psychic surgeons suffered relapses when they returned home to their own friends and colleagues who planted doubts in their minds as to the efficacy of the surgery.

The power of the mind to heal the body is clearly just as effective as the most potent pharmaceuticals that Western medicine can concoct, and psychic surgery is only the most extreme example of a wealth of healing modalities that continue to defy scientific explanation. In considering the power of psychic energy—indeed, of all psychic phenomenon—we should perhaps focus our attention not on why these practice should not work as on what it is that does make them work—at least for certain people under certain conditions. As Barbara Brennan points out, the problem is not whether or not these healing modalities are effective, but rather finding a context into which they fit:

A lot of this stuff was known before, in ancient history, but nobody had the basis of the scientific method to test it. And now we have both. . . . You use the scientific method to support the phenomenon. Rather than saying the phenomenon isn't real, the true scientist says, "Oh, here's a phenomenon, now let's find out what's going on here. What is this phenomenon about?"

It doesn't mean there's chaos, it simply means we don't understand it now; we don't have the theory to support what the phenomenon is. So we observe a phenomenon, we start a whole theory, then we set up experimentation to support the theory. If it works or doesn't, we set up other experimentation or we change the theory. That's the scientific method. And then we can honestly entertain a way of incorporating it into our daily lives.

How do you communicate with somebody? You find common ground and you communicate with them. If someone's a surgeon, I can talk about tumors, if they're a Buddhist, I can talk about the *Brahma* and the *Maya*. If they're a Christian, then I can talk about guardian angels. If they're a solid physicist, then I talk about energy fields and holograms. Lots of communication levels—same phenomenon.

In deciding to visit a psychic healer, you should determine the ways in which these techniques appeal to your own sense of truth and direct your attention to those aspects of yourself that you think would respond to such treatment. Remember: no one is going to "fix" you simply by "zapping" you with energy.

What you should be seeking when you look for a psychic healer is a way of looking at health and disease that makes the most sense to you and that therefore will give you additional tools to get on with the job of healing yourself.

As a final note of caution, bear in mind that psychic healers are no substitute for adequate conventional medical care. If you are suffering from a serious condition, it is important that you have it properly diagnosed and that the range of treatments—both conventional and alternative—is explained to you before you decide on a course of action. If you decide to be treated by a psychic healer, your doctor should be informed of this and your condition constantly monitored to note any improvement or deterioration. It is only in this way that you and your psychic healer will be able to determine the effectiveness of the treatment.

CHAPTER FIVE

How To Prepare For Your Visit

It's clear that the type of psychic you are planning to visit will affect both your expectations and the way you prepare for your reading. But there are aspects of preparation that are common to all readings; these will enhance both what you experience during your visit to a psychic and what you can get out of that visit afterward.

Cooperation vs. Exploitation

The first thing to realize is that the responsibility for a successful visit rests as much with you as with the psychic you have chosen. (Actually, that responsibility began the moment you decided to visit a psychic—in examining what you hoped to achieve from your reading and the type of person who might best meet your needs.) Be aware that you are not attending a performance. Rather you are consulting a professional (in some cases, a very expensive professional), whose job it is to supply you with a service. Imagine what kind of results you would get if you went to consult a lawyer you had never seen before and didn't say a word the whole time you were there!

If you are visiting a psychic for either help with a problem or a psychic healing, then it's obvious that you will have to cooperate in the same way you would with a doctor or therapist—assuming you want to get something out of your visit. But even if you're just "in it for the fun," remember that an attitude of openness is essential. It is a rare person who can enjoy a film after reading a scathing review of it. Chances are, though, that you found your psychic after a thorough screening process or a positive recommendation from a friend, so your thoughts should already be heading in the right direction.

Use that as a starting point. Ask your friend again what it was that she liked so much about this particular psychic. How did she feel when she left? What was it about the psychic that sparked the recommendation? You've probably already asked these questions, but take the time to go back and think about the answers once again. What you are focusing on here are the *results,* not the whys and wherefores. It can be fascinating and even enlightening to dwell on the more philosophical aspects of psychic phenomena. But this is the time to put those thoughts aside and just be ready to *experience.*

Skepticism

This is also the time to try to put aside your reservations. I haven't met anyone yet—psychics included—who didn't have occasional doubts about what it all means. But if you indulge your skepticism at this point, bear in mind that you put yourself in the position of evaluating the reading rather than experiencing it. The difference is in thinking about something rather than living it. We think in the past; we experience in the present. Let yourself be "present" for the hour or so you are with your psychic. You can do your postmortem later (especially if you've taped the session). One client described his attitude this way:

> I'm very skeptical of all of them. It's kind of a contradiction: I go there wanting to like them, yet I walk in with a major wall up—"Prove it to me"—an unspoken challenge: "Make me believe in you." So partly, I think, that wall keeps me from getting all the information I might be open to. Because I do have this challenge, so if I can't immediately link what they are saying with something about the way I see myself or perceive myself, then my mind starts wandering, and I miss half the stuff that they're saying. So if I continue to see other psychics, I know that's something I'll have to hold back on.

Keeping an open mind doesn't mean you have to make any great "leap of faith," or that you should let yourself get suckered into a phony put-on. It merely means that for the time being, you will gently put aside your doubts until later (at which time, you assure yourself, you will be free to indulge in a glorious explosion of righteous indignation). For now, open yourself up to whatever happens, whether with the psychic or within yourself. If something you hear doesn't make any sense to you, file it away for later review. Remember, nobody's perfect, and that includes psychics. They make mistakes just like anyone does. But if you focus on what seems wrong rather than what seems right, you may miss something important.

More than that, you may misinterpret something of significance. As mentioned earlier, the nature of psychic information is that much of it comes in symbolic images or feelings and must be interpreted. It is just as much your job to interpret these images as it is the psychic's. The psychic has to translate what he receives into words in order to communicate to you. Since words have different connotations to different people, something that initially doesn't make sense to you may click later on. By keeping an open mind and focusing on what seems accurate, you'll make it easier to receive the knowledge the psychic is giving you.

All this should be going through your mind *before* you go for your reading. It's a good idea to start thinking this way from the minute you make your appointment. It's important that you don't feel as though you're suppressing your natural skepticism. The shift in attitude should be gentle and ongoing. So the sooner you begin thinking this way, the easier it will be. You will, of course, have a great many thoughts during the time leading up to your appointment. Dwell on the positive ones, gently brush aside the negative ones. Try to foster an attitude of openness, curiosity, and above all, adventure. Approach your reading with the same degree of expectation you would have for an exciting trip. The only difference is that on this journey you will be discovering yourself.

Fear of the Future; Fear of the Unknown

Another consideration you may have is fear. Time and time again people have said to me, "I'd like to go to a psychic, but I'm afraid of what he might tell me." We all share some degree of fear when it comes to psychic phenomena. What is it, exactly, that we are afraid of? For one thing, just about everyone is afraid of hearing that something bad will happen either to himself or someone close to him. In response to this, I can make what is perhaps the only unequivocal generalization in this book: No reputable psychic will tell you that something bad is going to happen to you if it can't be prevented.

Aha! you say. I knew they were all making it up! Not exactly. As we saw in the last chapter, most psychics open themselves up to only that which they feel is "for the highest good of all involved." Does this mean they only receive good news? No. It means that anything that occurs in life, even if it seems like a tragedy at the time, can be used as a growth experience. Call it karma, call it fate, call it maturity, life is the process of learning to deal with good and bad. Viewed in that light, bad experiences become good lessons. So even though a psychic may see something that objectively seems bad, it will be perceived by her as a good opportunity for your personal growth. And she will communicate it that way to you.

Most psychics share the view that nothing is preordained. The idea of karma cannot be divorced from the idea of free will. Therefore a bad experience can almost always be avoided if the right steps are taken: that is, if you identify those aspects of yourself that need strengthening in order to overcome the difficulty. This is the primary role of the psychic: to help you in that process of searching yourself. The growth is up to you. Again, this is why you should view your visit to a psychic as a dual responsibility. The psychic will help you see where you are and why. It's up to you to do something with that knowledge.

But what if there is no way out? A fatal disease, perhaps, or a parent dying of old age. Again, I know of no psychic who will give that information to a client. If there is an ethics of this profession, then this is where it is to be found. For one thing, no psychic I have ever met has had the arrogance to be that sure of his ability to "condemn" someone to a terrible fate. Each one of them understands the responsibility he has taken on in doing psychic readings and will not bear the burden of life and death issues. On another level, if the real purpose of gaining psychic knowledge is to grow and better yourself through self-knowledge, then in most instances, knowing that someone is going to die is of little use.

I know of one case where a very skilled healer saw that one of her friends was going to die from cancer.

Rather than try to help the woman by warning her, she made a clear decision to hold on to that knowledge, suggesting instead that her friend return to her hometown to spend time with her husband. It was up to the doctors who later diagnosed the disease to give the woman the bad news, at which point the healer friend was able to help her face the possibility of death.

The point to remember is that you are visiting a psychic not to be told the future, but to find out more about yourself. If you approach it properly, it can be one of the most positive things you do in your life. Rest assured that you will be given only that information that is good for you and that is right for you at this time in your life.

It should also be pointed out that fear, like skepticism, can interfere with your reading. Fear implies resistance, which puts up a wall that some psychics will have difficulty reading through. No reputable psychic will be comfortable giving you information if he senses that you aren't ready to receive it, so he will be forced into censoring what he says, and perhaps feeling that he's forcing the information on you. Even a process as seemingly mechanistic as palm reading can be undermined by fear, as palmist Nat Altman explains:

> When I'm reading your hands, you're sending out a big dose of energy—it's like Kirlian photography— and I'm picking it up. So, if you don't want me to read you, then your energy might be held in, making it more difficult for me to read. Some people don't want

me to do it, or they have their own turmoil—they're afraid, so it's more difficult for me to get the information out. Others are sometimes forced into it by friends or relatives, and it comes out when you're reading that they really don't want [a reading]. Whereas with other people, who are genuinely interested, it is a pleasure, it is easy, no problem at all.

Another aspect of fear that we all share is fear of the unknown. Psychic phenomena are notorious for scaring people out of their socks. Ghosts, poltergeists, dead spirits—all come under the heading of "psychic." And although the chances are slim that you will encounter any ghosts during your visit to a psychic, many of them do use spirit guides or entities from the astral plane that are not clearly defined. Whether you consider them merely aspects of the psychic's higher consciousness or disembodied spirits of people who have lived and died, the fact remains that the mechanism for receiving psychic knowledge is still not understood. And anything which cannot be understood makes people uneasy.

Again, there are two points to remember. The first is that nothing occurs during your visit that is not intended to be beneficial to you; even spirit guides are perceived by psychics to be loving, caring, and protective. The second is the previous suggestion that you focus not on the process, but on the result; don't worry so much about where the knowledge comes from as about what it means to you. There are also steps you can take to prepare for your visit that will lessen your anxiety and enable you to make the most of your reading.

Before You Call

If you're a little apprehensive about your visit—and even if you're not—it's a good idea to learn as much as you can about the process your particular psychic uses for readings (see Chapter Four). There will be plenty of surprises without having to worry about what the psychic is going to do. The more you know what to expect, the more you'll be able to focus on what is being said. You'll also be able to prepare yourself both emotionally and intellectually for the experience.

If you received a recommendation from a friend or business associate, begin your search for information with that person. Ask him to describe, in as much detail as possible, exactly what happened during the course of the reading. Where did the reading take place? What does the psychic's home or office look like? Are there trappings of a psychic nature around? What was the psychic like personally? Was there an opening meditation or prayer? Did the psychic spend some time either before or after simply chatting? Many people will ask their friends what the reading itself was like, but they may neglect to ask about these more mundane matters. But this is the kind of information that will give you a feel for where you are going and thus help to remove some of your apprehension. After all, you are going into an encounter with the unknown; why not fill in all the details that *are* knowable?

What You Need to Know

Continue your inquiry with the psychic himself. (In some cases, you won't be able to speak directly to the psychic, but to his agent or secretary.) At the time you phone for an appointment, take a moment to ask the psychic (or agent) what method he uses to perform readings. Don't ask for a detailed description, just casually express your interest in knowing beforehand. If you already know the method from speaking with your friend, say something like "I understand you use psychometry. Should I bring a piece of jewelry?" or "I was recommended by so-and-so, who said you are a channeler. Do you have a specific spirit guide you use?" Most psychics love to talk about what they do and will most likely be glad to take a few minutes to respond to your question, especially if you sound like you've done a little homework and at least know the terminology. Even if you can only speak to a representative, you may gain some useful information or be surprised by something you hear.

In any event, there are certain practical questions you should be sure to ask in order to be fully prepared. First, double-check the fee (assuming you already know it), and if you would prefer to pay by check, make sure that that is acceptable. Ask whether there is a cancellation period (some psychics are as heavily booked as physicians and should be treated with the same professional courtesy).

Then find out if you need to make a list of questions (more about that in a minute)—some psychics prefer to respond to specific questions rather than give a more general reading. Ask if you can bring a tape recorder or, if the psychic uses one, whether you should bring your own blank tape and what length it should be. And be sure to find out the address! A psychic may assume that if you were referred you already have the address. And you may forget to ask. It's also a good idea to give the psychic your phone number, in the event she has to cancel.

If you are making an appointment with an astrologer, she will need to know in advance your exact date and time of birth (down to the nearest four minutes) as well as the place where you were born. A numerologist will need to know your birthdate and the exact spelling of your full name as it appears on your birth certificate. Be sure to have this information ready when you phone for an appointment.

Finally, before you hang up, ask "Is there anything else I should know?" This shows the psychic that you are interested and looking forward to your visit and goes a little further toward establishing a rapport. I always make a point of asking this question, and more times than not, the response gives me a good feeling for the type of person I am dealing with and sometimes an indication of how the psychic views her ability.

Although there are quite a few books on the market concerning psychic phenomena, most are written from a particular point of view—generally one person's experience. As a result, if you try to generalize from them, you may end up with misleading expectations. Each psychic is completely different from the next, even if similar methods of reading are used. If you read a description of channeling in, say, Shirley MacLaine's books, you might expect to have the same kind of spirit guide speak to you, or have the same kind of questions answered. My experience has shown that the kind of information each psychic offers is unique to that person. (That is part of the beauty of exploring yourself through psychic means.)

What you are trying to do, at least at this point in preparing for your visit, is to get an idea of the specific experience *you* will have. I heartily recommend reading as many books on psychic phenomena as interest you from a philosophical or intellectual perspective, but leave them behind when you go for your reading. Again, simply open yourself up to whatever is being offered. Taking intellectual baggage with you will only help to create false expectations. And if you spend your session trying to figure out why the spirit guide is talking about your past lives, when all you wanted to know was whether or not you should take that new job, you'll find yourself at odds with what is occurring. One woman I know waited six months to get an appointment with a well-known New England trance medium, paid $75, and drove two hours to reach his rural home. The one thing she did not do is a little research. As she described it:

I really didn't know what to expect. From what I had read in Shirley MacLaine's book, her psychic experiences were very personable. But this guy was so cosmic. I expected more of a conversation back and forth. But he gave a whole reading, much of which I didn't understand. And then at the end, when I was supposed to ask questions, I was afraid I was going to ask something he already answered. And being that I didn't understand so much of what he said, I didn't know what to ask. I was afraid of offending him.

You can avoid this pitfall if you do your homework first and then take the time to organize your thoughts about what it is you would like to know. Actually, the ideal time to do this is before you choose a specific type of psychic, but since many people will be going on one or two recommendations, not having the luxury of handpicking someone, now is the time to make sure that you at least structure your questions in a way that makes sense, given your psychic's particular style.

Organizing Your Thoughts

We have already discussed possible reasons for visiting a psychic. And presumably you have chosen your psychic according to what it is that you would like to get from the experience. Now is the time to put these considerations into more of a framework. In organizing your thoughts you should pay attention not only to what it is you would like to know *at this point in time*, but which issues are most important to you in general.

It's possible that since the time you first decided to consult a psychic, the aspects of your life that most concerned you have changed. Rather than trying to recapture your original motivation for wanting to go, think about where you are now and what it is that you find yourself thinking most about during the course of your day. These are the issues you should address during your reading. It doesn't make much sense to ask questions whose answers don't get at the heart of your concerns. In this way you have a great responsibility. It's up to you to know yourself and focus the direction of the reading—or at least of your attention. Although some psychics will home right in on what is really on your mind, if you are looking for other answers, you will miss the real response.

On the other hand, you may have wanted to visit a psychic for very specific reasons. Perhaps someone close to you just died, and you're having a hard time coming to terms with that. Or maybe you just started a new job and it doesn't feel right. In that case think back to what it was specifically about that situation that made you want psychic help and ask yourself what kind of answers would help you deal with it. Chances are, your reactions are based upon other issues in your life that you haven't yet resolved, and examining this specific case may help you confront something you've been avoiding.

In either case, if you've done your research—spoken to friends, made an appointment, chatted with your psychic—you're sure to have a much greater understanding of the process and what a psychic can and cannot do than you did before. It's possible that, in light of this new knowledge, the way you look at your problems has also changed from the time you first thought about going for a reading, and the information you are looking for may now be different. Tune in to this subtle shift and nail down exactly what it is you would like to happen at your reading.

It will help you to organize your thoughts if you write things down. Words have very precise meanings, and by trying to find the right word, you'll be forced to define for yourself exactly what it is that concern you about a particular issue. You don't have to be literary or poetic. Simply jot down words that you think capture the essence of what you are looking for. These are the words that will best convey to the psychic precisely what it is you would like to know.

Now look at your notes. Decide which issues, or aspect of a particular issue, concern you most, and number them in order of priority. Bear in mind that you may run out of time during your reading and not be able to cover everything on your list. Put the most important things first, so you'll be sure to have them answered. In addition, you may find that during the reading you'll want to know more about something being said. So if you begin with your most compelling thoughts, you'll leave yourself plenty of time to discuss or fully clarify those issues.

Preparing a List of Questions

Next comes your list of questions. As mentioned earlier, some psychics require you to provide specific questions. Most, however, do not. Usually you will be given a choice. It's a good idea to draw up a list in any event, at least for yourself, in order that you have something to fall back on should the reading drag or the psychic "dry up." In the case of a psychic healing or a general astrology chart, you can dispense with specific questions and simply keep in mind those issues (or ailments) that concern you most.

The questions can be in any form, but it's probably better to avoid simple yes/no queries. For one thing, many psychics will not give you simply a yes or no answer. They will want to explore aspects of yourself or others upon whom the outcome depends, rather than predicting your "fate." Also, if you force yourself to formulate more introspective questions, you'll benefit from the self-reflection it entails and help the psychic to isolate those aspects of the subject that concern you most.

For instance, instead of asking, "Will I get the new job I interviewed for?" try writing it down as "I am worried about the new job I interviewed for. Although the interview went well, I can't help but feel I'll be turned down." The psychic may focus on the fact that you always feel rejected after job interviews or the fact that you lack confidence in general. Or maybe you don't really want the job at all, but feel you should make a career move right now and are just going through the movements.

Or you might want to ask something like, "Will my relationship with Clem work out?" Try rephrasing it as, "I want to be with Clem all the time, but he says he needs his own space. It makes me worry that we won't stay together." In this way the response could deal with anything from your constant feelings of rejection in relationships or the fact that you look to others to fulfill all your needs, to Clem's fear of taking responsibility or his preoccupation with his work to the detriment of other aspects of his life.

The point to remember is that most outcomes are not written in stone. They depend upon you and the way you think of them. By phrasing your questions in this way, you are acknowledging the fact that your life is what you create, not something that simply happens to you. You'll find that one of the wonderful things about psychics is that they can often isolate aspects of yourself—and others involved in your life— that you haven't fully acknowledged to yourself. Use this ability to your advantage when you ask your questions.

How many questions should you prepare? That depends. If your questions all deal with different aspects of one or two subjects, then prepare a lot. Chances are that those aspects will be covered without your having to actually ask about them, but your list will make a good checklist to see that everything that concerns you is covered. In this case, ten to 20 questions would not be a bad idea.

If, however, there are many issues you would like to cover, each question will open up much more discussion, so you will need fewer of them. It's easy to fill up an hour-long reading with as few as five questions if they all concern different subjects. Let your thoughts be your guide. If you have strong feelings about an issue, it will probably take up much of the reading time. If it is simply something you wouldn't mind knowing about, a few sentences may be enough of a reply.

Your questions should be clear and concise—and make sure they are in a form that is easily legible. You don't want to waste valuable time either trying to interpret what you really meant or deciphering your own scrawl. Go over your list a few times to acquaint yourself not just with the issues you'll be dealing with, but with the way the questions are phrased. They should come naturally to you and sound like your voice.

Whether your list is five questions long or 50, take another few minutes when you're all done to think of any other issues at all that figure in your life. It's a frustrating feeling to have all your questions answered by the psychic with 15 minutes remaining in your reading (especially when you are paying for it). So jot down a few backup questions that you may not really care so much about, just in case you need to fill in some time. They may be more significant than you think!

What You Need to Bring

So now you are ready for your reading. You know enough about your psychic and her method to enable you to feel comfortable with the process, and more important, you know enough about yourself to maximize the value of your reading. Having organized your thoughts, it's time to gather together some essentials. First, your list of questions and any notes you might have made that you think would be helpful. These should be clear and concise. Although you don't want to forget to cover anything, burying your head in a pile of notes will only distract you from the reading.

Next, select any items you might need if you are going for a particular kind of reading. For instance, a psychometrist will need a personal object—preferably something that you bought for yourself and that you have owned for at least three months. Some readers require that it be something made of metal—a piece of jewelry or a pair of eyeglasses, for example. Many psychics can also read photographs of other people. If you want to ask about another person, try to find a shot of that person alone; other people in the picture will only cause confusion in the event the psychic tries to read from the print. If you don't have a photograph, you might think about bringing a letter that was signed by the person you want to know about, or anything that once belonged to him or was in his possession for a while. Such items can aid a psychic in tuning into people who aren't present during the reading. When you call for your appointment, ask the psychic which if any of these objects might be helpful, then place them with your list of questions so you won't forget to bring them.

Most psychics will ask you to bring either a 60-minute or 90-minute blank cassette for recording the reading. Follow their instructions closely; many psychics rely on the length of the tape to tell them when the session is over and will not appreciate a deviation from routine. If the psychic doesn't generally record the session, you should ask if you can bring your own tape recorder and cassette. There will be a lot of information given to you at the time of the reading, much of which may not make sense right away. You will also want to be able to check the accuracy of any predictions that are made, and a tape is an infallible record.

A note of caution here: you should be leery of any psychic who refuses to let you tape a session. Claims of "it interferes with the spirit vibrations" or similar metaphysical mumbo jumbo should trigger a little warning bell in your head. Any reputable psychic will not only agree to taping the session, but encourage you to go back and listen to it many times to discover new insights or information you might have missed. The exception to this, of course, is a 15-minute storefront reading, or a one-flight-up "quickie," which you are probably indulging in more for fun than anything else. Use your judgment. If you're shelling out $75 and have spent several hours preparing, then beg, borrow, or steal a suitable tape recorder so that you can review the session at your leisure in the quiet of your own home. And bring extra batteries.

Finally, if you are visiting a psychic healer, you may need to know certain pertinent medical information about your condition. You won't need to bring doctor's records, but jot down the history of the specific condition you are going for. When did it start? What type of treatment have you received? What changes have occurred? You may also be asked about your sleep habits, nutrition, drinking habits, drugs, what vitamins or supplements you take, and your spiritual development. The healer may also want to know about common childhood diseases, injuries, accidents, and anything else you consider relevant to your condition. Remember, a psychic healer is not a licensed doctor; if you are receiving medical treatment for your condition, it's a good idea to tell the healer about it in as much detail as possible for both of your interests.

An astrologer will have taken down your date, time, and place of birth when you called for an appointment, but some other psychics may use your astrological sun sign as a adjunct to their primary method of reading. So it isn't a bad idea to remember to take this information with you when you go. Similarly, a numerologist may not need your name until the time of your visit. Be sure you know exactly how it appears on your birth certificate, even if you go by a nickname.

Dealing with Last-Minute Doubts

Well, you are as ready as you will ever be. As you pack up your materials and head for your reading, allow your mind to continue to cultivate the feeling of openness and anticipation you began when you called to schedule your appointment. By the time you reach your destination, you should be thoughtful, focused, and above all, excited. There is a good chance, however, you will have last-minute doubts, especially as you make that climb "one flight up." "What am I doing here?" you may ask yourself. "I'm a fully rational, mature person, who can certainly work out my own problems without the help of some fortune-teller."

Gently remind yourself that you are not there to pass judgment on the psychic or to evaluate the authenticity of what you are about to experience (at least not until later). You are there simply as a way of finding out more about yourself, and you want to avail yourself of whatever mechanisms make that possible, whether they can be scientifically explained or not. More than that, you are looking for adventure and are willing to open yourself up to new dimensions of yourself and of human consciousness in general. Above all, remind yourself that you are going to have fun.

CHAPTER SIX

How To Interpret Your Reading

Now that you've found the perfect psychic, had your reading, and returned home with your cassette, you are no doubt a bundle of questions and confusion. On one hand you may have heard a lot that didn't make sense to you right off the bat. On the other hand you may have had a profound experience, having heard things about your personality that you may have been keeping hidden even from yourself.

Whatever your reaction—and it may range from a feeling of deep inner peace to anger and frustration—you are probably wondering what the next step is. You have a tape with between 30 and 90 minutes of intense psychospiritual information. Now what are you going to do with it?

The first thing to realize is that a psychic reading is not an *event*—it is a *process*. As we have stressed before, by going for a psychic reading, you have taken on the responsibility for your own growth, and growth is an ongoing process. Part of your confusion following your reading is that you may have expected something to *happen*, some kind of immediate and significant transformation. At the very least, you probably expected to be impressed by displays of mind reading and future predictions. If you came away from your reading feeling anything less than awed, you may feel cheated. Relax. The journey has only just begun.

Part of the problem we have in American society is that we expect immediate results. We tend to see everything as a commodity to be paid for, used, and thrown away. Even services, such as those of doctors and lawyers, are to be used for a specific purpose and then forgotten about. We visit the doctor, pay our bill, and expect to be cured as a result. If we can take a pill, so much the better. Even personal growth has begun to be marketed as a quick spiritual fix—"enlightenment in the fast lane," as one psychic put it. Weekend workshops and growth seminars advertise such things as "opening the chakras" and "connecting with the higher self" in just two days.

The psychic reading itself is just the beginning point for investigating yourself. Particularly if you have visited a psychic healer, you will have been given a great deal of work to do in order to cure yourself. Marilyn, whom we mentioned earlier, had sought help for an inner ear problem. A year later she is still working on herself:

> Things did get better. But I realized after the second time that this was not a matter of "being fixed," that it was a matter of going through a process. I'm still

going through the process. I still have some dizziness. But I have a different attitude toward it now. . . . What I realized is that it's *all* a process—there's no product to it, there's no end. And I will just keep growing and changing with it.

So now that you have had your psychic reading and you're wondering why you don't feel different, try to adjust your attitude and prepare to evaluate what you have received in the larger context of your whole life. It's possible that the psychic you visited has already taken the time to go over some of the material he gave you and helped you to see how it can lead to your continued growth. But even if he hasn't, it's up to you to do the work.

Having a psychic reading is actually a four-stage experience. First, there is the reading itself, during which you should listen to what the psychic says without trying to analyze it and should try to feel the energy she is tapping into at that moment. Second, there is the review process—going home and thinking about it, reexperiencing it, and seeing what surfaces from the memory of the experience. Third, you should sit down and listen to your tape, see what you missed and what now seems most important to you, and try to determine ways in which you can apply it to your life. Last, you have to do something about it. It is only after you actually take some action and try to effect changes that you will come to see the real value of psychic readings. We will consider each of these steps in order.

How to Evaluate Your Reading

The first point at which you begin to take in information is during the reading itself. The way in which this information is conveyed to you varies from psychic to psychic. In many cases, however—especially with channelers—the psychic will tap into his right-brain perception to "read" you. As a result, the information he gives you may be communicated in a primarily right-brain mode. This means that what you receive is not meant to be evaluated through an analytical process, which is a left-brain function. You may even feel yourself getting a little "spacey," since you may also respond from a right-brain, nonanalytical point of view. Martin is a computer software salesman in Boston who found that he was particularly sensitive to the energy surrounding certain psychics, as he recalls:

It was at a psychic fair, where I paid for a 15-minute reading with this psychic. I sat down across the table from this very heavy man, and he had me hold a crystal in my hand. . . . He told me to picture a place in which I felt very comfortable. So I pictured a beach I had been to that I liked. First, my neck was twitching, then my shoulders were hunching up just like there was electricity running through me. It was like every muscle in my upper torso twitching at the same time. And then I felt like I'd left—just for a couple of minutes, but that I'd left. It was probably the most peaceful feeling I've ever felt in my entire life. I felt like I was floating in a pool, but it went beyond that.

I sensed I was up in the clouds, or something. It wasn't long enough to get a deep sense, but it was lasting. I remember the sounds, the smells, the temperature, and I felt like I'd gone there [to the beach] and come back.

In some cases, the words themselves may be inadequate to convey what you are meant to receive. Some psychics have recalled sessions in which they channeled energy to the client by using sounds, or even sessions where they made no noise whatsoever but simply transmitted pure energy. The important thing at this initial stage is not to judge but simply to listen and to feel. One of the reasons you have taped the session is so that you can go back and analyze it later. Carl, whom we mentioned earlier, recalls a visit to a numerologist during which he was trying to analyze everything that was being said:

I'm not good at listening half the time. Because the numerologist just went on and on and on, while I was trying to specifically relate some of the things he was saying to my life. Let's face it, if something doesn't pop up right away, it's just listening to someone babble. Without having a specific thing to relate it to, it's hard to know what he was talking about.

Such a thorough stream of information is not always inadvertent on the psychic's part. Even if the information does strike a chord in you right away, you may find difficulty in focusing on all that is being said. More often than not, you will bombarded with information about yourself, about your friends and relatives, and about the world as a whole. Margo Schmidt explains one reason why this is so:

> A lot of information comes through my work. That's why I ask people to bring a tape. I tend to be a fast talker. I've tried to slow my pace down, but I get a headache. So I asked, in my meditations, why is this happening? Do I need to adjust here? Give me some guidance. And I was told that one of the reasons that that happens is that it really blows people out of their left-brain modality. They're being inundated, because they're not supposed to try to figure out every word. They're supposed to be marinated in the energy that's coming through. They have the tape to listen to later. You're not supposed to try to figure out and understand, you're supposed to experience it.

All this is not to say that you should shut off your brain completely. A good psychic will expect you to respond to what you are experiencing, on whatever level. Indeed, you should be evaluating what is taking place, so you can decide if it feels right. But that process of evaluating is one that takes place on a deeper level than logical analysis. What you should be trying to do is tap into your own intuition, just as the psychic is tapping into hers, because in the final analysis, the veracity of what you are experiencing is totally up to you. The most important thing to bear in mind is does it *feel* right? If not, then either the information you are hearing, or the psychic herself, are not right for you. Anne, whom we mentioned earlier, visited quite a number of psychics, but only one seemed to strike the right chord in her:

> I just had a great sense of trust—a good feeling about her. I felt that we were relating to each other, and that there was a lot of goodness in the room. Now, we could dissect all of this and say, Anne, you obviously fed her a lot of information. But I just felt that it all came together. There seemed to be a point when she actually started flowing, and she was just going and going and going with it. It was like she was wishing me Godspeed—goodness. I said to one of my friends that [the psychic] made my day, that day.

As in any relationship, a lot of what takes place during your psychic reading cannot be analyzed from a totally rational point of view. Nevertheless, you will have to evaluate what takes place using both your heart and your mind. There is a difference between thinking and feeling, and your psychic reading is a beginning point for learning to differentiate between the two. If a psychic's energy is strong, and you are "blown out" of your left-brain mode, as Margo Schmidt puts it, you will find it easier to avoid making analytical judgments. On the other hand, you want to avoid being blinded by "the trappings" of psychic phenomena. Susan Edwards graphically describes the need to learn to trust your own sense of truth:

> Very often a person will come to you and because you're "The Psychic" they become very stupid. The psychic tells you your left hand is your right hand,

and you say, "No kidding." In the end you have to try out [the information] and see if it's true, and if it's not true for you, you have to build up your courage and say, "Well, the psychic said this, but it's not true for me." Be very clear with yourself.

The Catch-22 of all this is the fact that the very skill you need to evaluate your psychic reading while you are experiencing it—i.e., trusting your intuition—is actually an ability that you will begin cultivating as a *result* of your visit. Connecting with your inner knowingness, learning to tap into the inner source of knowledge that we all have, trusting your inner self— all of this is the basis of the work you will be doing on yourself after your reading.

It is important to consider where to put your attention during your reading. In view of the fact that you are experiencing something completely new—and perhaps witnessing an impressive display of psi—you will be tempted to focus on the process itself rather than the information being given to you. Try not to get caught up in the presentation, no matter how unusual it may seem. When it comes to psychic readings, the medium is *not* the message.

Kevin Dormeyer, co-owner of Together Bookstore in Denver, points out that the Eastern spiritual traditions have long recognized the value of intuitive insight, but that such spiritual "tricks" as channeling are considered means to an end, not goals in and of themselves. For the most part, among Eastern adepts, their use is discouraged. The danger, he says, is that when these *siddhis,* as they are known, are used without adequate spiritual development, they result in the growth of the ego and the exercise of power over people.

Both Dormeyer and his partner, Craig Steele, caution against visiting psychics who are too flamboyant, who put on a good show. The danger for a culture such as ours, which lives on television, is that we will get lost in the spectacle and overlook the deeper insight we are being given.

How to Evaluate the Information

The next step in utilizing your psychic reading is to evaluate the information you have received. You can first do this simply by rehearsing in your mind all that took place and letting the fullest truths—those that speak to you directly—rise to the top, so to speak. You should contemplate not only the information you were given, but the feelings you had during and after your reading, as well. Susan is a 35-year-old writer who recalled that even the smallest details of her reading were good indicators that the psychic was on the right track:

A lot of what she said made sense to me, about what I'm going through and things that I want to happen. It was really right on the money. She told me that in the next month I was going to be so busy that I'd be running around like a chicken without a head—that's the story of my life. She said that there would be a job change in four months, which was good, because

311

I'd like to find a new job. And she brought up a lot of other things that were minor, but which were interesting. She told me to wear bright colors, even though I had black on that day. I usually do wear bright colors, so that was really interesting to me. When I asked her specific questions about friends of mine, she said, "You know, you're really coming into your own. You're surrounded by a lot of friends, but for the first time, you're really picking and choosing. You're realizing that maybe some of them aren't so necessary in your life, and you're starting to pull back." And that was really true.

Although a lot of this kind of information may sound trivial, these are indicators that the psychic is tapping into the right source of information. After all, if you were told that you are a very social person, when in reality you prefer to stay at home most nights watching television, there would be little reason to also believe that you are about to get a big job promotion just because a psychic said so. Many psychics do make small, seemingly unimportant observations about you during a session. Use these to your advantage in getting a sense of her accuracy.

The next thing you'll want to do is listen to your tape. It's probably a better idea not to do this the minute you get home; spend at least a day or two with the information that's in your head before you go back and reexperience the entire session. It might also be a good idea to recount your reading to a close friend, someone whom you consider a good sounding board.

In the process of retelling the experience you will remember things that had slipped your mind, see others in a new light, and most likely come to some new insights about yourself and the information you received.

It is interesting that in some instances people have received information that was only meant for the moment—in other words, that should not have been taped. I have been told stories by several psychics in which tapes were inexplicably blank when they were played back, in which video tape failed to record images, and in which tape machines refused to operate when specific tapes were put in them. Barbara Rollinson recalls one such incident:

I've found it very interesting when there have been blanks. We've had everything from heartbeats to blanks to all kinds of things. I think the most dramatic for me was with a couple I had known in California. They came for a reading and what happened was that my son, who had passed over, came through. The information [he gave] was that he would greet me next time on the earth plane and that I was not to be concerned about this—that he would not leave as he had left before—and that my interaction with him was to be as my new grandchild.

And then all this other information came through for [the clients]. They were blown away. And so they were telling me the exact words that were said. Well, needless to say, I was feeling all this emotion. They said, "You've got to listen to this," and they went back and the whole tape was blank. The only thing we heard was "Testing, one, two, three, four."

So things like that do occur. It was not supposed to be recorded. Afterward, I was a little upset, because all their information was lost as well, but they looked at each other, and they said, "You know, we didn't need to record that." They knew also.

Whether you believe these were instances of tele-kinesis or simply technological glitches, the point is that in some cases a psychic reading is most effective primarily during the reading itself and only with respect to the information that sticks in your mind. So be sure you rehearse the material as thoroughly as possible in your mind before sitting down to listen to your tape. When you feel you're ready and want to further clarify those things that you can recall only marginally, play your tape.

The beauty of having the tape is that you'll be able to dwell upon those aspects of your reading that do seem significant and try to decipher those that don't. As one New York psychic put it:

People hear what they want to hear. It's like a mother who tells a child ten times, "Don't touch that," and the child finally learns. If you let somebody record [a session], they can hear it ten times till it sinks in. That's why I love people to record what I say. A lot of psychics don't like it, but I think when you go home and you listen to that tape again, you get much more out of it. And sometimes something that you per-ceived the first time isn't quite what I said, but the second or third time you *hear* it. It makes it better for you, it makes it better for me. If someone's having a problem [with something they heard], I'll say, "Bring in the tape; lets talk about it."

When it comes to sifting through the information itself, it's important to try to drop your preconceptions. The truth comes in many forms. You may be expecting a simple yes-or-no answer to some questions but in reality receive a great deal more insight into the problem. However, because you are only focused on being told what decision to make, you overlook the wisdom you are actually being given.

You also have to be open to the truth in whatever form it presents itself, although you may want a "quick fix." If you want a lot of money, for instance, you may be hoping that the psychic will tell you that you are going to win the lottery. Instead you hear a lot about how to work on getting a job promotion, what career paths would prove most lucrative for you, and how, if you focus your efforts in a particular way, you will be rewarded with financial security. Because you are focused solely on whether money is simply going to fall into your hands, you may miss the advice that might actually help you attain your goals. The odds against winning the lottery are huge, and visiting a psychic won't change those odds. The most a psychic can do is tell you how to go about implementing change in your life in a way that can maximize your possibilities. Just because you don't like the advice, it doesn't necessarily follow that it was a bad reading.

There is a deeper, spiritual component, however, to the way in which information may be presented to you. Andrea Hinda explains the mechanisms of psychic insight in this way:

> You have to understand that the specific answer you're looking for may not be the answer [you get], and that what you hear may not be what you really want to hear— and may not be what you're expecting. Because often [clients] ask, "Will I get married?" or "Will I marry this man?" "Will this career work out for me?" And what happens is the answer has to do with some block or some pattern in their own personal being that they first have to look at in order to create that happening. That's what you get: you get the truth.

Another problem that arises in trying to understand the information you receive in a psychic reading is, as we have mentioned throughout this book, that knowledge accessed from the right brain is often transmitted in symbols. And those symbols may be very personal to you, not following any standardized system, making it difficult for a psychic to interpret them.

Suzanne Kluss is one psychic who recognizes the difficulty in interpreting such symbols and therefore considers her role to be more of a facilitator than a counselor:

> Any kind of awareness comes through the symbols that you [the client] understand. If someone said

[following a meditation], "I saw a house, what do you think that means?" I couldn't possibly interpret that, because I don't have a history of what a house means [for that person]. If I was a little kid who had been beaten repeatedly in a house, the symbol of a house coming up would mean something entirely different [than it would for] someone who always used to get away in the summers to a house.

The symbols work within one's own structure. So what you can teach people to do is to listen and interpret and to trust their own senses, but you can never impose your interpretation mechanisms on somebody else.

The opportunity to interpret your own symbols is clearly easier when someone is channeling for you, or guiding you through a focused meditation or visualization. But what if you are sitting with a clairvoyant and he is telling you things that don't necessarily ring true? Craig Steele suggests that you probe a little further into what the psychic is seeing or feeling that leads him to those conclusions. For example, he says, take the case of a tarot reader:

If I see that a person doesn't even know the [tarot] symbols, I'll know something about their skill as a psychic. Don't be afraid to ask, "Your judgment that I'm heading that way is based on what?" They've got to have something that they're going by: for example, a tingle on their left shin means you're going to have an accident, a tingle on their right means you're going to fall in love.

According to Steele, "Sometimes you'll have a better grasp of the information than the psychic." If the psychic shares with you the image he is seeing, then you will both be able to compare notes, so to speak. In this way, says Steele, "it's like overlaying screens—maybe the truth will drip through."

The problem that arises when a psychic begins interpreting what she sees or feels is that it becomes difficult to separate her own ego from the process. This is one reason why trance channelers may not need as much experience as clairvoyants, for example—they aren't interpreting anything but instead are attempting to remove their ego from the equation so that the information flows directly to you, the client. Nevertheless, even that is no guarantee of an unclouded reading, as Gordon recalls of a reading he had with a channeler while on a business trip:

> The thing was, he kept bringing up the issue of sexuality—not just sexuality, but whether I was gay or not and my need to come to terms with that. Well, I've never had any inclination that way, so it surprised me, to say the least. That is, until I found out that it had been a big issue for him in his own life.

Ego involvement isn't the only problem. Many psychics have spoken about the difficulty of knowing where to stop—of resisting the urge to embellish when they are not completely sure of the significance of the information. This temptation is fed by the attitude of the client, who generally wants more specifics. Because professional psychic work is, after all, a business, a reader will feel a great deal of pressure to give the customer what he wants, even if that means stretching the truth a bit.

One New York psychic who is very critical of the level of work being done in her field claims that the ego problem is quite widespread:

> A lot of psychics feel that because they're psychic they have to know everything. So if you ask a question, and they're not getting a valid feeling, they'll answer you anyway. I will say to people, "I don't know. I'm not picking it up." And they usually will accept it. I can't tell you how many psychics I've gone to who made a mistake or who couldn't answer a question and instead of saying, "I don't know," second-guessed it. That turns me right off. They could've been right on nine other things, but because they couldn't be honest with me, I don't want to hear the rest of what they have to say.
>
> A lot of people, when they get going in this, start becoming very blown out of proportion. They think they have the right to sit across the table and say, "I *know* this and I *know* that." When you get to that point, you should retire. And if you ever go to a reader who does that, and if they don't like you contradicting them, ask them to do it again. And if they don't want to hear you, then you don't need the reading. You say, "I'd rather not do this. Thank you. Good-bye." And do not pay for the services.

In addition to the problem of ego, there is also the problem of judgment on the part of the psychic. Especially with those readers who feel they have evolved to a certain spiritual level, you may detect a slight holier-than-thou attitude. Presumably you have researched your psychic carefully and won't be exposing yourself to someone with a bad attitude. Nevertheless, it's something to bear in mind, as Susan Edwards points out:

> That's something you have to watch in psychics—the judgment that might just sneak in there. It's a self-awareness experience. If someone tells you something that really makes you feel bad—if you feel like they're judging you—that's their problem. It's something I have a hard time with. Ever so often I'll go to [another psychic] just to see what they're doing. And the judgment is incredible. So I don't recommend [going to a] reader unless you interview them and get a feeling for their judgmental attitudes about life.

Another aspect of the judgment problem is that a good psychic will have tried to empathize with your situation in order to relate the information more directly to your circumstances. It is difficult for a psychic to establish that connection with a client while trying to maintain an objective outlook in interpreting the images she is receiving. It's a delicate balancing act, at best. So when you are evaluating your reading, be sure that the information you were given is objective truth, as far as the psychic knows it, and not something she thought you *wanted* to hear.

On a more positive note, there are a number of ways in which you can apply specific criteria to what you have heard that will help you separate the gold from the dross. One test for the veracity of the information

"Okay, maybe that's because I need this time right now to work on my career. So I'm not going to let myself get involved." In other words, it's giving you a direction in which to focus your energies so that they will bear the most fruit.

One of the common difficulties with psychic readings—especially future predictions—is the element of time. Many psychics get a clear picture of what will be occurring but have trouble pinning it down to a specific time frame. Very often they may even get a number, for example, "six." But they won't know if that means six days, six months, or six years. This is why you have to look into your own situation deeply enough to try to determine when something might be relevant for you. A psychic cannot possibly know enough about your life to determine an exact sequence of events—only you can make that judgment, based upon your own analysis of the situation.

Psychics differ among themselves as to whether the information that comes through is only relevant for the immediate present or may be applicable later. Some feel very strongly that what you hear should be usable at this moment. Others disagree. They feel that it may take a while for the information to settle in and for an individual to come to an understanding of what he has been told. This generally relates to the more spiritual information a person receives, as Margo Schmidt explains:

Interestingly, people will come to me, and they don't know what the hell I'm talking about. And then years later—maybe two years later—they will call me up or write me a letter and say, "I thought you were so off the wall, but everything you said makes sense now." Sometimes my work is an instigator for *them* to do the work and do the experiential stuff so then they have a context [to put the reading in]. So that I, as a co-creative channel, open their energy.

Even concrete predictions can be astoundingly accurate but relate to a different time period in someone's life. One psychic tells the story of a reading she did for a close friend of hers. She told her friend to join a particular health club because it would be at that club that she would meet her future husband. She told her exactly which hours to go to the club, and that she should hang around the swimming pool. She also mentioned that this would be a man the friend already knew casually from her past. After a year of attending the health club, the friend let her membership expire, and the psychic had to admit she was wrong. Three years later, however, the friend met the man in a different context. It turned out he *had* been swimming at that club at those particular times, but that, although he had been very close to getting divorced, he was still married. Thus, by some strange "quirk of fate" the two had never actually met, even though they were at the same place at the same time.

How to Use the Information

Once you have gone over your tape and sorted out which information strikes a true chord in you, which information seems logical but not entirely clear, and which doesn't seem to relate to you at all, you should sit down and decide in what ways you can actually use it to enhance your life. Depending upon the type of psychic you went to and what your major concerns were, you will have different goals. It may be a simple question of finding a better job, or you may have been given specific steps to take to enhance your own spiritual growth. What you do with the information you were given is clearly a very personal thing, and it will probably involve more than one aspect of your life. Nevertheless we can break down specific uses of psychic insight into several categories.

On the simplest level, a psychic can be helpful in pursuing creative problem-solving. As we mentioned earlier, sometimes a problem you are having gets "jammed up" in your left brain through overanalysis of the situation. In such cases, just having someone to bounce the problem off can be a great help, but if that person happens to be psychic and is able to process the data through right-brain intuition, so much the better. In this way a psychic can let you see possibilities you may not have seen before.

A psychic also has the benefit, as do all therapists, of not being intensely bound up with the emotions attached to your personal problems. Very often, simply by getting an objective view on the situation, divorced from your own desires for a particular outcome, you can make a more informed choice. That kind of insight, coupled with the fact that it is coming from a total stranger, will often be enough of an impetus to get over the logjam of emotional angst.

Pat, an editor at a national magazine, just happened to drop in on a storefront palm reader for a lark. When she came out 15 minutes later, she had been given a great deal of insight into an emotional entanglement she was involved in:

> The thing was, she was able to pick up on the things in my life that I'm confused about without getting obscured by the emotional turmoil that I'm feeling. She really didn't tell me anything I didn't know, but hearing my own thoughts about the situation come back to me from a total stranger gave them a clarity that I couldn't find within myself. It was better than hearing it from a friend or a relative, because someone who's close to you, who cares about you, is also bringing a whole emotional context to the situation. They know what is important to you, and they know what something means in the scope of your whole life, so it's also difficult for them to separate out what is objective from what is going on on so many different levels.

Still, not all problems yield such immediate results. Often they are there for a purpose, and if your psychic reading has been successful, you will be able to discover reasons for the problems you have been experiencing, especially if they seem to fit a particular pattern. Numerologist-astrologer Stephen Calia sees problems as growth opportunities. As such, they need to be accepted and not avoided:

The Devil in the Bible is better translated as "adversary." It deals with strengthening. Our problem with things that we consider evil lies is not seeing them rightly. We need to be thankful for those opportunities rather than be mired in them. Use them as "irksome limitations"—that's what they're called—and learn to see them as opportunities given by God; opportunities to get out of our old patterns. It's all for us to use.

Most problems have deep roots, of course, and it is rare that a psychic will be able to give you a quick and easy solution to something that has been troubling you. More likely she'll be able to isolate those aspects of yourself that relate to the problem and that in some cases may actually be the cause of the problem. Very often it is really only how we look at something that gives it the power of a true block. By identifying those inner blocks, a psychic can help you clear your particular path of inner growth.

Personal growth takes many forms. The best place to begin is with an affirmation of who you are. Chances are, if you really resonated with the psychic you visited, you will already have felt a very strong sense of affirmation. Many channelers are particularly good at transmitting this kind of energy during the course of a session. But this is a skill that every true healer, whether spiritual or psychological, should possess. Diane Brook Gusic, who is an astrologer and numerologist as well as a psychospiritual counselor, points this out:

I think the only thing you ever get from someone else is acceptance and encouragement—that's the wisdom of the practitioner across the board. A good therapist should be able to do it, a good psychic should be able to do it. And someone poor in those fields, no matter how well trained, won't be able to get that, so they create a dependency. They're not going to give what I think is the highest form of giving, which is acceptance and encouragement.

Laverne, the New Jersey textile designer we mentioned earlier, began her spiritual search by attending channeling sessions and soon found that she wanted to pursue her own spiritual path, built around visualizations and meditations. She is very clear on what it has done for her:

> What it's given me is [the awareness] (a) that I have to believe in myself (which a good therapist would tell me), but (b) that my self is a lot bigger than I thought it was. And it's not as egocentric. Because I really believe that I am a part of this whole God thing.

In addition to giving you personal affirmation, a good psychic reading can offer you direction in your life. With the phenomenal pace of life today, we all seek some safe anchor in the stormy sea of survival. What we hope to gain from a psychic reading is an indicator of where we are going—as Linda Hill describes it, a "signpost along the way." The way she sees it, she enables people to put their life experience into a specific context, perhaps a context that they had not seen previously. "They pick the context," she explains, "but I help them to look at it in different ways."

This idea of the psychic as a "signpost" is common to all good psychic work. A psychic can offer you guidance but, as we have pointed out again and again, he can never make decisions for you. The ultimate responsibility for your choices in life rests with you. What you should hope to get from a psychic is simply more data to use in making your decisions.

The last point to remember about personal growth is that it is ongoing—if you don't take responsibility for changing yourself, you won't be ready for the next step. Many psychics consider their readings to be "homework" for their clients. These psychics are all too aware that many people go from psychic to psychic looking for a way out of taking responsibility for themselves. Many such people will hear the same message from a wide variety of sources, while they continue to reject their role in the process.

There are many psychics who will refuse to accept an appointment with clients they know have not taken on responsibility for their own growth. Some people try to get around this by visiting channelers, because they figure they will benefit from hearing from different spirit guides with each visit. This doesn't always work, however. Hossca Harrison, channeler of the spirit entity known as Jonah, says that until a client has decided to undertake the work Jonah gives him, he isn't ready for another session. He recalls several such occasions:

> That has occurred a few times, and Jonah won't talk to them. If people have a session, and they use the in-

formation and they grow with it—that is, they've grown to another level of awareness, and they need some more advice—he'll talk to them. But if someone has come for a session, and [Jonah] has [already] given them advice but they didn't do anything with it, and they're sitting in the same state they were in before, then he may come through and say, "The information has already been given. You need to work on it. Good-bye." Or sometimes he won't even come through.

The problem of dependency is a great one with regard to any type of counseling, whether it is psychological or spiritual. Most good psychics will be aware of their clients' needs and gently try to discourage constant consultations. It is a fine line between giving someone encouragement to make changes in his life and making him depend upon that encouragement before he takes the next step.

The parallels between psychic readings and psychotherapy run much deeper than the problem of dependency. There are forms of psychological counseling that now take into account the spiritual aspect of the human being. Transpersonal psychology and psychosynthesis, for example, seek to achieve a true healing on all levels: emotional, mental, and spiritual. These forms of work are usually undertaken by trained psychologists. But it is clear that much of the work being done by people who have psychic ability clearly qualifies as what I have termed "psychic-therapy."

Traditional psychologists have to rely upon the words you use to describe what you are feeling and thinking. A psychic, on the other hand, can tap directly into those aspects of yourself that most affect the way you are in the world. In doing so, parts of yourself may be revealed that you admit rarely to yourself, let alone to another person. So in listening back to your tape it is important to recognize those insights that a psychic may have made that perhaps make you uncomfortable but which nevertheless strike a chord. In some ways, the more effective your psychic reading, the more resistance you may find yourself putting up to the information you are given, because it represents a threat to your psychological defense mechanisms.

Free Will

In the final analysis, psychic information boils down to free will. The issue is taking control of your own life. Rather than seeing things as predetermined and trying to find out what will happen in the future, you should be seeking to find out the ways to *make* things happen. As Stephen Calia puts it, "Either you do your life or your life does you." The question you have to ask yourself is whether you want to put yourself in the role of victim. If you do, then a psychic reading can easily be used as a means to justify inaction and lack of growth. If, however, you want to put yourself in the position of personal power, then a psychic reading can be a valuable tool.

Unfortunately, psychic readings are often seen as excuses for not achieving the best that we are capable of. We like the idea of giving away our power to "unknown forces," whether we call them karma or fate or destiny. Astrologers come up against this problem quite a bit, since things can always be blamed "on the stars." Linda Hill is critical of those people who check their astrological chart every day before making a move in order to see that the planets are all lined up right:

> To me there's no growth in that. There's no power in it. To me that's the misuse of astrology. Also, people who do that usually use astrology as a way to justify their behavior: "Well, what can you expect from me? I've got Saturn on my moon right now so therefore I can't be expected to do x, y, and z." The most common misuse of astrology is to use it as a way to justify not growing. None of my clients is familiar with that way of operating.

Personal power doesn't come from trying to change reality but rather learning how to accept it. Problems in and of themselves don't exist as a part of reality, they only exist when we—as human beings with free will—interact with reality. In other words, the degree to which we perceive the world as difficult depends upon the way in which we experience it. As Margo Schmidt explains, "We can't always choose to make things happen the way we want them to, but we can always choose whether we're reacting or responding. That's where your empowerment always is."

When we *react* to a situation, we put ourselves in a position of opposition to it, and more often than not, we have reacted before we have even realized what it is we are reacting to. A *response*, on the other hand, comes from a position of power—we respond to a situation only *after* we consider precisely what the appropriate response should be. The great mystery of free will is that by responding appropriately we seem to be able to change the character of events, if not the actual physical events themselves. The knowledge necessary to make an informed, appropriate response can be gained through psychic insight.

On a more profound level it seems that exercising your free will can actually alter the course of events. Since everything that happens in your life follows from what came before, decisions you make now will alter the path that your life may take. This may be one reason why psychic prediction is not as accurate as we would all like it to be. We all have a choice at every moment of every day, and whether we choose A or B will affect very significantly what follows thereafter.

Ron Havern tells several stories of readings that were uncannily *in*accurate, but which may have been the result of free will altering the outcome of possible events. As he tells it:

In one case, I had a woman come [for a reading], and I told her, "I see your husband in a car wreck, and it's very tragic. He should be very careful." And I gave her a specific time frame. And she said, "Well, it's not going to happen." So I asked her why not. And she said, "Every single psychic I have ever gone to has said, 'I see your husband dying in a car wreck,' describing it exactly the same way and within the same time period." Over a ten-year span, they had all given her exactly the same description of what was going to happen the following month.

Someone's explanation is that you get things that were meant to be. How things were *supposed* to happen. And there can be rearrangements of events somehow. Another example was a woman who had three children. I described all the children and their lives. Well, the first one was accurate, the third one was accurate. But the woman only had two children. Now, I had a whole career for the middle one just as clearly as the other two. Then it came out a week later, when she called me, that she had had an abortion of a third, middle child. So I apparently got what would have happened to the child.

All a psychic can really tell you is the outcome of some of your possible choices. And since those choices are truly unlimited, a psychic can never know exactly what will occur. When you evaluate your reading, bear in mind that everything you hear is contingent upon a very special set of circumstances being played out. If you accept the fact that simply by making different choices—choices from a place of knowledge and personal power—you can change those predictions, I think you'll find it a liberating experience. And rather than being disappointed in the accuracy of the psychic reading, you will be pleased at the prospect of your new-found freedom.

Following Up

The last thing you will want to consider when evaluating your reading is whether you feel you would benefit from a follow-up visit and exactly when that visit should be. There are two aspects to seeing a psychic the second time around. The first is one of clarification. If you heard something on your tape that doesn't make complete sense to you, or if you have a question that you forgot to ask with regard to the information you were given, you might consider calling your psychic on the phone. Not all psychics welcome phone calls, and many won't remember you or your reading. But others feel—and rightly so—that they have a responsibility, like any professional, to follow up personal visits or clarify nagging questions.

One New York psychic I know takes phone calls both at her office and her home; although she discourages dependency, she doesn't hesitate to make herself available to clients who may be experiencing a crisis in life. The fact that she is also able to read people over the phone makes this a valuable service. As she sees it, a responsible psychic has an obligation not to leave a person hanging:

> You should have the right to call that psychic up and say, "I'm having a problem with this. Could you help me with it? Could you explain this to me? Could we talk?" You should always have the right to go over [your reading]. Not too many psychics are willing to do that. But it's important, because you're playing with people's lives. A psychic can be a major help in somebody's life or enough to make him pull the plug. You can go one way or another with this.
>
> It's not your place to take control of somebody's life, but it is your place to explain the advice you have dumped in somebody's lap if they don't know what

to do with it. Who else are they going to talk to about it if they can't come back to the psychic? I really care about the people I read for, and I don't want it to become a business that's so overwhelming I can't handle it.

I have sat in this particular psychic's office and seen her take phone call after phone call, giving people bits of advice, calming down those who are panic-stricken, and telling others to get a hold of themselves and take responsibility for their own lives. On the other hand, I've met psychics who can only be reached through an agent and whose own telephone numbers remain a guarded secret. No one way is necessarily better than another. Professional psychics are clearly still considered a fringe element, and many feel that they have to protect their privacy. But if you have been for a reading and felt a rapport with the psychic, you should feel free to ask whether you can call if you have any further quesions and what the best time would be to do so.

But it should also be stressed that a psychic is not there to consult with every time you have to make a decision about something. There are plenty of people who won't make a dinner date without calling their astrologer first. This is not only an abuse of a reader's skills but can demonstrate a crippling dependency. Most psychics, therefore, will act right away to discourage such behavior as soon as they see the signs.

It's up to you to use your psychic's availability wisely. Try to decipher your reading yourself. If you have problems, discuss them with friends. Finally, if you simply can't arrive at a satisfactory answer yourself, try calling back with a short, clear question. Above all, avoid calling your psychic with questions that you might have forgotten to ask during your reading, such as "What is going to happen to my career?" (That's what you prepared your list of questions for—to make sure you didn't miss anything, remember?) Be specific, and show the reader that you have thought about the question thoroughly and simply need one or two pieces of clarification.

Another approach you might take to trying to clarify something in your reading is to see a different psychic. If your readings are accurate, you should hear the same kinds of things, even if they are presented in different ways. This is probably the best kind of confirmation you could get, especially with regard to predictions, which you could not otherwise verify—at least not without waiting for them to oc-cur. Getting similar information from two different psychics proves that they are getting some form of ob-jective input from outside themselves, and that they are not clouding their interpretations with aspects of their own ego.

One psychic, who does both medium work and clairvoyance, stresses how important it is to double-check the information you are given:

> If you go to a psychic, and he gives you a certain amount of information, go to another psychic. It has to be exactly the same. It's like a doctor. Because you have only one story in your life, and whether I see it,

or somebody else sees it, it should be identical. In fact, yesterday, a friend of Mary's [another psychic] called and said, "Mary is too close to the subject. Could you please do a reading?" And as I finished giving her the information, she started laughing. And she said, "Every single thing Mary told me you told me, down to the minutest details." Well there you go, you have to double-check.

Any reputable psychic should be glad to have you go for a "second opinion." And many psychics will be happy to give you a referral for another reading. If a reader seems threatened by the idea of you consulting someone else, or tells you not to discuss your reading with anyone, that should be a clear sign that you are in the presence of a fraud, or at least of someone whose ego is getting in the way of his readings.

Assuming that you have understood most of what you were told during your reading and have found ways to apply that knowledge to specific areas of your life, you'll most likely be thinking about your next visit. If you liked your psychic and enjoyed your reading, then there is no need to look for a different psychic, unless you simply want to explore other kinds of readers and get a feel for another person's way of working.

Many people find that after going for one particular kind of reading, they want to sample something else, usually something a little more "far out." For instance, you may have started with an astrologer, a type of reading that is more "scientific" than the others. Having had a successful experience, you may now feel you're ready for a tarot reader and later on, perhaps a channeler. Eventually, you will discern the different strengths of each approach to accessing psychic information and know when a certain reader is more suited to a particular problem you have.

A lot of people find, however, that it pays to return to the same reader. If the psychic has taken an interest in you, she may even ask you to check back with her in a few months to let her know if the reading has been of help and whether her predictions were accurate. By returning to the same reader, you will be building upon past experiences and may benefit from her previous knowledge of your circumstances. You will also feel more comfortable with the psychic, will know what to expect, and will be better informed about how to formulate your questions and follow up on the answers. In short, you will become familiar with your reader's style and be able to focus more on the message and less on the process.

As to the question of when to make your next appointment, no one can give you the answer to that. It all depends upon your rate of growth and the degree to which your life changes in the interim. You should not go back to your psychic for another reading until you feel you have exhausted the information you were already given and found ways in which to apply it to your life. Once you begin to make changes in the way you approach the world, circumstances may change dramatically, and you may feel the time is right for a further consultation.

The majority of psychics will not tell you when to

return for a visit. Obviously, if you have an astrology chart that only covers the next six months, or a numerology reading that is for the next year, you will simply want to book your next appointment for when those readings run out. Or if you have visited a psychic healer for a specific ailment, she may have already given you an appointment for another treatment (contingent on signs of improvement). Other than those cases, however, most psychics will leave the issue of future visits solely up to your own awareness. So again, it's matter of trusting yourself. If you have understood the value of psychic information and have begun to use it in positive and productive ways, you will soon be more able to tune in to yourself and your needs, and you'll know when the time is right.

If you do decide to return to the same psychic, and you feel that you've grown a great deal in the interim, be sure the information you are given differs from that of your previous reading. Just as you are constantly changing, so, too, should the information you are being given vary with your life circumstance and your inner growth processes. Many fraudulent psychics have a routine that they stick to, and you will be all too aware of that routine if you get sold the same bill of goods the second time around.

All this brings us around to where we began this chapter—with the reminder that psychic readings are an ongoing process. The process is a fluid one that changes with time and circumstance, but mostly with growth. If you come to see your life in this way—as an ever-changing, fluid intersection of events and choices—then you will also see the way in which psychic readings can become an integral, and equally dynamic, part of your life, rather than a mere evening's entertainment or a static excuse for avoiding responsibility in your life. Use psychic readings as you would any tool—in a way that justifies not only your time and your money, but most important, your attention.

CONCLUSION

No matter where you go, there you are.
　　　　　　　　　　　—Buckaroo Banzai

We have looked at a full range of psychic experience, both from the point of view of the professional psychics and from their clients. What is probably most apparent by now is that even within each particular type of reading there are as many different styles and approaches as there are psychics. Simply trying to categorize them is difficult, because many psychics don't fall easily into one single category, with respect either to the methods they use or to their goals in working with people. For some psychics, doing readings is simply using a gift that they were given, much like someone would play the piano or paint a picture. For others, psychic ability has grown out of a deep and significant spiritual search, sometimes resulting from years of meditation and study. The way in which they approach their work and the service that they are able to provide to others will depend upon where they see themselves on the intuitive continuum.

Today we are in a unique situation. Divination is being accepted again, not because of its ability to "wrestle with the forces of nature" or its parlor-game diversion value, but as part of the recent shift toward New Age thinking, which emphasizes the value of nonrational intuition and the ability of each one of us to heal ourselves. It is a philosophy that Hinduism, Buddhism, and the shamanic traditions have held onto for thousands of years and that we in the West are only just rediscovering from our own past. But because of our unique place in the history of science, we may be able to make breakthroughs that neither science or religion alone can accomplish. Psychic phenomena are only a part of that larger transition. If we close ourselves off to the "unexplained" just because we're uncomfortable with it, we may be giving up the chance of a lifetime.

On an individual level, each one of us has to decide not only what the implications of psychic phenomena are for our own world view, but also what psychic ability has to offer in terms of our personal growth. As a consumer, you have to acquaint yourself with what is available so that you can make an intellectually informed choice. As a human being, you have to search yourself for those aspects of yourself that will benefit most from a psychic reading and choose a style and reader accordingly. Just as each psychic is an amalgam of skills and experiences, so, too, is each of us a combination of spiritual, mental, emotional, and physical attributes that become manifest in a totally unique way. Your job as a psychic consumer is to find the proper fit between you and the world of psychic experience.

Every psychic reading that was excerpted in this book was done for one person: me. Over the course of a year, I had over two dozen different psychic readings, ranging from a ten-minute palm reading in a Brooklyn storefront to a three-hour channeling session in the foothills of the Rocky Mountains. I was given a number of predictions, a good many of which never came true. Some occurred within a few weeks of the forecast date, others a year later. Still others materialized in ways that were often so subtle or "disguised" that it was only months later that I recognized them for what they were. What soon became clear to me is that we can never fully know reality, and to sit back and wait for our lives to happen in a particular way simply because someone says so is a psychological and spiritual dead end. No matter how much we would like to order our lives into a predictable series of specific events, reality remains too much a product of the interplay of diverse energies and convergent intentions to ever be fully foreseen by anyone, no matter how impressive their abilities.

What was significant about these psychic readings is that each and every psychic I visited told me something about myself. Sometimes they were things that I already knew and simply enjoyed hearing confirmed. At other times I was described in ways that had never occurred to me before, but which seemed accurate and which opened up new insights for me into myself. And then there were readings that portrayed a self I couldn't identify with, but which nevertheless seemed to ring a still, small bell somewhere deep inside me, and which for some reason weren't easy to simply brush off as "misses."

As I think is apparent from reading the excerpts presented in this book, each of these psychic readings described me in a completely unique way, tuning in to a different frequency of my self, sometimes focusing on the more mundane aspects of my life, other times on the more subtle, spiritual levels of my experience on planet Earth. I discovered that the more I was willing to examine myself and the various roles I take, the more each of these readings made sense. By putting myself into relationship with each of these psychics for a particular period of time, I took on a new role and watched and listened as that role was examined and described by that psychic. Sometimes the differences were a function of the method being used, other times it was simply a question of personality. But if I was willing to *listen*, then there was always something to take with me when a session was over.

After all the reading, searching, and sifting is done, whatever psychic you choose will have something to give you—if you are willing to take it. And although you should make every effort to locate someone with whom you feel at ease and who challenges your concept of yourself, in the end it isn't so much where you go or what you hear as what you do with it. Because wherever you are now *is* your reality. If you wish to change that reality, you first need to know exactly what it is you're trying to change. In the process of evaluating the psychic as a person and the message she has for you, you will also have to examine *yourself* as a person and the assumptions that you live by. By determining where those two sides of the equation meet—or how you can *make* them meet—you will begin to create a blueprint for how you want to be in the world and how you can best create that reality. In doing so, you will discover how psychic ability can help you to make the most of your life, your dreams, your self.

APPENDIX A

A Brief History of Psychic Phenomena

The history of psychic phenomena is probably as long as that of the human race itself, and, in the past hundred years, certainly as detailed. It is difficult to know, however, exactly which phenomena throughout the ages come under the heading of "paranormal." We do know that foretelling the future was a common practice in the ancient world, specifically because the Old Testament warns against consulting "soothsayers, enchanters, or sorcerers," and "resorting to ghosts or familiar spirits." In addition, there are the stories of prophets—too numerous to mention—who experienced revelations, saw "visions," and heard "voices." Others, such as Joseph, received premonitions in the form of dreams.

The ancient Greeks were also not immune to the lure of trying to predict the future. Their penchant for consulting oracles for a host of situations is common knowledge. What may be less well known is that the philosophers themselves pondered the nature of psychic phenomena. In several of Plato's writings he discusses the role of prophecy and the laws concerning soothsayers, magicians, and diviners. Perhaps more startling is his assertion that the highest form of knowledge can only result from a direct knowing by the soul, not the intellect. Aristotle, the father of Western logic, argues that a lack of human understanding is insufficient grounds to dismiss the role of dreams in foretelling the future.

At around the same time that Plato and Aristotle were speculating on psychic knowledge, the Eastern traditions were making practical use of that knowledge. In China, the *I Ching*, or *Book of Changes*, was being formulated by the Taoist and Confucian sages. It explained how, by throwing yarrow stalks or coins, one could forecast future events. And in India the Vedas, in a tradition that was already 2,000 years old, explained how the practice of yoga could lead to knowledge of past lives and future events, not to mention freeing the astral body from the physical self.

In the West, however, the first millenium of the Christian era put a damper on public reportings of psychic experiences because they were considered unholy, or the work of demons. By the time of the Renaissance, however, philosophers and theologians had found ways to explain psychic experiences in religious terms, mainly through various forms of mysticism. In Italy, tarot cards appeared, not just as a way of foretelling future events, but as a metaphor for describing a person's spiritual journey through life. In the rest of Europe and the Middle East, numerology, astrology, and kabbalism also flourished. Christian, Jewish, and Islamic mystics practiced meditation and reported having out-of-body experiences, hearing voices, and receiving prophecies.

The most well-known psychic of this time was Nostradamus, a French physician, counselor, and astrologer to the king. He not only made startlingly accurate predictions of events in his own day, but forecast cataclysmic happenings in world history that reached into the twentieth century. In addition to predicting the death of Henry II, he foresaw the decline of the Church as a political force and gave detailed accounts of the French revolution and the Napoleonic period. Most amazing of all, though, was his prediction, in 1555, of World War I, which even included a description of airplanes as "a flock of ravens . . . throwing fire from the sky."

By the seventeenth century, psychic experiences were firmly woven into the fabric of popular Western culture (they had never been absent in the East). William Shakespeare, for one, made liberal use of ghosts, "portents," and various spirits. Another popular author, Daniel Defoe, was the Stephen King of his day, terrifying readers with the first real ghost stories to appear in modern English. He was also a professional journalist, however, and one of his stories, *A True Relation of the Apparition of One Mrs. Veal*, purports to be the true story of a psychic apparition who returned from the dead one fine autumn day in 1705. Henry More, the English philosopher, writer, and poet, also took it upon himself to record instances of spirit apparitions, poltergeists, and possession that he claimed were beyond "all suspicion of either Fraud or Melancholy [hallucination]" in his work *Antidote Against Atheism*.

But the most famous psychic of the early eighteenth century was Emanuel Swedenborg, a Swedish scholar with expertise in a wide range of disciplines, including philosophy, literature, theology, engineering, and the natural sciences. In what has become one of the best documented instances of clairvoyance ever recorded, Swedenborg "saw" a fire, which was sweeping through his home town of Stockholm (and which he "watched" halt within three doors of his own), while visiting the city of Göteborg, 300 miles away. The story of the fire captured the imaginations of Europe's most distinguished minds, including the philosopher Immanuel Kant, who wrote the 20,000-word treatise *Dreams of a Ghost Seer*, in 1766, in an attempt to make sense of the incident.

The Enlightenment, or Age of Reason, which began in the seventeenth century with Newton's physics and Locke's philosophy, gathered momentum well into the eighteenth century, when materialism and the belief in a rational, scientific world overshadowed other-worldly concerns. It is perhaps because of this shift in European thought that the Golden Age of Spiritualism exploded not in England or on the Continent, but in the New World.

The Salem witch trials of 1692 provided one of the earliest recorded incidences of "unexplained phenomena" in American history. Although there is some question as to how much of those occurrences were the product of political or social vindictiveness, their origin has never been satisfactorily explained. In any event, by the time Edgar Allan Poe was writing his tales of terror in the 1840s, psychic phenomena were back, and in a big way. In the words of the nineteenth-century German philosopher Arthur Schopenhauer, "the despised ghosts," which the "super-clever past century" had sought to banish, had been "rehabilitated."

The Golden Age of Spiritualism began on March 31, 1848, in Hydesville, New York, where the Fox sisters, Kate and Margaret, lived with their parents. Although the girls were not yet teenagers, they found they could receive communications from dead spirits in the form of raps, which followed them around throughout the house. One such spirit claimed to be a peddler who had been murdered with a butcher knife while spending a night in the house. The spirit raps led the family to the cellar, where they eventually unearthed some human remains, which had lain undetected under five feet of earth. The rest of the skeleton was not discovered for another 56 years, when a cellar wall was opened up.

The Fox sisters not only became the first professional mediums, touring the country and giving demonstrations, but they were the subject of extensive scientific inquiry as well. Horace Greeley, editor of the New York *Tribune*, was one of their staunchest supporters, and his articles fed the Spiritualism craze that swept the country. Suddenly séances were "in." Mediums put on public demonstrations and held private sittings. Self-proclaimed psychic "investigators" exposed frauds at every opportunity. Famous thinkers went on record, either for or against. There were even White House séances, where Mary Todd Lincoln, and some say the President himself, looked for guidance from mediums. The Lincoln Papers in the Library of Congress include a letter purportedly written to him by the dead spirit of Edward Baker, a close friend. The letter, allegedly the product of "automatic writing," is five pages long, written in reverse so that it can only be read in a mirror reflection.

The mediums of the Golden Age were the superstars of their era. And like the superstars of today, they toured Europe as well as the States. The most famous of these was David Dunglas Home, who was born in Scotland but raised in the United States. Home has been called "the greatest physical medium in the history of modern spiritualism." He had his first vision at the age of 13. His second prophecy predicted the death of his mother to the hour. The physical phenomena Home is alleged to have produced included handling live coals, setting various objects in motion, levitating himself out one window and in another, and making an accordion float around the room and play by itself.

Home became the darling of European royalty, holding séances for the likes of Napoleon III, the King of Bavaria, the King of Naples, the Emperor of Germany, and the Queen of the Netherlands. Alexandre Dumas, author of *The Three Musketeers*, was a witness at his wedding, and many of the writer's stories came from his association with Home. Another literary fan was Elizabeth Barrett Browning, whose favor toward Home enraged her husband, Robert, and led him to write the scathing poem, "Mr. Sludge, The Medium."

Even more bizarre than floating accordions were the manifestations of the medium known as Mrs. Guppy. She was a particular favorite of Alfred Russel Wallace, the naturalist, who, concurrently with Darwin, developed the concept of evolution. Wallace reported that he saw Mrs. Guppy, who was a large woman, levitate off the top of a table while seated in a chair, make a variety of musical sounds without instruments, and, most unusual of all, produce exotic fruits and flowers from nowhere, in the dead of winter, "all absolutely fresh as if just gathered from a conservatory." Other witnesses claimed that they saw the medium produce not only snow falling in the room, but prickly cactus, butterflies, sea water, live starfishes, eels, lobsters, and sand. Wallace's work with Mrs. Guppy led him to write *On Modern Miracles and Spiritualism*, in 1881, and to declare therein that psychic phenomena "are proved quite as well as any facts are proved in other sciences."

Some of these claims were, at the very least, exaggerated. And it was just such exaggeration that fueled

the fires of controversy over the Spiritualist movement. Two of the best known antagonists in the ongoing debate were Sir Arthur Conan Doyle and Harry
Houdini. Doyle, who is known for his brilliant
Sherlock Holmes fiction, spent the last decade and
a half of his life proclaiming the validity of psychic
phenomena. Known as "the St. Paul of Spiritualism,"
Doyle began as a skeptic, but after attending a séance
where he received a very personal message from his
wife's brother, who had been killed in World War I
two years before, he became a believer and embarked
on a career of investigating, writing, and lecturing
about spiritualism that took him to four continents.

Harry Houdini was a completely different case. A
magician of such magnitude and skill that many
believed his tricks to be the result of psychic abilities,
he began his investigations with an open mind. After
numerous unsuccessful attempts at contacting his
dead mother through various mediums—during
which he unmasked many cases of blatant fraud—
he became an arch enemy of the Spiritualists, exposing trickery whenever he could. It has been suggested
that Houdini's crusade was more the result of
publicity-hunting than moral outrage, but whatever
the motive, he pursued his "witch hunt" with the same
fervor that Doyle showed in proclaiming psychic
authenticity.

The two men had been fast friends, but the intensity of the debate eventually took its toll on their
friendship, until they finally stopped speaking to one

another, except in public proclamations made in newspaper stories, through magazine articles, and on the lecture circuit. While Doyle publicly endorsed one medium after another, Houdini continued to demonstrate the ways in which séances could be rigged to produce apparitions, voices, and physical manifestations. Houdini's biggest coup, however, was being appointed to a committee of five selected by *Scientific American* magazine to investigate claims of psychic phenomena. A prize of $2,500 would be awarded to any medium who the committee agreed had truly demonstrated psychic abilities. More often than not Houdini was the sole dissenter, refusing to believe what was in some cases exhaustive evidence. The committee was dissolved and the prize left unclaimed when the magician was caught using test apparatus he had designed in order to "frame" mediums he could not otherwise expose.

The list of notables who entered the psychic fray is long. William Thackeray, author of *Vanity Fair*, was an avid supporter of D.D. Home and visited séances with the Fox sisters. (Charles Dickens, in the opposing camp, continually attacked Home in the magazine *Household Words*.) Victor Hugo spent two years on the isle of Jersey, claiming a constant stream of communication with spirits. Mark Twain considered himself telepathic, claimed that his wife's cure from partial paralysis was due to a psychic healer, and asserted that he had had a dream foretelling his brother's death in a riverboat accident.

The extent to which psychic phenomena were entrenched in ninteenth-century American culture is exemplified by Nathaniel Hawthorne's story about the ghost of "old Doctor Harris," seen regularly at the town reading room, always in the same chair, perusing the Boston *Globe*. Hawthorne recalled that the ghost was clearly "interested in me," but that he refused to speak to the apparition because he and Doctor Harris had never been properly introduced prior to the minister's death. As Hawthorne put it, "I was not aware that social regulations are to be abrogated by the accidental fact of one of the parties having crossed the imperceptible line which separates the other party from the spiritual world."

But the Golden Age of Spiritualism was not completely divorced from the Industrial Age. The two came together most elegantly in the workshop of Thomas Edison, the inventor of the electric light bulb, the phonograph, motion pictures, and hundreds of other devices that brought him the title of "America's Most Useful Citizen." In an interview with *Scientific American*, Edison admitted to having worked on a device to contact the dead, although the plans for it were never found. He based his work on the assumption that "if personality exists after what we call death, it's reasonable to conclude that those who leave this earth would like to communicate with those they have left here." He felt, however, that if communication could be achieved, it would not be through mediums and séances, which he considered "crude, childish, and unscientific," but through purely mechanical means. Needless to say, this was one "useful" device that never came to fruition.

Edison was not the only member of the scientific community who took an interest in psychic phenomena. The Golden Age gave rise to a new scientific discipline: psychical research. It was probably Sir William Crookes, one of the leading scientists of his day, who initiated formal scientific inquiry into the "unexplained." Crookes was a Fellow of the Royal Society, was knighted in 1897, and received the Order of Merit in 1910. His psychic investigations began in 1870 with D.D. Home, whom he investigated thoroughly and concluded to be genuine. The scientific community refused to accept his findings, which is not so surprising in light of Crookes's own ambivalence: "Even now, on recalling the details of what I have witnessed, there is antagonism in my mind between reason ... and the consciousness [of] my senses."

On February 20, 1882 the Society for Psychical Research was founded in London. Its objectives, among others, included: "an examination of the nature and extent of any influence which may be exerted by one mind upon another, apart from any generally recognized mode of perception," and "an inquiry into the various physical phenomena commonly called spiritualistic." The society's first president was Henry Sidgwick, Knightbridge Professor of Moral Philosophy at Cambridge (and brother-in-law of Lord

Balfour, who later became prime minister). In years to come presidents of the society would include three Nobel laureates, ten Fellows of the Royal Society, one prime minister, and, as Arthur Koestler put it, "a galaxy of professors, mostly physicists and philosophers."

Three years later, the American Society for Psychical Research (ASPR) took root in Boston, mainly due to the efforts of William James, who was not only a leading force in twentieth-century psychology, but a pioneer in exploring the relationship between psychology and religious experience. James served as the society's president from 1894-95, but was its intellectual leader from its inception. At the time, James was professor of psychology at Harvard. Through his mother-in-law he was introduced to Mrs. Leonore Piper, who has been called "the foremost trance medium in the history of psychic research." In an analogy that has become famous, James said, "to upset the conclusion that all crows are black, there is no need to seek demonstration that no crow is black; it is sufficient to produce one white crow." Mrs. Piper was James's "white crow."

In 1920, ten years after James's death, his former chair was taken over by William McDougall from Oxford. McDougall had antagonized his colleagues in England by challenging their mechanistic concepts of the mind. He continued to do so at Harvard, especially with behaviorists. In 1927 he accepted a position at Duke, where he later hired J.B. and Louisa

Rhine to head up the Parapsychology Laboratory. McDougall drew a distinction between psychical research, which he envisioned going on in the lab ("strictly experimental") and parapsychology, which was the larger whole, and which included "obscure warnings and premonitions, veridical phantasms of the living and the dead, and other sporadic manifestations of mysterious origins," the study of which would be left to "extra-academic groups."

In view of this vivid turn of phrase, it should come as no surprise that McDougall was responsible for the first issue of the *Journal of Parapsychology* in 1937. Two years earlier, the Duke laboratory had become a separate department within the university, gaining recognition for the "Pearce-Pratt experiments," which relied heavily on statistics and were "scientifically clean." Because of his success at Duke, McDougall was at least indirectly responsible for the establishment of parapsychology departments in universities throughout Western Europe and the Soviet Union. J.B. Rhine continued his tireless advocacy of applying scientific objectivity to psychic phenomena right up until his death in 1980.

No survey of psychic phenomena would be complete without mentioning Edgar Cayce, "the Sleeping Prophet." From 1901 until his death, in 1945, Cayce underwent a daily regimen of trances, during which his "spirit guide" would diagnose the illnesses of thousands of people who had written to Cayce, usually as a last resort. From their names and addresses alone, Cayce's spirit guide would describe the ailment in minute detail and prescribe specific treatment, which in some cases violated conventional medical tenets. In addition to these "physical readings," Cayce was capable of doing "life readings," which related in detail the past lives a subject had lived and the reason for his present incarnation. Sometimes these would lead to psychological evaluations, which the Cayce entity found inextricably intertwined with a person's spiritual dimensions.

Finally, Cayce's contact in the spirit world went on to expound upon a host of subjects, including history, science, religion, psychic phenomena, and particularly the legendary continent of Atlantis. Today, the full opus of Cayce's readings— all 14,246 of them, which were recorded exactly—are on file at the Association for Research and Enlightenment in Virginia Beach, Virginia.

Despite ongoing and quite varied psychical research, as well as exhaustive data compiled by groups like the ASPR, skepticism in the mainstream scientific community remained steadfast, and public interest in psychic phenomena waned from the 1930s on. The next 40 years were punctuated by "sensational" events, such as the medium Arthur Ford's report to Mrs. Houdini that he had received a coded message from her dead husband, and Jeane Dixon's prediction, in the May 13, 1956, issue of Parade magazine that John Kennedy would be assassinated.

In the early 1970s there was a resurgence of interest

in psychic phenomena, typified by astronaut Edgar Mitchell's telepathy experiments in space, aboard Apollo 14. Using card techniques similar to those developed at Duke, Mitchell tried to "send" the images to four psychics here on earth, one of whom, Olaf Jonsson, was featured in *Life* magazine at the time. The results, according to Mitchell, were "statistically significant" to the point where the laws of chance were "bypassed." The astronaut went on to found the Institute of Noetic Sciences, in 1973, whose goals are "to support research and education on human consciousness," and "to broaden knowledge of the nature and potentials of mind and consciousness, and to apply that knowledge to the enhancement of the quality of life on the planet."

The 1970s also saw the return of mediumship, now called "channeling." Jane Roberts led the way with several volumes of "Seth" material, purported to be the spiritual wisdom of a discarnate spirit. Teachings such as "A Course in Miracles," a collection of lectures from the spirit of Jesus Christ, gave rise to spiritual counseling groups, classes, and workshops. The number and range of people using psychic ability grew, along with a steady flow of books, newsletters, audio cassettes, and videotapes, all promising spiritual growth. Suddenly psychics were "in," not just as cheap Saturday night entertainment, but, as Shirley MacLaine's books suggest, as an integral part of the lifestyles of the rich and famous.

Today, parapsychology is the subject of study at major universities throughout the world. In 1982 the Chinese Academy of Sciences sponsored a public hearing on psychic phenomena. A survey in the *American Journal of Psychiatry* a few years back revealed that 58 percent of doctors interviewed favored teaching parapsychology in medical school programs. At New York University nurses learn the healing art of "therapeutic touch," a new form of the age-old technique of the "laying on of hands."

Meanwhile, psychics are popping up in some of the strangest places. One Los Angeles psychic earns up to $1,000 a day as a "business specialist" and writes a regular column of economic predictions. Another psychic, in Canada, specializes in locating ancient archeological finds and dating artifacts, in some cases accomplishing in 20 minutes what might take an archeologist three years to do. There is even a group called Professional Psychics United, which claims an 87 percent success rate in helping the police with unsolved crimes. And the FBI academy in Washington, DC, offers its trainees a presentation on "How Psychics Can Be Useful." Perhaps not so surprising is the revelation that ABC-TV employed a psychic for two years, at a salary of $54,000, to advise the programming staff.

Even the struggle for global power is not free from psychic involvement. In a series of columns published in April 1984, columnist Jack Anderson reported that the Pentagon has used psychics to "spy on the Soviets by projecting their minds out of their bodies," and that psychic abilities are "almost universally accepted in the intelligence community." And a recent report by the Congressional Research Service claims that whereas the United States is spending only half a million dollars on psychic research, the Soviets are spending "tens of millions."

This explosion of interest in psychics, channelers, crystals, spirit guides, extraterrestrials, and the like is all part of what has been termed the "New Age." Previously the domain of the counterculture, the New Age went mainstream with the publication of Shirley MacLaine's *Out on a Limb,* in which the actress described her own discovery that life has a spiritual component, and reached a crescendo on August 16, 1987, with the "harmonic convergence," when New Age adherents around the world gathered in "power places" to meditate on world peace, hoping to usher in a new era of spiritual awareness. Even such bastions of mainsteam journalism as *The New York Times* and *The Wall Street Journal* regularly run articles on everything from tea rooms to psychics who do readings for pets.

The concept of a "New Age" actually has its roots in astronomy. Because the earth wobbles on its axis as a result of the gravitational pull of the sun and moon, the North Pole actually describes a circle roughly every 26,000 years. This "precession of the equinoxes," as it is known, places the pole in a different constellation every 2,000 years or so. (It is also the reason why the astrological "signs" don't line up with their respective constellations any longer.) As a result, the earth as a whole enters a new astrological age every two millenia. Thus the earth entered the Age of Taurus around the time that Moses received the Ten Commandments on Mount Sinai; the Age of Pisces dates back to the time of Jesus Christ; and we are currently entering the Age of Aquarius, which is the "New Age." (No one knows the exact date the earth will enter the Aquarian Age; some people claim it has already begun, while other estimates range ahead as far as the year 2020.)

Each astrological age is marked by certain characteristics that are reflected in the events and values of the time. Contrary to popular belief, it was the Piscean Age, not the Aquarian Age, that embodied the idea of universal oneness. It was characterized by the emotions—ruled by the heart, not the mind. The Age of Aquarius, astrologers tell us, brings with it universal brotherhood as well as individual expression, so that people will not be labeled or placed under banners that overshadow their individuality. Interestingly, Aquarius is also the sign that rules technology, which is very mind-centered: hence, the significance of the computer.

The New Age marks a turning point in human history—an end to old values and a search for new ones. This is perhaps the reason for the interest in psychic ability and the power of the mind at the same time that we are experiencing an unprecedented explosion of technology. As a result, new paradigms are being formulated in every field, from medicine to economics, while older systems of thought, such as the Eastern religions, are being reevaluated for their relevance to a twentieth-century Western lifestyle.

Astrologers also tell us that another mark of the Aquarian Age is the advent of democracy and the idea of the rights of the individual. It is therefore not surprising that the center of this great confluence of ideas is located here in the United States. It is also fitting that the New Age should be expressed in a uniquely American way: with a great deal of entrepreneurship, marketing, and glitz. Everything, it seems, including spirituality itself, is fair free-market game, and even though no one has been able to figure out how psychic ability works, that hasn't stopped anyone from making a buck off it.

No matter what the astrologers say, the New Age, for better or worse, is already upon us. It has been picked up by mainstream America and landed on the cover of *Time* magazine. Whether this obsession will go the way of the Spiritualist movement of the last century remains to be seen. Only time will tell if this is indeed a new era in human thought or simply another apocalyptic fad marking the end of a millenium.

APPENDIX B

List of Resources

Psychics and Others Quoted

NATHANIEL ALTMAN
169 Prospect Park West
Brooklyn, NY 11215
Palmistry

ELWOOD BABBITT
P.O. Box 25
Wendell Depot, MA 01380
Mediumship

BARBARA BRENNAN, M.S.
331 East 71st Street, #1C
New York, NY 10021
*Psychic Healing; Channeling:
"Heoyan"*

STEPHEN PAULO CALIA
215 West 90th Street, #12D
New York, NY 10024
Numerology, Astrology, Tarot

LINDA CHAGNON
P.O. Box 380
Greenville, RI 02828
Psychic Healing

YVONNE CIARDULLO
807 Kendall Street
Lakewood, CO 80214
Clairvoyance

JUDY DAMRON
HCR-1, Box 4A
Boiceville, NY 12412
Channeling

SUSAN EDWARDS
844 19th Street
Boulder, CO 80302
Tarot, I-Ching

PAT EINSTEIN
765 Greenwich Street
New York, NY 10014
Psychometry

PAUL GALLAGHER
Deer Mountain Taoist
Academy
R.D. 3, Box 109A
Guilford, VT 05301

I-Ching, *T'ai Chi Chu'an,*
Taoist Healing Arts

MICHAEL GOODRICH
Cosmic Contact Psychic
Services
26 East 13th Street, 5 C
New York, NY 10003

DIANE BROOK GUSIC, M.A.
241-20 Northern Blvd.
Douglaston, NY 11363
Astrology, Numerology, "A
Course In Miracles"

HOSSCA HARRISON
P.O. Box 1559
Boulder, CO 80302
Channeling: "Jonah"

J. RONALD HAVERN, M.Div.
150 East 7th Street
New York, NY 10009
Tarot

ELLEN HENDRICK
13067 Calais Street
New Orleans, LA 70129
Psychic Healing, Voodoo

LINDA HILL, M.A.
46 Great Jones Street
New York, NY 10012
Astrology

ANDREA HINDA
962 11th Street
Boulder, CO 80302
Psychic Counseling

BRIAN HURST
12418 LaMaida Street
North Hollywood, CA 91607
Channeling

PETER JANNEY, Ed.D.
17 Fresh Pond Parkway
Cambridge, MA 02138
Psychotherapy, Spiritual
Counseling, Nutritional
Counseling

ROCK KENYON
40 MacDougal Street
New York, NY 10012
27 South Street
Lily Dale, NY 14752
Channeling

SUZANNE KLUSS
2675 West Highway 89A, #126
Sedona, AZ 86336
Channeling

JANET MACRAE, R.N., Ph.D.
834 Union Street
Brooklyn, NY 11215
Therapeutic Touch

BROOKE McADAM
476 Broome Street
New York, NY 10013
Channeling

ROLLA NORDIC
121 West 72nd Street
New York, NY 10023
Tarot, Rune Stones

CHRISTINE RAKELA
166 West 75th Street
New York, NY 10023
Astrology, Palmistry

BEATRICE RICH
14 Horatio Street
New York, NY 10014
Clairvoyance, Psychometry

BARBARA ROLLINSON, M.S.
P.O. Box 7381
Boulder, CO 80306
Channeling

MARGO SCHMIDT, M.Ed.
2678 Massachusetts Avenue
Lexington, MA 02173
Spiritual Counseling

MARIA TADD
7 Dix Terrace
Winchester, MA 01890
Psychic Healing

DIANA VELAZQUEZ
Centro de las Familias
75 Meade
Denver, CO 80219
Curanderismo, Psychic Healing, Spiritual Counseling

Astrology Organizations and Services

AMERICAN FEDERATION
OF ASTROLOGERS
P.O. Box 22040
Tempe, AZ 85282
Sponsors biannual convention; publishes monthly bulletin for members.

ASTRO COMPUTING
SERVICES
P.O. Box 16430
San Diego, CA 92116.
Complete astrological services by mail; publishes ephemerides and books on a wide variety of astrological and psychic subjects, including numerology, palmistry, and channeling;

Publishes quarterly
newsletter.

NATIONAL ASTROLOGICAL
SOCIETY
205 Third Avenue, #2A
New York, NY 10003
Sponsors workshops, special publications, and an annual conference for serious students of astrology; publishes quarterly journal.

NEW YORK ASTROLOGY
CENTER
63 West 38th Street,
Suite #505
New York, NY 10018
Complete astrological ser-

vices by mail; prepares personal astrological charts; offers private readings; maintains bookstore and library.

PARA RESEARCH
85 Eastern Avenue
Gloucester, MA 01930
Complete astrological services by mail; offers chart calculation services for astrologers, as well as interpretive charts for beginners; publishes a number of books on astrology, numerology, metaphysics, and meditation.

Psychic Referral Services

COSMIC CONTACT PSYCHIC SERVICES
26 East 13th Street, #5C
New York, NY 10003
National psychic referral service; fee charged.

PSYCHIC CONNNECTION INTERNATIONAL
13067 Calais Street
New Orleans, LA 70129
Organization for people interested in psychic and spiritual pursuits; offers free psychic referral service; publishes listing of members and monthly newsletter.

Spiritual Support Groups

ROCKY MOUNTAIN SPIRITUAL EMERGENCE NETWORK
935 Spruce Street
Boulder, CO 80302
Local chapter of national organization (see below); operates phone line for support and referrals; sponsors educational programs for professionals and "persons experiencing spiritual emergence."

SPIRITUAL EMERGENCE NETWORK
Institute of Transpersonal Psycholog·
250 Oak Grove Avenue
Menlo Park, CA 94025

Founded in 1980 by Stanislav and Christina Grof, the developers of "holotropic therapy"; national headquarters of nonprofit network consisting of 40 U.S. regional coordinators; promotes the Grofs' philosophy of spiritual emergence; operates referral service to callers experiencing spiritual crises; conducts workshops and training programs.

SPIRITUAL SCIENCES
INSTITUTE
330 East Canon Perdido
Suite B
Santa Barbara, CA 93121
Nonprofit healing and teaching center founded and directed by channeler Verna V. Yater, Ph.D; conducts lectures, seminars, and healing clinics; organizes traveling workshops across the U.S.; operates Blue Mountain Center, a spiritual learning center and power spot in Colorado Springs; publishes quarterly newsletter.

New Age Learning Centers and Bookstores

THE BODHI TREE
BOOKSTORE
8585 Melrose Avenue
Los Angeles, CA 90069

GOLDEN LEAVES BOOK
MART & METAPHYSICAL
CENTRE
211 Phlox Avenue
Metairie, LA 70001
Sponsors classes, groups, lectures, and private sessions in the New Orleans area, including meditation, yoga, hypnosis, crystals, astrology,

Tarot, palmistry, massage, "Course in Miracles", etc.; sells psychic and spiritual books and paraphernalia; publishes calendar of events.

INTERFACE
P.O. Box 860
Watertown, MA 02172
"An education center founded 13 years ago to explore those trends in health, personal growth, science, and religion which excite and encourage us to seek new ways

of living, expand personal horizons, and join with others to help create a better world"; runs courses, lectures, and workshops in the Boston area.

NEW YORK OPEN CENTER

83 Spring Street
New York, NY 10012
Offers lectures, courses, and workshops in a wide range of subjects, including metaphysics, Eastern thought, psychic ability, tarot, the *I-Ching*, psychic healing, bodywork, transpersonal psychology, holistic health, etc.; runs bookstore; offers discounts for members on books, audio tapes, and crystals.

NEW YORK THEOSOPHICAL SOCIETY

Quest Bookshop
242 East 53rd Street
New York, NY 10022
Offers lectures, classes, and workshops in metaphysical topics; runs metaphysical bookstore; maintains library for on-premise use; publishes calendar of events; also see Theosophical Society in America, below.

TOGETHER BOOKS

2220 East Colfax Avenue
Denver, CO 80206
Sponsors psychic fairs, private psychic readings one day a week; offers classes, lectures, and groups in yoga, T'ai Chi Chu'an, zen, polarity therapy, reiki, numerology, astrology, tarot, channeling, etc.; full line of metaphysical books and crystals; publishes monthly newsletter and calendar of events for the Denver area.

WAINWRIGHT HOUSE CENTER FOR DEVELOPMENT OF HUMAN POTENTIAL

260 Stuyvesant Avenue
Rye, New York 10580
"Non-profit, non-sectarian center for education dedicated to the development of human potential in a changing world"; sponsors lectures, workshops, and programs in various areas, including psychology, health and healing, spiritual development, global issues, business ethics, creativity, and the arts; offers personal counseling with qualified professionals; makes referrals; runs bookstore with discounts for members.

374

Spiritual Retreat Centers

ESALEN INSTITUTE
Big Sur, CA 93920
Founded in 1962 as a small
college dedicated to the
study of consciousness; today, presents more than 500
workshops, seminars, and
conferences annually on
various subjects, including
spiritual practice, bodywork,
creativity, exceptional functioning, social action, Gestalt
awareness training, and
group work through "direct
experiences"—physical, emotional, cognitive, and
spiritual.

LILY DALE ASSEMBLY
5 Melrose Park
Lily Dale, NY 14752
"A community dedicated to
metaphysical education,"
founded in 1879; offers
private readings and healing
sessions, as well as lectures
and workshops on psychic,

spiritual, and New-Age
themes.

NEW YORK PATHWORK
CENTER
61 Fourth Avenue
New York, NY 10003
New York branch of the
Phoenicia Pathwork Center;
see below.

PHOENICIA PATHWORK
CENTER
Box 66
Phoenicia, NY 12464
"An educational and spiritual
center" in the Catskill Mountains of New York State (and
home to 18 residents); hosts
programs on self-
transformation, workshops
on personal and professional
growth, retreats, conferences,
and intensives, based on 258
spiritual lectures channeled
by Eva Pierrakos.

Research Organizations

ACADEMY OF PARA-
PSYCHOLOGY AND
MEDICINE
P.O. Box 36121
Denver, CO 80227
Organization for promoting

the use of parapsychology in
healing; publishes sym-
posium transcripts and
technical reports; provides
referrals.

AMERICAN SOCIETY FOR
PSYCHICAL RESEARCH
5 West 73 Street
New York, NY 10023
One hundred-year-old
organization dedicated to
parapsychology research and
investigation of the paranormal; maintains a substantial
library on psychical research
and related subjects; sponsors lectures and workshops;
publishes quarterly journal.

ASSOCIATION FOR
RESEARCH AND
ENLIGHTENMENT
P.O. Box 595
Virginia Beach, VA 23451
Organization dedicated to
perpetuating the work of
Edgar Cayce; maintains
library with complete
transcripts of all 30,000
Cayce readings; sponsors
psychic research; runs lectures, classes, and work-
shops; maintains network of
health care professionals
using Edgar Cayce cures;
publishes bimonthly
magazine.

ASSOCIATION FOR
TRANSPERSONAL
PSYCHOLOGY
P.O. Box 3049
Stanford, CA 94305
Organization for profes-
sionals and others interested
in the field; sponsors annual
conference; publishes profes-
sional journal.

CENTRAL PREMONITIONS
REGISTRY
P.O. Box 482
Times Square Station
New York, NY 10036

FOUNDATION FOR
RESEARCH ON THE
NATURE OF MAN
Box 6847
College Station
Durham, NC 27708
Nonprofit organization that
conducts and encourages
research in parapsychology,
extrasensory perception,
psychokinesis; maintains Institute for Parapsychology,
which conducts workshops
and seminars; maintains
reference library; conducts
summer study program;
operates mail-order book service; publishes journals and
books.

INSTITUTE FOR NOETIC
SCIENCES
475 Gate Five Road,
Suite 300
Sausalito, CA 94965
Founded in 1973 by Apollo
astronaut Edgar Mitchell "to
broaden knowledge of the
nature and potentials of
mind and consciousness, and
to apply that knowledge to
the enhancement of the
quality of life on the planet";
publishes bimonthly *Bulletin*,
quarterly *Review*, and
periodic reports on research;
offers discounts for members
on related books, publications, and audio tapes.

MOBIUS SOCIETY
4801 Wilshire Boulevard,
Suite 320
Los Angeles, CA 90010
Nonprofit research corpora-
tion dedicated to the scientific study of consciousness;
maintains library (open to
the public by appointment);
holds workshops; publishes
quarterly newsletter.

PARAPSYCHOLOGY
FOUNDATION
228 East 71st Street
New York, NY 10021

Research center and non-
profit organization founded
by psychic Eileen J. Garrett
in 1950; maintains extensive
library (open to the public
for on-premise use); sponsors
annual scholarship award,
grant program, and annual
international conference;
publishes bimonthly journal,
single-topic monograph
series, and annual information guide.

THEOSOPHICAL SOCIETY
IN AMERICA
P.O. Box 270
Wheaton, IL 60189-0270
Founded in 1875 "to form a
nucleus of the universal
brotherhood of humanity,
without distinction of race,
creed, sex, caste, or color; to
encourage the study of comparative religion, science, and
philosophy; and to in-
vestigate unexplained laws of
nature and the powers latent
in man"; maintains branch
chapters in various cities,
which sponsor lectures,
classes, and workshops in
spiritual and psychic
disciplines; publishes books
on metaphysical topics;
maintains lending library at
Wheaton headquarters;
publishes monthly journal.

Publications

American Astrology
475 Park Avenue South
New York, NY 10016

The American Theosophist
P.O. Box 270
Wheaton, IL 60189-0270

Astrology Guide
355 Lexington Avenue
New York, NY 10017

Astrological Review
Astrologer's Guild of
America
54 Mineola Boulevard
Mineola, NY 11501

**Body, Mind, & Spirit
Magazine**
(formerly **Psychic Guide**)
P.O. Box 701
Providence, RI 02901

Brain/Mind Bulletin
P.O. Box 42211
Los Angeles, CA 90042

The Common Boundary
7005 Florida Street
Chevy Chase, MD 20815

Consciousness Connection
432 Altair Place
Venice, CA 90291

Heart's Journey
P.O. Box 7381
Boulder, CO 80306

Horoscope
P.O. Box 4800
Marion, OH 43302

New Age Journal
342 Western Avenue
Brighton, MA 02135-9907

New Realities Magazine
P.O. Box 17877
Austin, TX 78760-7877

**Metapsychology: The Journal
of Discarnate Intelligence**
P.O. Box 3295
Charlottesville, VA 22903
(Back issues only)

**Parabola: The Magazine of
Myth and Tradition**
656 Broadway
New York, NY 10012

Pursuit
P.O. Box 265
Little Silver, NJ 07739

Spirit Speaks
P.O. Box 84304
Los Angeles, CA 90073

Yoga Journal
2054 University Avenue, #302
Berkeley, CA 94704

GLOSSARY

Akashic Records

A "cosmic data base" of all knowledge of human events, past, present, and future, accessible on the astral, or spiritual, plane; often consulted for information about individual past lives

Alpha State

An altered state of consciousness characterized by alpha brain waves produced during deep relaxation, meditation, and hypnosis; used by many psychics to access intuitive information

Apparition

A visible image of a deceased person's physical body; usually the result of either a strong emotional link to the physical body at the time of death, or a state of spiritual confusion resulting from a sudden or violent death

Astral Body

See *Soul*

Astral Plane

A higher vibrational level than the physical plane, populated by the souls of the deceased and various other spirit entities

Astrology

A system of divination that uses the movement of the planets through the constellations to determine and predict human characteristics, tendencies, and events

Aura

A constantly fluctuating bioenergetic "shell" that surrounds and interpenetrates all living beings; and that some psychics claim to be able to see (see *Chakras*)

Automatic Writing

A means of channeling or mediumship in which a spirit entity uses a channel's hand to write or type a message; usually done in trance

Bilocation

The ability to "be in two places at once" by sending the astral body, or soul, to another physical location, usually during a trance state

Chi

The Chinese "life force," or vital energy, that travels throughout the body along specific pathways, animating living beings and ensuring vitality

Chakras

The energy centers of the human auric field (see *Aura*), which vibrate in varying intensity and colors and roughly correspond to the human endocrine system

Channeler, Channel

A psychic who is used by spiritual entities as a means of communication, generally by going into a trance; also known as a medium

Chiromancy

See *Palmistry*

Collective Unconscious

Carl Jung's concept of a shared level of knowledge that is common to all humankind, consisting of mythological images (archetypes), standard patterns of behavior, and instinctual responses

Clairaudience

The ability to access psychic information by using the sense of hearing, including either external or internal sounds

Clairguscience

The ability to access psychic information by using the sense of smell

Clairsentience

The ability to access psychic information through an emotional or physical feeling

Clairvoyance

The ability to access psychic information by using the sense of sight, including either external visions or internal images

Control
A spirit entity who acts as "gatekeeper" and guide for a channeler or medium who seeks to contact other spirit entities on the astral plane

Crystals
Naturally occurring rock formations, generally quartz, which are thought to possess certain physical properties that aid in the manipulation of spiritual energy; different colors are thought to have different spiritual properties

Death
The moment at which the soul, or astral body, leaves the physical body, and the "connecting cord" is severed

Divination
Any method whereby information about the future outcome of an event is sought

ESP
See *Psi*

Extraterrestrial
A being from another planet, galaxy, or dimension of space-time; such beings may exist in nonphysical form and may communicate through spiritual means; also known as "space brothers"

Ghost
See *Apparition*

God Consciousness The highest level of spiritual awareness, in which the individual self is merged into a profound state of Oneness with all things

Horoscope A chart prepared by an astrologer that fixes the positions of the sun, moon, and planets at the time of a specific event, e.g. birthday, business deal, marriage, etc. (see *Natal Horoscope*)

Hypnosis An externally induced altered state of consciousness, similar to meditation and characterized by deep relaxation, alpha brain waves, and access to the subconscious; often used for recalling deeply rooted memories or past lives

I Ching The ancient Chinese *Book of Changes*, which is a compendium of Taoist and Confucian wisdom used in conjunction with coins or yarrow stalks to determine the best course of action in a particular situation

Intuition The ability to perceive information about a person, thing, or event through a nonrational "sense of knowing"; similar to a hunch or "gut feeling"

Kua The Chinese name for the hex-

agrams used in consulting the
I Ching

Karma

The Hindu concept of cosmic
cause and effect: that every action one does in a single
lifetime is balanced by what occurs in other lifetimes, both
past and future

Law of Correspondences

The metaphysical belief that
"what is above is reflected
below"; that the forces affecting the larger, natural world
(such as the movement of
planets) also determine the
course of human events

Laying On of Hands

Psychic healing achieved by
sending energy through the
hands into an ailing person's
body, or working with that person's own energy field at the
location of an injury or pain
(see *Therapeutic Touch*)

Left Brain

The left hemisphere of the
brain, which expresses itself
through logical, linear thought
and deductive reasoning

Master

A human being or spirit entity
who has attained the highest
level of spiritual enlightenment
and who has chosen to use that
knowledge to aid humankind

Materialism

The belief that only what can
be apprehended using the five

senses (or instruments extending their range) is real; and that all matter is made up of elementary particles that behave according to known laws (see *Spirituality*)

Meditation

A self-induced altered state of consciousness characterized by deep relaxation and a quieting of the mind enabling a person to contact nonrational levels of the subconscious and subtle spiritual energies

Medium

See *Channeler*

Metaphysics

The branch of philosophy that deals with spiritual, cosmological, and existential aspects of reality

Mysticism

Religious practices that seek to bring the subject into a direct knowing of God or a true perception of spiritual reality (see *God Consciousness*)

Natal Horoscope

A horoscope prepared for a person's birthdate and time, from which personal characteristics, karmic lessons from past lives, and future tendencies can be determined (see *Horoscope*)

Numerology

A system of divination that uses numbers derived from a person's name and birthdate to determine personal characteristics and karmic lessons from past lives and to predict at what periods during that person's life those issues will be most prominent

Palmistry

A means of determining personal characteristics and predicting life patterns by looking at the shape, texture, mounds, and lines of the hand; also known as chiromancy

Paranormal

Events that cannot be explained by the known laws of physics; any information or knowledge that is gained without using normal means of communication involving the five senses

Parapsychology

The branch of psychology that deals with the paranormal, extrasensory perception, and mediumship

Paraphysics

The branch of physics that seeks to discover both the means by which paranormal events take place and the mechanisms by which psychic information is transmitted from one person to another

Past Life

A person's existence in a previous incarnation, in which the same soul inhabited a different body, either on Earth or elsewhere (see *Regression*)

Prana   The Hindu concept of a "life force," or vital energy, which is taken in with the breath by means of specific exercises, such as yoga; similar to the Chinese concept of *chi*

Precognition   The ability to predict future events

Progressions   The different levels of existence, each of which vibrates with a different frequency of energy, ranging from the lowest, the physical, to the highest, the causal or Godhead; often said to number seven in all

Psi   The technical term for psychic ability; also known as extrasensory perception (ESP)

Psychic   A person who can access information about a person, thing, or event without using normal means of communication or sensation; also, a person who can receive communications from those who are deceased or any spirit entity

Psychic Healer   A person who can cure illness or relieve pain by sending healing energy to a patient, with or without the use of direct touch

Psychic Surgery   The process of opening the body and removing diseased tissue or foreign objects without the use of sterile surgical technique or anesthetic; sometimes attributed to the intervention of spirit entities or "doctors"

Psychometry

The ability to access information about a person, thing, or event simply by holding an object or photograph in the hand

Regression

The process of using an altered state of consciousness, such as hypnosis or meditation, to "remember" a past life

Reincarnation

The belief that the soul, or spirit body, leaves the physical body at the time of death and eventually inhabits a new body at the time of conception

Retrocognition

The ability to recall past events in a person's life that are otherwise unknown to the psychic, including information about past lives

Right Brain

The right hemisphere of the brain, which expresses itself through intuitive, nonrational thought and inductive reasoning; it seems to be particularly active during altered states of consciousness

Rune Stones

A method of divination using pieces of stone, wood, or clay

inscribed with letters from an ancient Nordic alphabet to predict the outcome of specific events

Séance
A gathering of a sitter or group of sitters together with a medium or channeler, with the express purpose of contacting the souls of deceased people

Sensitive
A person who can see—or sense in some way—spiritual energies, including human auras, chakras, and spirit entities

Shaman
A spiritual leader, a "witch doctor" or "medicine man," who acts as psychological counselor, medical doctor, and spiritual guide to a group of people with traditional, naturalistic beliefs

Sitter
A person who receives a psychic reading

Soul
The nonphysical aspect of the human being, which contains the essence of the self—including all one's memories and experiences—and which leaves the physical body at the time of death; also known as the astral body (see *Astral Plane*)

Spirit
The nonphysical, nonpersonal

part of the human being that contains the Divine essence or God Consciousness

Spirit Guide

A spirit entity who watches over and helps a particular person who is living; similar to a guardian angel

Spiritualism

A system of thought dating back to the ninteteenth century, which propounds belief in survival of the soul following bodily death, in reincarnation, and in the ability of mediums to contact those souls who have already "passed over"

Spirituality

The belief that reality is made up of more than the physical universe, and that human beings possess a nonmaterial component that can exist apart from the body (see *Materialism*)

Synchronicity

Carl Jung's concept of two independent events that are somehow connected in a non-causal way

Tarot Cards

A method of divination that uses a tarot deck to analyze the various aspects of a problem or question, or a particular period in a person's life; also used as a "book" of ancient spiritual wisdom in pictorial form

Tea Room

A place in which a group of

psychics, usually card readers and palm readers, do short, inexpensive readings for customers on a walk-in basis

Telepathy

The ability to receive a thought that is sent by another individual who is not present and not in direct communication with the psychic

Therapeutic Touch

A contemporary version of the laying on of hands, in which the patient's energy field is manipulated or "smoothed out" using the hands, developed by Dolores Krieger and Dora Kunz in the early 1970s (see *Laying On of Hands*)

Third Eye

The chakra point located in the center of the forehead, which is thought to be the seat of spiritual wisdom

Trance

An altered state of consciousness in which psychic information can be accessed, spirit entities contacted, and paranormal feats performed; also the process by which the consciousness leaves the physical body in order to make room for a spirit entity (see *Channeler*)

Transpersonal Psychology

The branch of psychology that deals with higher states of being, altered states of consciousness, and the spiritual component of the human being

Vibrations See *Progressions*

NOTES

Chapter One

1. Arthur Koestler, *The Roots of Coincidence,* 2nd ed. (London: Picador/Pan Books, Ltd., 1972), p. 130.
2. Brendan O'Regan, "The Emergence of Paraphysics: Theoretical Foundations." In *Psychic Exploration: A Challenge for Science,* edited by Edgar Mitchell (New York: G.P. Putnam's Sons, 1974), p. 448.

   For a good summary of some of the work that has been done in the area of paraphysics, as well as other scientific reasearch into psychic phenomena, I refer the reader to Mitchell's book, which contains one of the most comprehensive treatments of the subject available in one volume.
3. See David Bohm, *Wholeness and the Implicate Order* (London: Routledge & Kegan Paul/Ark Paperbacks, 1983).
4. Koestler, p. 76.
5. See John J. Heaney, *The Sacred & the Psychic: Parapsychology & Christian Theology* (Ramsey, N.J.: Paulist Press, 1984), p. 43.

   Heaney also points out that in the Old Testament books I Kings and II Kings, the prophet Elijah and his disciple Elisha each perform miracles by multiplying food and bringing the dead back to life, just as Jesus is credited as having done.
6. Swami Nikhilananda, *Hinduism: Its Meaning for the Liberation of the Spirit,* 2nd ed. (Mylapore, India: Sri Ramakrishna Math, 1982), p. 141.

7. Paramahansa Yogananda, *Autobiography of a Yogi* (Los Angeles: Self-Realization Fellowship, 1946), p. 178.
8. Psychic healing is discussed in detail in Chapter Four; for present purposes it should simply be mentioned that Chinese medicine is based in large part on the same idea of balancing internal energies. Acupuncture, which is now in wide use in this country, actually works by stimulating or blocking these various energy pathways with needles or, in the case of acupressure, with pressure from a finger or blunt instrument.

   In addition many Western researchers are now convinced of the existence of a very subtle yet measurable "bioenergetic" field that is produced by the individual cells of the body and can be used in the process of healing.

Chapter Four

1. Ronald C. Davison, *Astrology* (New York: Arco Publishing Co., 1963), p. 22.
2. See Appendix B for a list of some excellent chart calculation services that can be used in preparing your own horoscope.
3. For more on the history of psychic phenomena, specifically channeling and mediumship, see Appendix A.
4. Corinne McLaughlin, "Tuning In to the Best Channel," *New Realities* Magazine (July/August 1987).
5. See Elwood Babbitt and Charles H. Hapgood, *Voices of Spirit* (Turners Falls, Mass.: Fine Line Books, 1975) for such evidence, as well as for transcripts of conversations with Albert Einstein, John F. Kennedy, Adlai Stevenson, Abraham Lincoln, Mark Twain, William Wordsworth, and Louis Armstrong, among others.
6. See Elwood Babbitt and Charles H. Hapgood, *Talks with Christ and His Teachers* (Turners Falls, Mass.: Fine Line Books, 1981) for the transcripts of these sessions with Jesus Christ, as well as with Luke, Joseph, Pontius Pilate, and others.
7. Excerpted from Katherine Martin, "The Voice of Lazaris," in *New Realities* (July/August 1987).

8. Andrew Weil, *Health and Healing: Understanding Conventional and Alternative Medicine* (Boston: Houghton Mifflin Co., 1983), p. 41.
9. Quoted in "Beating the Odds," by Judith Glassman, *New Age Journal* (November, 1985), p. 32.

BIBLIOGRAPHY

Abell, George O. *Exploration of the Universe.* 3rd ed. New York: Holt, Rinehart and Winston, 1975.

Altman, Nathaniel. *The Palmistry Workbook.* Wellingborough, Northamptonshire, England: Aquarian Press, 1984.

Anderson, Harry. "Business Psychic." *Newsweek* February 19, 1979.

Blum, Ralph. *The Book of Runes.* New York: St. Martin's Press, 1982.

Brandon-Jones, David. *Practical Palmistry.* Reno, NV: CRCS Publications, 1986.

Bohm, David. *Wholeness and the Implicate Order.* London: Routledge & Kegan Paul/Ark Paperbacks, 1983.

Bro, Harmon Hartzell. *Edgar Cayce on Religion and Psychic Experience.* New York: Warner Books/Association for Research and Enlightenment, 1970.

Campion, Nicholas. *The Practical Astrologer.* New York: Abrams, 1987.

Capra, Fritjof. *The Tao of Physics.* Boulder, CO: Shambhala Publications, 1975.

— — —*The Turning Point.* New York: Simon & Schuster, 1982.

Carey, Ken. *The Starseed Transmissions*. Kansas City, MO: Uni*Sun, 1983.

— — — *Vision*. Kansas City, MO: Uni*Sun, 1985.

Cerminara, Gina. *Many Mansions*. New York: New American Library, 1950.

Chang, Stephen T. *The Great Tao*. San Francisco: Tao Publishing, 1985.

Christopher, Milbourne. *Houdini: The Untold Story*. New York: Pocket Books, 1970.

Cleary, Thomas, trans. *The Taoist I Ching*. Boston: Shambhala Publications, 1986.

Davison, Ronald C. *Astrology*. New York: Arco, 1963.

Ebon, Martin. *They Knew the Unknown*. New York: World Publishing, 1971.

Fodor, Nandor. *An Encyclopaedia of Psychic Science*. Secaucus, NJ: University Books, Inc., The Citadel Press, 1974.

Friedrich, Otto. "New Age Harmonies." *Time* December 7, 1987.

Gerus, Claire. "A Feel for the Past." *MacLeans* September 22, 1980.

Gittelson, Bernard and Laura Torbet. *Intangible Evidence*. New York: Simon and Schuster, 1987.

Glassman, Judith. "Beating the Odds." *New Age Journal* November 1985.

Goodrich, Joyce. "Science and Psychic Healing." Lecture at the New York Open Center, June 12, 1987.

Gray, Eden. *A Complete Guide to the Tarot*. New York: Crown, 1970.

Greeley, Andrew. "Mysticism Goes Mainstream." *American Health* January/February 1987.

Hapgood, Charles H. and Elwood Babbitt. *The God Within: A Testament of Vishnu.* Turners Falls, MA: Fine Line Books, 1982.

— — —. *Talks with Christ and His Teachers*. Turners Falls, MA: Fine Line Books, 1981.

— — —. *Voices of Spirit*. 2nd ed. Turners Falls, MA: Fine Line Books, 1986.

Harary, Keith. "The Mind Race: Inside American and Soviet Psychic Research." Lecture at the New York Open Center, February 6, 1987.

Harner, Michael. *The Way of the Shaman*. New York: Bantam Books, 1982.

Heaney, John J. *The Sacred & the Psychic: Parapsychology & Christian Theology*. Ramsey, NJ: Paulist Press, 1984.

Jakobson, Cathryn. "The Booming Soothsayer Biz." *New York Woman* November/December 1986.

Javane, Faith and Dusty Bunker. *Numerology and the Divine Triangle*. Gloucester, MA: Para Research, Inc., 1979.

Karagulla, Shafica. *Breakthrough to Creativity*. Marina Del Rey, CA: DeVorss & Co., Inc., 1967.

Kitman, Marvin. "Out-Psyching the Neilsen's." *The New Leader* May 1981.

Koestler, Arthur. *The Roots of Coincidence*. 2nd ed. London: Picador/Pan Books, Ltd., 1972.

Krieger, Dolores. *The Therapeutic Touch: How to Use Your Hands to Help or to Heal*. Englewood Cliffs, NJ: Prentice-Hall, 1979.

Krippner, Stanley and Alberto Villoldo. *The Realms of Healing*. 3rd ed. Berkeley, CA: Celestial Arts, 1986.

Kunz, Dora. "The Invisible Worlds Around Us." Lecture given at the New York Theosophical Society, September 26, 1987.

— — —, ed. *Spiritual Aspects of the Healing Arts*. Wheaton, IL: Theosophical Publishing House, 1985.

LeShan, Lawrence. *The Medium, The Mystic, and the Physicist*. New York: Ballantine Books, 1966.

Line, David and Julia. *Fortune-Telling by Dice*. Wellingborough, Northamptonshire, England: Aquarian Press, 1984.

Macrae, Janet. *Therapeutic Touch: A Practical Guide*. New York: Alfred Knopf, 1987.

Macrae, Ron. *Mind Wars: The True Story of Secret Government Research into the Military Potential of Psychic Weapons*. New York: St. Martin's Press, 1984.

Martin, Katherine. "The Voice of Lazaris." *New Realities* July/August 1987.

McGuire, T.M. "Edgar Cayce's Legacy of Holistic Health." *East West* September 1987.

McLaughlin, Corrine. "Tuning in to the Best Channel." *New Realities* July/August 1987.

"M.D.'s and Magic." *Science Digest* May 1982.

Mitchell, Edgar D., ed., *Psychic Exploration: A Challenge for Science*. New York: Putnam's, 1974.

Needleman, Jacob. *Lost Christianity: A Journey of Rediscovery*. New York: Harper & Row, 1980.

Nikhilananda, Swami. *Hinduism: Its Meaning for the Liberation of the Spirit*. 2nd Ed. Mylapore, India: Sri Ramakrishna Math, 1982.

Payne, Phoebe D. and Laurence J. Bendit. *This World and That: An Analytical Study of Psychic Communication*. Wheaton, IL: Theosophical Publishing House, 1950.

"The Pentagon, The CIA, and the Psychics." *Discover* June 1984.

Pollack, Rachel. *Seventy-Eight Degrees of Wisdom: A Book of Tarot*. Part I and Part II. Wellingborough, Northamptonshire, England: Aquarian Press, 1980.

"A Psi Gap?" *Discover* February 1984.

Psychic Magazine, ed. *Psychics*. New York: Harper & Row, 1972.

Quinn, Janet. "Therapeutic Touch." *New Realities* May/June 1987.

Ralston, Jeannie. "Can Psychics See What Detectives Can't?" *McCall's* February 1983.

Raphaell, Katrina. *Crystal Enlightenment.* New York: Aurora Press, 1985.

Rodegast, Pat and Judith Stanton. *Emmanuel's Book.* New York: Bantam Books, 1987.

Rogo, D. Scott. *Exploring Psychic Phenomena: Beyond Mind and Matter.* Wheaton, IL: Theosophical Publishing House, 1976.

Rudhyar, Dane. *The Practice of Astrology.* Boulder, CO: Shambhala, 1978.

Russell, Eric. *Astrology & Prediction.* Secaucus, NJ: The Citadel Press, 1972.

Scholem, Gershom. *Kabbalah.* Jerusalem: Keter Publishing House, 1974.

Skutch, Robert. *Journey Without Distance.* Berkeley, CA: Celestial Arts, 1984.

Sogyal Rinpoche. "Survival of Consciousness: A Tibetan Buddhist Perspective." *Institute of Noetic Sciences Review* Summer 1987.

Stern, Zelda. "The Healing Touch." *Childbirth Educator* Summer 1985.

Stevenson, Ian. "Changing Fashions in the Study of Spontaneous Cases." *The Journal of the American Society for Psychical Research,* Vol. 81, No. 1.

Svoboda, Robert. *The Hidden Secret of Ayurveda.* Weed, CA: Trishula Publications, 1980.

Talbot, Michael. "Beyond the Quantum." Lecture at the New York Open Center, April 3, 1987.

Targ, Russell. "The National ESP Test." *New Realities* September/October 1987.

Truzzi, Marcello. "China's Psychic Savants." *Omni* January 1985,

Vaughan, Alan. "Channeling." *New Realities* January/February 1987.

Waite, Arthur Edward. *The Pictorial Key to the Tarot.* New Hyde Park, NY: University Books, 1959.

Weil, Andrew. *Health and Healing: Understanding Conventional and Alternative Medicine.* Boston: Houghton Mifflin, 1983.

Wilhelm, Richard and Cary F. Baynes, trans. *The I Ching.* Princeton, NJ: Princeton University Press, Bollingen Foundation, 1950.

Willis, Tony. *The Runic Workbook.* Wellingborough, Northamptonshire, England: Aquarian Press, 1986.

Yogananda, Paramahansa. *Autobiography of a Yogi.* Los Angeles: Self-Realization Fellowship, 1946.

Zimmer, Heinrich. *Myths and Symbols in Indian Art and Civilization.* Princeton: Princeton University Press, Bollingen Foundation, 1946.

Zukav, Gary. *The Dancing Wu Li Masters.* New York: Bantam Books, 1979.

INDEX